Conquering the Highlands

A history of the afforestation of the Scottish uplands

K. Jan Oosthoek

Conquering the Highlands

A history of the afforestation of the Scottish uplands

K. Jan Oosthoek

World Forest History Series

Australian
National
University

E PRESS

Published by ANU E Press
The Australian National University
Canberra ACT 0200, Australia
Email: anuepress@anu.edu.au
This title is also available online at http://epress.anu.edu.au

The **World Forest History Series** publishes authoritative histories analysing the institutional, intellectual and environmental impacts of professional and state forestry, with a special but not exclusive focus on colonial forestry and its legacies. Each book, published in hardcopy and available as an electronic copy for download, is available free to scholars and the public around the world. The World Forest History Series has long been a dream of many foresters and historians who wanted a single series to document and analyze the unique global and local histories of forestry. The World Forest History Series is dedicated to the foresters who played a seminal roles in starting and directing the global environmental movement; because of these efforts many of the world's forests still remain.

Series Editors: Gregory A Barton, Research Fellow, Centre for Environmental History, The Australian National University; Brett M Bennett, Lecturer in History, University of Western Sydney.

National Library of Australia Cataloguing-in-Publication entry

Author:	Oosthoek, Jan.
Title:	Conquering the Highlands : a history of the afforestation of the Scottish uplands / Jan Oosthoek.
ISBN:	9781922144782 (pbk.) 9781922144799 (ebook)
Notes:	Includes bibliographical references.
Subjects:	Afforestation--Scotland.
	Afforestation--Environmental aspects--Scotland.
	Forests and forestry--Scotland.
	Sustainable forestry--Scotland.
	Scotland--History.
Dewey Number:	634.95609411

Cover image: *Ploughing in Achray Forest, ca. 1951*. David B Paterson, from http://forestry-memories.org.uk with permission.

Cover design and layout by ANU E Press

Printed by Griffin Press

Contents

List of figures

List of tables

List of maps

List of acronyms

APRS   Association for the Preservation of Rural Scotland

CPRE   Council for the Preservation of Rural England

FC   Forestry Commission

FLD   Friends of the Lake District

NCC   Nature Conservancy Council

NNR   National Nature Reserve

NTS   National Trust for Scotland

PAWS Plantations on Ancient Woodland Sites

RSPB   Royal Society for the Protection of Birds

SNH   Scottish Natural Heritage

SNP   Scottish National Party

SSSI   Site of Special Scientific Interest

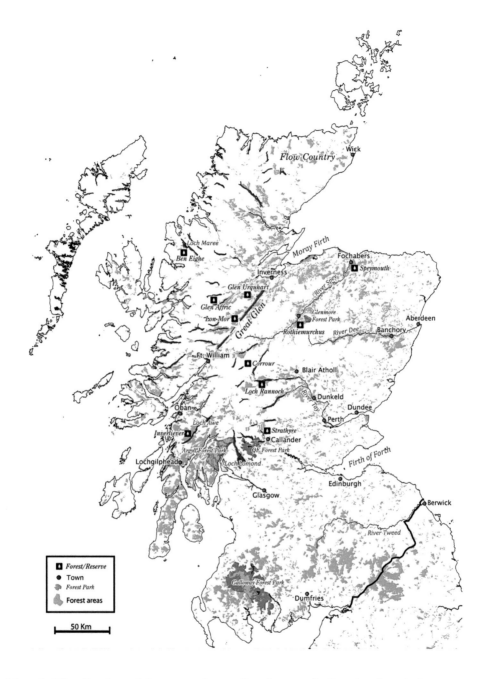

Map 1. Distribution of forest and woodland cover in Scotland and places mentioned in the text.

Source: Map by author. Forest distribution based on National Forest Inventory supplied by the Forestry Commission of Great Britain.

Preface

The moment that this book began can be clearly pinpointed. It was July 1992 and I was on a hiking holiday with a good friend in northern Scotland when we stumble upon Loch an Alltan Fheàrna in Sutherland. The water table had fallen dramatically because of the unusual dry weather, exposing part of the lakebed. These conditions revealed the remains of tree trunks and stumps normally concealed by the water of the loch. It was clear evidence that once a massive forest had flourished at this location where no trees can be found today. My curiosity was awakened and I wanted to find out what had happened to these lost Scottish forests.

A couple of years later I spent six months in the Department of History at the University of Hull in England as part of a student exchange programme. It was here that I discussed the problem of the lost Scottish forests with Professor Donald Woodward, who advised me to contact Professor Chris Smout in St. Andrews if I wished to study Scottish woodland history. I followed this advice up and contacted Professor Smout, who invited me over for a discussion of what I wanted to do. My initial idea was to make a study of the ancient forests of Scotland but Professor Smout suggested I look at the recent past and to make a study of the Forestry Commission. It was this suggestion that put me on the course that would ultimately result in this book.

Most of the research for this book was undertaken at the University of Stirling in Scotland as part of my PhD studies. Initially the idea was to focus on the conflicts between the Forestry Commission and environmentalists over the creation of monoculture forestry plantations. Conservationists believed that forestry plantations were devastating the landscape and the surviving native woodlands. During the initial research and learning more about the Scottish environment and the background of British forestry policy it became clear that environmental factors were crucial in explaining the nature of modern forestry plantations. In addition, while interviewing retired foresters, it became clear that many of them disliked the monoculture plantations. They were quick to point out that these plantations were the only type of forest that would survive on the land available for forestry. In fact, it seemed that many foresters were very ecologically minded and that the narrative of narrow-minded foresters who only wanted to create monoculture plantations was too simplistic. What emerged was a story of discussion, self-doubt, experimentation and adaptation within the forestry community that was worth telling. That story highlighted that the appearance of modern Scottish forest plantations is not so much the result of the foresters' lack of interest in nature conservation and landscape preservation but the social, economic and political pressures that underpinned their creation as well as the Scottish physical environment. Although others have studied the Forestry Commission in Scotland, I hope that this book will contribute to a better understanding of Scotland's forests by approaching the topic from a different perspective.

Many people have provided intellectual support for this project over the years and I would like to offer all of them my heartfelt thanks. I am particularly grateful to my mentors at the University of Stirling Fiona Watson and George Peden for their time, encouragement and critical comments that have shaped large parts of this book. I am also grateful to Chris Smout for his support and the many stimulating discussions we have had over the years. This book is very much inspired and shaped by these discussions and his work on Scottish forest history in general.

During my time at Stirling I was also fortunate to meet the late John Matthews[1], emeritus Professor of Forestry at the University of Aberdeen, who taught me how to look at forests and woodlands and their development from a forester's perspective. The meetings and field trips of the Native Woodland Discussion Group were equally inspiring and introduced me to the management problems of the native woodlands of Scotland. Equally important were the annual meetings of the Scottish Woodland History Discussion group that helped to place forests and forestry in an historical context that not only covered recent history but also the deep past.

I also would acknowledge with great pleasure the help provided by the following people: Michael Phillips and Graham Tuley for providing insights into Scottish forestry that cannot be found in books or archives and for a very pleasant and interesting afternoon on the Black Isle. Mrs. Diana Stewart of the APRS for sending me photocopies of early annual reports. The staff of the Forestry Commission Library at Alice Holt near Farnham for providing me with a full run of Forestry Commission annual reports between 1949 and 1980, John Dargavel of The Australian National University in Canberra for providing comments on Mark Anderson and forestry at the University of Edinburgh during the 1950s and for the many inspiring discussions we have had over the years. Michael Osborn for his kind permission to consult the archives of the Royal Scottish Forestry Society, and the staff of the Highland Council Archive who allowed me to consult the Novar Papers while in the process of being catalogued. Also, Hugh Insley, Andy Little and Douglas Clark for providing me with the names and addresses of retired foresters and officers of the Forestry Commission, and André Bontenbal for an unforgettable motorbike odyssey around Scotland that enabled me to interview some foresters in remote corners of the Highlands.

---

1   Professor John D. Matthews passed away on 25 May 2005.

I would also like to thank the following people who were kind enough to allow me to interview them, or who provided written or oral comments: Sandy Cram, the late John Davies, Jim Atterson, Fred T. Donald, Dick Jackson, Dr William Mutch and George D. Holmes, Roger Bradley, John Berry, Mr T.A. Robbie, David Danbury, Ian M. Carrioch, Professor Charles J. Taylor, Mr E.H.M. Harris, George Dey and Arthur Cuthbert. These interviews and comments were essential to get a better understanding of forestry in Scotland during the second half of the 20th century.

A number of colleagues have read and commented on drafts of the book or individual chapters, have discussed the issues with me, and corrected the text. I am particularly indebted to the following individuals: John Dargavel and two anonymous referees for reading and commenting on an earlier draft of this book. Richard Oram generously shared his knowledge of medieval and early modern texts related to forestry. Richard Tipping for commenting on the section that explores the deep history of the Scottish woodlands and for making sure that my use of technical terminology used in the first chapter is correct. James Beattie for reading and commenting on the introductory chapter, making sure that the book gets off on a good start and for correcting some other parts of the text. Cath Knight for bringing a fresh and critical outsider look to several chapters of the book. Jill Payne for the lightening fast reading and commenting on chapter four and ten and Gwenda Morgan for casting her eye over chapter three. Finally I would like to thank Erin Gill for finding some time in her busy schedule to critically read a draft chapter. As with any publication, the remaining faults of this book are entirely mine.

I also like to thank the Director and members of the Fenner School of Environment and Society of The Australian National University in Canberra for their hospitality, civility and intellectual stimulation when I was fortunate enough to have a Visiting Fellowship there in the first six months of 2011. This enabled me to rework and complete the manuscript of the book. It was at The Australian National University that Greg Barton and Brett Bennett suggested that I publish this book with ANU E Press as part of their World Forest History book series. I would like to thank them for the opportunity to publish this book and their encouragement and assistance. A special thank you to Alan Pymont who provided us with a home while in Canberra and for all the support that he has given us throughout the years.

Above all I want to thank my wife, Justine and the rest of my family who gave me loving encouragement and for their patience during the long process that it took to get this book finished. And last but not least I like to thank my father for his unconditional support over the years. It was his interest in history, science and technology that aroused my interest in the past and the world we live in. I hope that he will enjoy reading this book.

K. Jan Oosthoek
Brisbane
October 2012

Introduction

In July 1800 John Leyden (1775 - 1811), the well known Scottish linguist and poet, travelled trough Glen Croe in present day Argyll Forest Park, next to Loch Long, in the west of Scotland. In his travel journal he described the glen as 'the most desolate place under heaven', and he added: '[i]t is completely covered with stones of different descriptions, which leave no room for vegetation'.[1]

Figure 1: Glen Croe with forest plantations ca. 2005.

Source: Gerald England, www.geraldengland.co.uk with permission.

The attitude of John Leyden was typical throughout the 19th century: the uplands of Scotland were regarded as unproductive, apart from sheep grazing, and certainly not suitable for any serious forestry. In the intervening two centuries Glen Croe has become less desolate and devoid of vegetation and today large blocks of conifer plantations grow in the glen. This indicates an historical shift in attitudes towards the Scottish uplands as well as some technical and scientific developments that made afforestation of the Scottish uplands possible. By the early 20th century, the perception of forestry in the Highlands moved

---

1   John Leyden, *Journal of a Tour in the Highlands and Western Islands of Scotland in 1800* (Edinburgh and London: William Blackwood and Sons, 1903), p. 22.

in a direction in which forests, and the land on which these were planted, were perceived as spaces of production, through the introduction of conifers and the practice of 'scientific forestry'. By the second half of the 20th century, the Highlands of Scotland had become an ecotechnical environment, with the main aim to produce timber as efficiently as possible. Production forestry created a hybrid or composite landscape that at the same time is natural and man made.[2]

By the late 20th century the 'machine model' of forestry in Scotland was very much under pressure as a result of conflicts between forestry interests and conservationists. Consequently the remit of the Forestry Commission widened to formally include socio-cultural as well as environmental values, shifting Scottish forestry away from a machine model towards an organic model.[3] This transformation has drawn the attention of environmental historians and geographers and has led to a plethora of studies in the social cultural relations of wider society in relation to the work of the Forestry Commission and its past focussing on politics, aesthetics, cultural meaning, recreation and economic value.[4] However, more often than not it has been forgotten that forestry is not just a human story made out of the issues mentioned above, but also includes the environmental and ecological context in which forest policy and practice develops.

Similarly, foresters are often made out as technocrats who implemented forestry policy without much consideration for landscape and environment. It is often believed that during the 20th century foresters could not see the wood for the trees and regarded such values as nature conservation and landscape aesthetics or anything else that could undermine the smooth management of forest plantations as a threat to the efficient production of timber. Morton Boyd (1925 - 1998), a conservationist and former Scottish Director of the Nature Conservancy, expressed this perception about foresters eloquently:

> ...there is often an unwillingness [amongst foresters] to express [environmental values], since to do so, may smack of unprofessional practice or may put at risk the orthodoxy of tidy, economic forestry, trained into the forester from youth and consolidated by years of standard practice.[5]

---

2   Samuel Temple, 'Forestation and its Discontents: the Invention of an Uncertain Landscape in Southwestern France, 1850-Present', *Environment and History*, 17 (2011) 1, 13-34, p. 14.

3   J.M. Kennedy, M. Dombeck and N Koch, 'Values, Beliefs and Management of Public Forests in the Western World at the Close of the Twentieth Century', *Unasylva* 49 (1998) 192, 16-26.

4   These studies include: Donald Mackay, *Scotland's Rural Land Use Agencies. The History and Effectiveness in Scotland of the Forestry Commission, Nature Conservancy Council and Countryside Commission* (Aberdeen: Scottish Cultural Press, 1995); Judith Tsouvalis, *A Critical Geography of Britain's State Forests* (Oxford: Oxford University Press, 2000); David Foot, *Woods and People: Putting Forests on the Map* (Stroud: History Press, 2010). For discussion of the history and impact of the creation of forestry plantations of a particular locality see: Ruth Tittensor, *From Peat Bog to Conifer Forest: An Oral History of Whitelee, its Community and Landscape* (Chichester: Packard Publishing, 2009).

5   John Morton Boyd, 'Commercial Forests and Woods: the Nature Conservation Baseline', *Forestry*, 60 (1987) 1, 113-134, p. 131.

In reality the outlook of foresters from the early days of the Forestry Commission was much more nuanced than is suggested by Boyd. Many of them were interested in wildlife, landscape aesthetics and the natural functions of forests and many disliked the conifer monocultures they created. There was a realisation that the harsh environmental conditions of the Scottish Highlands made it difficult to initially do anything else than planting dense conifer forests and that this would be a necessary evil that was needed to create for a more diverse forest ecosystem some time in the future. These convictions and attitudes amongst many foresters within the Forestry Commission would prove vital in shifting from a machine model to an organic model of forestry in Scotland.

Purpose and focus of the book

The purpose of this book is to place 20th century Scottish forestry in its wider physical, ecological and historical context. British forestry history has in recent decades been dominated by the writings of Oliver Rackham in England and the work of Christopher Smout in Scotland.[6] Both authors have taken the long view and consequently twentieth-century forestry is often an afterthought. This book turns this view upside down and provides in the first two chapters an overview of the long history of the Scottish woodlands by summarising the work of these authors and others to provide a background for developments of the 20th century. The history of the native woodlands since the end of the last ice age is covered in more detail in: T.C. Smout, Alan R. MacDonald and Fiona Watson, *A History of the Native Woodlands of Scotland, 1500-1920*. This book does not place the 19th century developments in the wider context of the British Empire and, as the title suggests, focuses on the native woodlands and not the introduced species.

The 20th century work of the Forestry Commission has been the subject of other studies, in particular the work by David Foot and George Ryle,[7] which focus mainly on the institutional and social history of forestry. This book covers some of the same ground but from a different perspective. It tells the story of how 20th century foresters devised ways to plant the poor Scottish uplands, land that was regarded as unplantable, and to fulfil the mandate they had received from the Government and wider society to create a timber reserve, provide jobs in the highlands and to make marginal (waste) land productive. In addition

---

6   See: Oliver Rackham, *Trees and Woodland in the British Landscape: the Complete History of Britain's Trees, Woods and Hedgerows* (London: Phoenix Press, 2001); Smout, T.C., Alan R. MacDonald and Fiona Watson, *A History of the Native Woodlands of Scotland, 1500-1920* (Edinburgh: Edinburgh University Press, 2005); T.C. Smout, 'The Pinewoods and Human Use, 1600-1900', *Forestry*, 79 (2006) 3, 341-349.

7   George B. Ryle, *Forest Service. The First Forty-five Years of the Forestry Commission of Great Britain* (New Abbot: David and Charles, 1969); Foot, *Woods and People*.

the book will raise the question whether the adopted forestry practice was the only practical means to create forests in the Scottish Highlands by considering the discussions within the forestry community about the appearance of the forests and their long-term ecological prospects. Finally, the book will argue that the long held ecological convictions among foresters and modern ideas of environmentalists came together in the last decades of the 20th century in parallel with the still existing forces that called for an expansion of commercial forestry in Scotland.

Although the Forestry Commission is a United Kingdom wide body, the focus of this book is the work of Commission in Scotland. This geographically restrictive approach makes sense since more that half of all planting activity in the United Kingdom during the 20th century has taken place in the Scottish Highlands. From the inception of the Forestry Commission in 1919 it was believed that forestry would bring social benefits and be an engine of socio-economic development in rural upland areas: 'The districts which would benefit most are those which are now poorest and most backward, such as the hilly regions of northern England, Wales and Ireland, the Border Country and, most of all, the Highlands of Scotland'.[8] Furthermore, as the Forestry Commission began to acquire land, it could only afford to purchase cheap, marginal, upland areas that were dedicated mainly to grazing. In order to reduce the costs of forestry, the Commission also had to carry out land acquisition at a large-scale to reduce unit costs, and the only place where inexpensive large units of land was available was in the uplands. Because Scotland had the greatest extent of such marginal but plantable land available, 34 per cent of the land area of the United Kingdom (Table 1), it became the obvious focus of the afforestation effort.[9] This raised many technical difficulties because there was not much experience in the early 1920s with cultivating these lands for forestry on a large scale. As a result the Forestry Commission were concerned with problems arising from large-scale afforestation of upland peat and heath land during the inter-war period.[10] As a secondary consequence the Forestry Commission focused much of its early planting activities on the more fertile and easily accessible lands available in England and Wales and to a lesser extent in Scotland.

Percentage of plantable upland areas	
England	20%
Scotland	34%
Wales	28%

Table 1: Plantable areas in the UK's uplands.

Source: Tsouvalis.

---

8   *Final Report of the Forestry Sub-committee of the Reconstruction Committee* (Cmd. 8881) (London: HMSO, 1918), p. 27.

9   Judith, Tsouvalis, *A Critical Geography*, pp. 70-91.

10   H. M. Steven, 'The Forests and Forestry of Scotland', *Scottish Geographical Journal*, 67 (1951) 2, 110 -123, p. 118.

During the interwar period rates of land acquisition and afforestation in England and Wales was higher than in Scotland, peaking in the early 1950s, but soon began to decline (Figure 2). By that time the Commission was running out of land for acquisition in England and Wales because of its diminishing availablility. In the meantime the forestry Commission had developed and perfected techniques for mass cultivation of upland areas for forestry, which opened up the large land reserves for afforestation in Scotland. The result was that by the late 1970s afforestation and acquisition rates in England and Wales had plunged to less than 2000 hectares per year while from the 1960s through to the 1990s the overwhelming majority of the afforestation being done in Britain was taking place in Scotland.

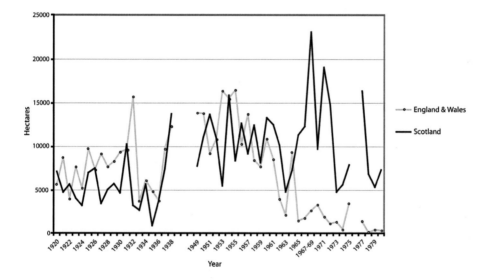

Figure 2: Acquisition of plantable land by the Forestry Commission in Scotland, England and Wales, 1920–1980.

Source: Forestry Commission Annual Reports.

Additional reasons for the focus on the Forestry Commission is the fact that it is the single largest landowner in Scotland and it acts as the Forest Authority, giving out advise and subsidies to private land owners by which it can influence the forestry industry. In many respects, the Forestry Commission is the spider in the web of the forestry industry, and defines its direction and development.[11] And because of the fact that the Forestry Commission is the largest landowner in the scenic parts of Scotland and in ecological sensitive areas it is also a major

---

11 Boyd, 'Commercial forests and woods', p. 115.

player in the nature conservation scene in Scotland. Furthermore, Scotland is both in terms of environment and landscape, as well as culturally, quite distinct from England and Wales. For this reason the wider UK aspects are discussed in this book where appropriate.[12]

This also applies to the international context of Scottish forestry and developments in the global forestry community and issues such as climate change will be discussed whenever relevant. In addition, Scottish foresters were part of and heavily influenced by the informal international network of foresters and the flow of forestry ideas within this network, that has existed since at least the early 19th century. Although some aspects of these forestry networks have been explored in the past they are far from all-encompassing and there are many overlapping stories that are not being told in these histories.[13] In order to tell these cross-border stories, it is necessary to produce national forest history that provides both hooks to wider international histories by embedding them in an international historical context and at the same time stress the unique properties of national forestry practice, policy and environmental conditions.

This is also important in order to produce internationally comparative histories based on common themes. In the case of the Scottish uplands such an overarching theme is the attempt to plant trees in locations not immediately conducive to afforestation, which could form the basis for comparative studies with locations around the globe where forestry has been developed in places hostile to tree growth. Examples of such studies are the work of David Moon on forestry on the Russian steppes and by Vimbai Kwasirai on afforestation attempts in the arid region of Matabeleland in Zimbabwe.[14] These studies could pave the way for international histories analyzing and comparing the reasons why, in quite different societies and in different social, economic, political and environmental contexts, people have tried to plant trees in locations that were not obviously conducive to afforestation. In addition such studies could analyse and compare the methods and tree species that were used, why these methods and species were adopted, and the success or otherwise of the attempts.

---

12   For the historical background of the Forestry Commission in England and in a UK-wide context see the following two publications: Sylvie Nail, *Forest Policies and Social Change in England* (Dordrecht: Springer Science, 2008); E.G. Richards, *British Forestry in the 20th Century: Policy and Achievements* (Leiden: Brill, 2003).

13   Examples of papers examining networks are: Peter Vandergeest and Nancy Lee Peluso, 'Empires of Forestry: Professional Forestry and State Power in Southeast Asia, Part 1', *Environment and History*, 12 (2006) 1, 31-64; Michael Roche, 'Colonial Forestry at its Limits: the Latter day Career of Sir David Hutchins in New Zealand 1915-1920', *Environment and History*, 16 (2010) 4, 431-454; James Beattie and Paul Star, 'Global Influences and Local Environments: Forestry and Forest Conservation in New Zealand, 1850s-1925', *British Scholar*, 3 (2010) 2, 191-218.

14   David Moon, 'The Environmental History of the Russian steppes : Vasilii Dokuchaev and the harvest failure of 1891', *Transactions of the Royal Historical Society*, 15 (2005), 49-174; Vimbai Kwashirai, *Green Colonialism in Zimbabwe, 1890-1980* (New York: Cambria Press, 2009).

Another area of comparison study is in the context of the British Empire, which the second chapter of this book provides in relation to British India. However, the context in which the Forestry Commission came into being is not unique and the experiences leading up to its creation were also felt in other parts of the Empire. From an early date, afforestation with exotic species was a distinctive response to forest scarcity not only in Scotland and the United Kingdom as a whole but also in New Zealand and Australia. In all three countries afforestation became a major preoccupation after the trade dislocation of the First World War and reinforced the need for timber self-sufficiency. The transformation of unproductive landscapes into plantations of fast-growing exotic softwood trees was largely the domain of the newly created State forest services created in response of the First World War.[15] So far no comparative studies exploring these similar developments and the dynamics within the forestry networks between the above-mentioned parts of the world have been attempted and this book could provide one of the building blocks for such a project.

Book structure

The structure of the book is largely chronological and focussed on the 20th century but the first two chapters deal with the long history of the Scottish forests preceding the implementation of forestry policy in Britain. Modern forests are the product of a very long history that, in the case of Northern Europe, stretches all the way back to the last ice age. In order to understand 20th century anxieties about low forest cover we must understand the natural and cultural dynamics that have led to such a situation and the response to any ecological changes that are caused by them. The chapter sets out with a description of the main physical factors that affects the extent and limits of tree growth in Scotland such as aspect and altitude, climate, and in particular wind exposure, as well as soil quality and the water balance. These environmental factors are important in understanding the difficulties that foresters faced in the 20th century when they had to afforest large upland areas that had not see a forest cover for at least hundreds of years. After a description of the physical environment, the chapter continues with a resume of the trends and events during the Holocene, until the 19th century. It discusses the development of the natural forests, the mix of native species and maximum extent and how over time it was decimated by a combination of human action and climate fluctuations. It will be pointed out that by the early modern period the forest cover of Scotland had stabilised at a very low level but was at the same time sustainably exploited by local users as well as the charcoal and tanning industries.

---

15 Brett J. Stubbs, Paul Star and Michael M. Roche, 'Editorial', *Environment and History*, 14 (2008) 4, 445-7, pp. 446-447.

The second chapter argues that two developments came together during the 19th century that led to increasingly vocal calls from landowners and foresters for the creation of national forestry policy in Scotland. The first development was the introduction of non-native conifers in Scotland and the planting experiments carried out by landowners all around Scotland. These experiments created a body of knowledge that formed the basis for the success of forestry plantations in the 20th century.

The second development was the influence on forestry in Scotland of empire forestry, and in particular the creation of an Indian forestry service. Scottish-trained foresters aided the adaptation of continental forestry models, mainly German and French, to the Indian conditions, drawing on their experience which they had gained in Scotland. Returning from their service in India they went on to advocate the creation of a forestry service in Scotland, which resonated with landowners who believed that forestry would make the Highlands more productive. The chapter ends with a discussion of a series of committees that advised the creation of a formal forestry policy and that laid down the main features on which Britain's forest policy would be based for most of the 20th century.

Chapter three is an overview of the development of forest policy in the interwar period, including the creation and role of the Forestry Commission, its influence on the shift in the composition and location of the Scottish plantations, the emergence of the widespread (and decried) Sitka spruce plantations, and the developments in ground preparation and forest management that accompanied these trends. The main argument of the chapter is that foresters were left with land that was hardly useful for large-scale forestry and how they devised methods to plant these areas successfully on a large scale.

Chapters five and six are an account of the post-war forest policy and the forces and considerations that shaped it, and how it adapted in the face of changing public attitudes, global strategic considerations, and UK micro- and macro-economic policy. It documents the shift toward multiple-use amenity forestry and open forests, as well as rising concern for wildlife and environmental considerations and the resulting internal conflicts. It shows the links between these developments and the development of large-scale afforestation in Scotland, with its contingent effects on the landscape, and on flora and fauna.

Chapter seven examines the interaction between culture and forestry with relation to Scotland. It addresses 19th and 20th century resistance to afforestation, its origins in the English Lake District, the clash between Wordsworthian romantic perceptions of nature and Scott's more utilitarian representation of a 'lived' landscape, in which afforestation is an improvement, albeit with native Scots pine. Scott foreshadows landscape forestry, while paradoxically influencing public attitudes sympathetic towards plantations. These attitudes meant that public resistance in Scotland was delayed and emerged only in the second half of the 20th century. The second half of the chapter addresses the feedbacks between public access to the forest estate, forestry policy, the involvement with the national parks movement, and the creation of a valuable public amenity asset in the setting aside of National Forest Parks. Finally the chapter discusses the formation of the Scottish conservation bodies in the interwar period, how these governed the direction of landscape forestry, and how their influence was moderated, or diluted, by the cross-over membership of elite groups, who had one foot in forestry, and another in conservation.

Chapter eight continues the story of the relationship between forestry, conservation bodies and the general public after the Second World War. It examines the institution of the Scottish Committee of the UK Nature Conservancy, and how the elites that served on it began to adopt policy positions in tension with the Forestry Commission, leading to a moderation of the Commission's planting programme in Scotland in the face of muted public concerns. But democratisation of conservation bodies as well as increased mobility from the 1970s onward accelerated the development of landscape forestry.

Chapter nine takes a step back in time and returns to the 1920s from where it sets out the evolution of 'ecological forestry' and amenity forestry in Scotland. It highlights the fact that many foresters and botanists disliked the geometric monoculture plantations from the early days of the forestry commission. The first part of the chapter focuses on the influential Scottish forester Mark Anderson and his ideas for a more natural treatment of the forests and a policy of sustainable forestry, as opposed to treating the forest as a crop. The second half of the chapter includes case studies that illustrate the uptake of these attitudes amongst Forestry Commission staff, and serves as a valuable history of such policy evolution driven by 'foresters on the ground' rather than from the top. It also highlights the discussion between proponents of ecological forestry and the more economical oriented foresters that accompanied it.

Chapter ten is a case history of the late 20th century evolution of forest policy toward formal sustainable forest management. It addresses multiple strands of policy development in the United Kingdom and Scotland and policy responses to domestic demands as well as international agreements, beginning with the United Nations Conference on Environment and Development (UNCED) Statement of Forest Principles. This agreement culminated in the UK Sustainable Forestry Programme and its expression in such instruments as the Forests and People in Rural Areas (FAPIRA) initiative, and the accompanying devolution to local community forestry, and the protection of native woodlands. This chapter also reveals the perverse consequences of policy instruments such as the system of tax concessions and grants of the 1980s, and how these outlived their relevance through opposition from conservationists in Scotland, and how it shocked forest policy to effect the shift to the broadleaf and sustainable forestry policies of the 1990s.

The final chapter is a brief contemporary history of the outcomes of 20th century forestry policy in Scotland interpretable against the background of the previous chapters. It accounts of the recent transfer of control of the publicly owned forests of Scotland to the Scottish Executive, and the subsequent evolution of a Scottish Forestry strategy. This involved the shift towards a broader, more inclusive multi-purpose forestry on the one hand and sustainable conservation on the other, dramatically reshaping Scottish forestry. Forestry in the 21st century is linked to the environment, preservation of biodiversity and above all climate change. The chapter illuminates that these developments depended on a younger generation of more conservation-minded foresters who had been educated during the 1980s and 1990s and who stood on the shoulders of previous generations of foresters who had advocated 'forestry on natural lines'.

1. The nature and development of the forests since the last ice age

Many tourists travelling through the Scottish landscape regard much of the treeless scenery as natural and do not expect to see extensive forests. The problem is that extensive forests grow at the same latitudes in North America and Scandinavia which suggests that the Scottish climate should be suitable for extensive tree growth. This chapter investigates the question why large parts of Scotland are not densely forested at present by putting this in the long historical context of the past 12,000 years. The first part of the chapter considers the physical environment of Scotland and how this impacts on the potential and distribution of tree growth. The second half of the chapter discusses the long history of forest decline caused by a combination of natural and human influences from the last glaciation up to the late 18th century. It looks at evidence for the abuse, use and careful management of the forests throughout the ages, which we need to understand the perceptions and practices that shaped Scottish forestry and forest policy during the 19th and the 20th century.

The physical environment

The main physical factors determining the suitability of an environment for tree growth are aspect and altitude, climate, in particular wind exposure, and soil quality and the water balance. Most of the high ground in the United Kingdom is found in Scotland, and to a lesser extent in northern England and Wales. The highest mountains are situated in the west of Scotland and on the Cairngorm plateau of the Central Highlands. The relief of Scottish Highlands north and west of the Higland line[1] tilts roughly from the north-west to the south-east, with the highest mountains in the north and west and rolling agricultural lands in the south and east. The Southern uplands of Scotland is an area characterised by a series of hills, many over 300 metres, with hills over 800 metres in the southwest, divided by broad valleys.

Scotland has a maritime or oceanic climate that is cool, with a low annual temperature range and high rainfall. This has a strong influence on the altitude at which trees will grow. The potential maximum altitudinal tree line in Scotland varies across the country and it is estimated that the tree line at it highest is somewhere between 620 and 650 metres in the Cairngorms. The tree line declines

---

1   The Highland line is the boundary between the highland and lowland Scotland and follows roughly the geological feature of the Highland Boundary Fault.

to about 520 metres in the northwest Highlands, 460 metres in the Western isles and is close to sea level in the most exposed areas of the northwest coast. In southwest Scotland the tree line is approximately at 460 metres but is estimated to reach 800 metres in parts of Southern Scotland. These are estimates of the upper limits of possible tree growth in Scotland but in practice most woodlands and plantations are found below 500 metres. Put in a global perspective, this in an anomalously low tree line and it is thought to be due to the harsh climate experienced in the Scottish uplands in combination with the growth of blanket peat and grazing pressures.[2]

In all regions of Scotland wind exposure is a limiting factor for both agriculture and forestry.[3] Because of the dominance of westerly winds the west coast is most vulnerable to strong winds but high slopes and mountain summits are also windy places. The orientation of valleys is another important factor with regard to wind exposure. Valleys with a west–east orientation are more vulnerable to wind exposure than valleys with a north–south orientation. It is therefore harder to predict which parts of the country are most vulnerable to wind exposure but we can make some generalisations. The west coast and the highest mountains are more vulnerable to high wind exposure that limits tree growth than the more sheltered eastern parts of the country, and inland areas are also less susceptible to strong winds than the coastal zone.[4]

Scotland's relief distribution is also reflected in the annual rainfall pattern with the highest annual means in the west, and declining towards the east (Map 1.1). This is caused by the fact that the mountains in the west catch much of the rain that comes with the prevailing westerly winds from the Atlantic.[5] It is no coincidence that the general soil distribution in Scotland roughly follows the relief and rainfall pattern (Maps 1.2 and 1.3). Four dominant soil types can be identified in Scotland: podzols, gleys, brown earth and peaty soils.

---

2 D.B.A. Thompson and Alan Brown, 'Biodiversity in Montane Britain: Habitat Variation, Vegetation Diversity and Some Objectives for Conservation', *Biodiversity and Conservation*, 1 (1992) 179-208, pp. 181-182; Richard Tipping, 'The Form and Fate of Scotland's Woodlands', *Proceedings of the Society of Antiquaries of Scotland*, 124 (1994), 1-54, pp. 13-14.
3 Wind exposure is not necessarily a limiting factor to natural woodland. Dwarfism is a successful adaptation to wind stress. An example of this is dwarf birch and willow growing in the Highlands.
4 A.S. Goudie and D. Brunsden, *The Environment of the British Isles. An Atlas* (Oxford: Oxford University Press, 1994), pp. 90-95; The Meteorological Office, *The Climate of Scotland. Some Facts and Figures* (London: HMSO, 1979), p. 20.
5 Goudie and Brunsden, *The Environment of the British Isles*, pp. 20, 60.

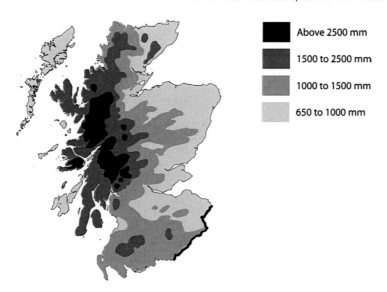

Above 2500 mm

1500 to 2500 mm

1000 to 1500 mm

650 to 1000 mm

Map 1.1: Average annual rainfall in Scotland.

Source: Meteorological Office, Climatological Atlas of the British Isles (London: HMSO, 1952), p. 72.

Podzols are usually associated with the wetter types of heath and with moorland vegetation. They are characteristic of any location where aerobic conditions prevail and water can percolate freely through the upper part of the soil profile. Because of the high rainfall and low evaporation levels in these areas, iron, aluminium and other minerals are washed down from the topsoil into the deeper soil layers, where the minerals precipitate to form clearly visible and very hard iron 'pan' which in turn prevents proper drainage. This is the so called iron-humus podzol, but the typical podzol found in more elevated and wetter locations is the iron podzol, in which the layer of organic material thickens until true peat forms, creating peaty podzols. Peaty podzols are widespread throughout the Highlands and Southern Uplands and found at all elevations from sea level to the summit of the Cairngorms. Under natural circumstances this soil is not of much value to forestry due to poor drainage and the iron pan that prevents root systems from developing properly. Podzols are generally of low fertility and are physically limiting soils for productive use.[6]

---

6   J. W. L. Zehetmayr, 'Afforestation of Upland Heaths', *Forestry Commission Bulletin*, 32 (London: HMSO, 1960), pp.1-2; The Macaulay Land Use Research Institute, *Exploring Scotland: Podzols*, www.macaulay.ac.uk/explorescotland/podzols.html Accessed: 21 February 2011.

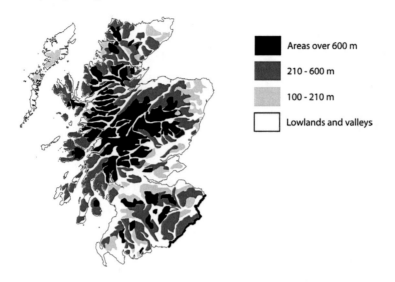

Map 1.2: Relief distribution in Scotland.

Source: A.S. Goudie and D. Brunsden, *The Environment of the British Isles. An Atlas* (Oxford: OUP, 1994), p. 21, with permission from the authors.

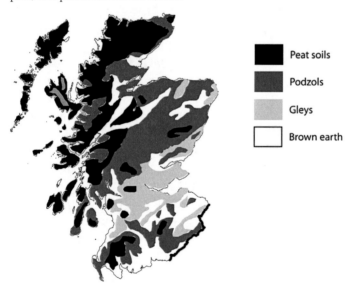

Map 1.3: Generalised soil types of Scotland.

Source: Goudie and Brunsden, *The Environment of the British Isles*, p. 149, with permission from the authors.

Gleys are widespread throughout the east coast, the Central Belt and the Scottish Borders and are found at all elevations. Gley soils develop under conditions of intermittent or permanent waterlogging. They result from the absence or very low levels of oxygen when iron compounds are changed chemically from their normal red and brown colours, to grey or green. Gleys are often confined to low lying sites or in depressions with poor drainage or where the soil is dense and water is prevented from moving through it. Under natural conditions gley soils support hygrophilous plant species and when cultivated they are used for rough grazing and forestry.[7]

The brown forest soils[8] are amongst the most fertile soils to be found in Scotland and used extensively for agriculture. Under natural conditions brown forest soils were formed on permeable parent materials under broadleaf forest conditions which promote the rapid decomposition of plant material and consequent recycling of plant nutrients. Brown forest soils are mainly restricted to the warmer, drier climate of eastern areas around Aberdeen, in Fife and the Lothians and parts of southwest Scotland.[9]

The soils of the Western and Northern Isles, the northern and central Highlands and elevated areas of southwest Scotland are influenced to a large extent by a moist and cool climate. The low temperatures and waterlogged conditions cause organic material to decompose slowly so that it accumulates in layers up to several metres thick to form peat. Many upland and low waterlogged areas of the West Highlands and northern Scotland are covered with blanket peat, which under semi-natural conditions provides grazing of low quality but has no other modern agricultural value, including forestry.[10] In the central Highlands and Southwest Scotland the same conditions exist on some elevated slopes and high plateaus.[11]

Historically the formation of blanket peat is regarded as one of the most important landscape transformations during the Holocene in Scotland.[12] Peat layers all over the Highlands contain the remains of tree trunks and stumps that testify

---

7   Alex Muir, 'Some Forest Soils of the North-east of Scotland and their Chemical Characters', *Forestry* 14 (1940) 2, 71-80, pp. 73-74; The Macaulay Land Use Research Institute, *Exploring Scotland: Gleys*, www. macaulay.ac.uk/explorescotland/gleys.html Accessed: 21 February 2011.
8   Brown earth is called brown forest soil in Scotland.
9   Andrew Taylor, et.al., *Soils, Scotland's Living Heritage* (Edinburgh: SNH, 1996), pp. 9, 16; The Macaulay Land Use Research Institute, *Exploring Scotland: Brown Earths*, www.macaulay.ac.uk/explorescotland/ brownearths.html Accessed: 21 February 2011
10   Until the 18th century the peatland supported a diverse economy, based on exploitation of the plant and scrub species that will grow there, and for the wildlife (birds' eggs, wildfowling etc).
11   John Whittow, *Dictionary of Physical Geography* (London: Penguin, 1984), pp. 389-390; The Macaulay Land Use Research Institute, *Exploring Scotland: Podzols*, www.macaulay.ac.uk/explorescotland/organic_ soils.html Accessed: 21 February 2010.
12   The Holocene is the present geological epoch that started at the end of the last ice age 10,000 years ago and that continues to the present day.

to this transformation. These tree remains indicate that large parts of Scotland were once covered with forests where there are no forests today. Until recently it was thought that the remains of these trees were the victim of invaders like the Romans, Vikings and later the English who felled these forests for timber, charcoal or for military reasons. It gave rise to the ideas that Scotland was once entirely covered with a pine and oak dominated Great Wood of Caledon that fell victim to invaders and that the forests were ruthlessly exploited for timber, charcoal production or burnt and cut down for military reasons.[13] But pollen analysis and carbon dating has shown that the remains of trees found in the peat were not felled in historical times but are over 4000 years old.[14] These trees, mainly Scots pine (*Pinus sylvestris*), were the victims of one of the most dramatic climatic and environmental changes that Scotland experienced since the last ice age, as will be explored in the next section.

Figure 1.1: Four-thousand-year-old tree remains at Loch an Alltan Fheàrna, Sutherland, northern Scotland.

Photo: Chris Zierleyn.

---

13   For a detailed discussion of the Great Wood of Caledon see T.C. Smout, Alan R. MacDonald and Fiona Watson, *A History of the Native Woodlands of Scotland, 1500-1920* (Edinburgh: University Press, 2005), Ch. 2, pp. 20-25.
14   J.H. Dickson, 'Scottish Woodlands: Their Ancient Past and Precarious Future', *Scottish Forestry*, 47 (1993) 3, 73-78.

Development and distribution of vegetation

The history of Scotland's modern forests began when the final phase of the last ice age, the so-called Loch Lomond Stadial, came to an abrupt end about 11,400 years ago (9400 BC).[15] By the end of the last ice age most of Britain was a tundra landscape, an almost treeless vegetation type characteristic of the Arctic region. This landscape looked very much like that found in present day Lapland, Alaska and northern Siberia, with many herbs, low shrubs such as willow, dwarf birch and juniper. Over the course of just a few decades the climate warmed to temperatures probably greater than today, making Scotland suitable for the growth of forests of trees.[16] When the temperature rose, trees such as hazel, birch, willow, pine and aspen relatively quickly replaced the tundra vegetation. Once established, the newly formed woodlands changed rapidly in appearance when the hardy pioneering species were joined by late succession species, migrating more slowly, lagging behind the climate change. These trees spread from the European continent, which was still joined to the British Isles by a land bridge, and through southern England. The process was gradual and deciduous trees such as oak, elm and alder arrived in Scotland only between 8,500 and 8,000 years ago (6500 and 6000 BC). Scots pine, the only conifer species that established itself in Britain after the last ice age, first appeared, surprisingly, in the northwest of Scotland around 9,000 years ago (7000 BC). It probably came from isolated populations in a now drowned ice-free area to the west of mainland Scotland. From there it spread across the Highlands as far South as the northern tip of Loch Lomond and Rannoch Moor. The pinewoods of South-west Scotland probably originated from populations invading from Ireland.[17]

The Scottish forests reached their fullest extent around 6,000 years ago (4000 BC) during the so-called Mid-Holocene Climate Optimum. Four broad woodland categories can be distinguished, which roughly follow the spatial distribution of modern natural woodland types. A mix of birch and hazel shrubs dominated the Outer Hebrides, the Northern Isles and Caithness and Sutherland. Woodlands in the Highlands were predominantly made up of pine and birch while the coastal areas of the west and east were mainly composed of a broadleaf mix of birch, hazel and oak. The southern part of Scotland was mainly composed of oak, hazel and elm dominated woodlands that covered all of the lowlands and much of the uplands.[18]

---

15   Throughout this chapter we use the Before Christ (BC) dating convention used by many historians. This does not refer to radiocarbon years but to calibrated calendar years.

16   J.J. Lowe, 'Setting the Scene: An Overview of Climatic Change', in: T.C. Smout, *Scotland Since Prehistory. Natural Change & Human Impact* (Aberdeen: Scottish Cultural Press, 1993), p. 7.

17   Smout *et al.*, *The Native Woodlands*, pp. 25-26; J.H. Dickson, 'Scottish Woodlands', p. 73.

18   Richard Tipping, 'Form and Fate', pp. 11-12.

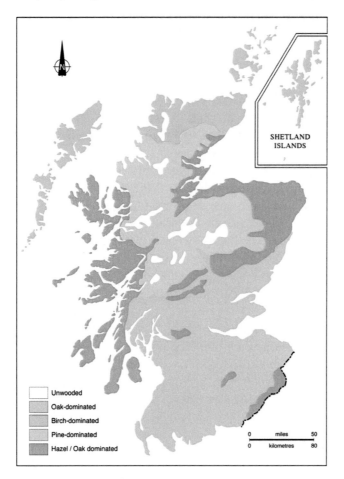

SHETLAND
ISLANDS

Unwooded
Oak-dominated
Birch-dominated
Pine-dominated
Hazel / Oak dominated

0	miles	50
0	kilometres	80

Map 1.4: The major woodland regions in Scotland ca. 6,000 years ago.

Source: Modified from R. Tipping, 'The form and fate of Scotland's woodlands', *Proceedings of the Society of Antiquaries of Scotland,* 124 (1994), 1-54. With kind permission from the Society of Antiquaries of Scotland/Richard Tipping.

This characterisation of the type of woodland and its spatial distribution was not as uniform as the descriptions suggests. The composition of forests is never uniform, and is made up of a varying mix of species and undergrowth and changes constantly over time due to climate variations and the fact that plant communities are dynamic. Huge variations also exist over short distances due to variations in topography, microclimate and soil quality. Nor should we think of these ancient forests as a closed canopy of trees covering Scotland from north to south and east to west. The precise extent of the woodland cover is difficult to estimate but an educated guess based on palynological investigations suggest that at least 60 per cent of the Scottish land mass was under some form of forest vegetation.[19]

---

19   Smout *et al.,The Native Woodlands,* pp. 26-27; Alexander Mather, 'Forest Transition Theory and the Reforesting of Scotland', *Scottish Geographical Journal,* 120 (2004) 1, 83-98, p. 83.

Cultural period	Year/period	Event
	9400 BC	End of last ice age
Mesolithic 8000–4000 BC	8000–4000 BC	Humans become active agents in the Scottish environment using crude land management techniques such as fire.
	7000 BC	Scots Pine established.
	6500–6000 BC	Arrival of deciduous trees such as oak, elm and alder.
Neolithic 4000–2500 BC	4000 BC	Woodland clearance for agriculture starting in the Western Isles and North of Scotland.
	4000–3000 BC	Mid-Holocene Climate Optimum: Fullest extent of Scotland's natural forests.
	2800 BC	Onset of woodland clearance for agriculture in southern half of Scotland.
	3000–2400 BC	Climate cooling and collapse pine forests.
Bronze Age 2500–700 BC	ca. 2200 BC	Woodland clearings become larger and more permanent.
Iron Age 700 BC–400 AD		Intensification of agricultural activity and further woodland clearing.
	Romans 80–400 AD	Arrival of Romans in Scotland. About half of the original woodland vegetation had been cleared. Scotland under 25% wood cover.

Table 1.1: Major events in the history of Scotland's woodlands during prehistory.

Source: Author's research.

The maximum extent was possibly reached during a warmer and drier period between 5,200 and 5,000 years ago (3200–3000 BC) when Scots pine advanced from its heartland and colonised the then dryer peat bogs in the north and west. Between 3000 and 2400 BC the climate turned wetter and cooler and in response the water table started to rise, drowning the root systems of the pines. As a result populations of pine trees collapsed all across Scotland, leaving large parts of country without big trees.[20] This was a climate-induced deforestation that happened just at the same time that agriculture began in Scotland. Some have suggested that the coming of agriculture, animal grazing in particular, contributed to the formation of blanket peat and the demise of the pine forests. This view is now much in doubt and it is thought that when early farming communities settled in the uplands from the later Neolithic period (app. 2000-3000 BC) many parts of the uplands were already buried under a blanket of peat in much the same way that they appear today.[21]

---

20   A.K. Moir et.al., 'Dendrochronological Evidence for a Lower Water-table on Peatland Around 3200–3000 BC From Subfossil Pine in Northern Scotland', *The Holocene*, 20 (2010) 6, 931–942; Smout *et al.*, *The Native Woodlands*, p. 29.
21   Richard Tipping, 'Blanket Peat in the Scottish Highlands: Timing, Cause, Spread and the Myth of Environmental Determinism', *Biodiversity and Conservation*, 17 (2008) 9, 2097-2113.

Prehistoric deforestation

Together with the forests and the varied animal species associated with it was another arrival that was to have a lasting impact on Scotland's forests: *Homo sapiens*. When human settlers moved into Scotland after the last glaciation they arrived in a birch-hazel woodland environment that was in many places gradually replaced with a more diverse and richer forest environment. The glaciers left behind a landscape of lochs and rivers, of hill-land, glen and mountain in which a diverse and mixed vegetation developed. This created rich resources and increased opportunities for humans to exploit them, including hunting, food gathering, and utilisation of stone and wood for tools and to build shelter. During this period of post-glacial settlement, called the Mesolithic (Middle Stone Age, 8000 - 4400 BC), humans became significant active agents in the environment, initiating processes of environmental change. Activities such as hunting, fishing and the first attempts to control watercourses and wild life disturbed the balance of vegetation. Based on his work in the North York Moors, geographer Ian Simmons has suggested that Mesolithic peoples altered their landscape through fire. This was a distinctive technique that marked them out from their predecessors and by doing so they created a more predictable environment for themselves.[22]

Burning grasses, heather and other vegetation rejuvenated environments over a period of 5-6 years, attracting game, especially if open areas were maintained near water sources. Fire also promotes the spread of under storey plants with edible fruits or berries. Even today, gorse, heather and the stubble of arable fields are burned as a means of land management in Scotland. However, it is taught that regular burning is a also a contributory factor in the creation of degraded upland environments with impoverished vegetation diversity, decreased forest cover and propensity to water-logging. In short, Mesolithic hunter-gatherers were very likely capable of altering and manipulating entire ecosystems. It was, however, a gradual process of a clearing here and burning there, but the repeated nature of these activities and a rising population resulted in a patchwork of open spaces and forest some 4,000-6,000 years ago (2000-4000 BC). This mosaic landscape is something that Simmons views as 'the most important environmental legacy of the British Mesolithic peoples'.[23]

In Scotland there is not much evidence that this kind of land management was practiced. However, it is not inconceivable that Mesolithic peoples used fire

---

22   James Innes, Jeffrey Blackford and Ian Simmons, 'Woodland Disturbance and Possible Land-use Regimes During the Late Mesolithic in the English Uplands: Pollen, Charcoal and Non-pollen Palynomorph Evidence from Bluewath Beck, North York Moors, UK', *Vegetation History and Archaeobotany*, 19 (2010) 5-6, 439-452.
23   I.G. Simmons, *An environmental History of Great Britain from 10,000 Years Ago to the Present* (Edinburgh: Edinburgh University Press, 2000), pp. 43, 45.

to manipulate their environments, in particular in the Southern Uplands of Scotland, which is in many ways very similar to environments found in the north of England. But it must be kept in mind that distinguishing between natural and human agency in vegetation changes is difficult. It has been suggested that hunter-gatherer penetration of Scotland's inland and upland areas away from the major river valleys is likely to have been too ephemeral to have caused detectable changes to the vegetation cover during the Mesolithic period.[24]

With the dawn of the Neolithic period (c.4000 BC), which signals the arrival of agriculture, evidence of forest clearance becomes more widespread and less ambiguous. Woodland clearance in the west and on the Western Isles started early in the Neolithic between 6,000 and 4,200 years ago (4000 BC and 2200 BC), depending on the location. On the Isle of Arran forest clearance started around 2600 BC and parts of the Isle of Skye were treeless by about 600 BC. The Orkney Isles off the north coast of Scotland were entirely cleared by 3,000 years ago and the woodlands never recovered.[25]

The west and north of Scotland seems to have been affected by woodland decline earlier than the more southern and eastern parts of Scotland. That was probably due to the fact that there was less forest vegetation to start with due to climate constraints. We must also keep in mind that this part of the country is very sensitive to climate fluctuations and that woodland clearance is almost certainly the result of an interaction of human and natural processes.

In the eastern Highlands Tipping has suggested that 'low-intensity grazing pressures sustained over long periods of time' effectively led to a serious decline of the woodlands long before the Romans arrived.[26] In the southern half of Scotland the onset of clearance for agriculture started sometime around 4,800 years ago (2800 BC) when semi-permanent areas for pasture and crops were established. These clearings appear to have been small and were maintained for a few decades or perhaps a century. Later, in the early Bronze Age, around 4,200 years ago (2200 BC), clearings became more permanent and persisted for hundreds of years. The Iron Age saw an intensification of agricultural activity from about 500 BC in the Southern uplands. This intensification coincided with a period of increased woodland clearance in other regions of Scotland.[27]

---

24   Kevin J. Edwards and Ian Ralston, 'Postglacial Hunter-gatherer Sand Vegetational History in Scotland', *Proceedings of the Society of Antiquaries of Scotland*, 114 (1984), 15-35.
25   Tipping, *Form and Fate*, p. 24.
26   Ibid., p. 30.
27   Smout *et al.*, *The Native Woodlands*, pp. 30-31; Tipping, *Form and Fate*, p. 33.

Historical period	Year	Event
Middle Ages 400 AD–1500	1000 AD	Woodland cover fallen to 20% of Scottish land area.
	13th century	Shortage of wood for construction in Perth due to exhaustion of woodlands in vicinity of the city. Building and firewood is increasingly sourced from remote Highland locations.
	14th century	Building wood is increasingly imported from overseas.
Early modern period 1500–1750	1503	Scottish Parliament passes two acts attempting to halting deforestation and encouraging reforestation.
	1611	Beginning of commercial exploitation of the oakwoods of western Scotland for charcoal to fuel the iron works at Loch Maree.
Modern period 1750–	Early 1800s	Charcoal production from coppiced oakwoods declined while the demand for tanbark increased rapidly.
		Exploitation of native pinewoods increases due to high timber prices and demand.
	ca. 1850	Timber prices collapse. In response Scottish landowners abandon forestry and turned to sport (hunting) and sheep farming as the main sources of income from their estates.
	1876	The last iron furnace at Bonawe closes putting an end to commercial charcoal production in Scotland.
	ca. 1900	Commercial exploitation of the coppice oakwoods of Western Scotland had all but ceased due to collapse tanbark market.
	1900	Woodland cover at a historic low of 6% of the Scottish land mass.

Table 1.2: Major events in the history of Scotland's woodlands during the historic period.

Source: Author's research.

By the time the Romans entered what is now Scotland in 80 AD, it is estimated that about half of the original woodland vegetation had been cleared. This means that about 25 per cent of the land was under some form of woodland cover, but there were large geographical differences.[28] The Highlands were much more wooded than the Lowlands, the Western and Northern Isles and the Southern uplands. The furthest extent of the Roman occupation closely followed the Highland Boundary Fault and included much of the arable district in southern and central Scotland that is classified today as first class agricultural land.[29] Here the Romans entered a largely cleared agricultural landscape while

---

28 Smout *et al.*, *The Native Woodlands*, p. 32
29 The Macaulay Land Use Research Institute, *Exploring Scotland: Land Capability for Agriculture*, www.macaulay.ac.uk/explorescotland/lca-arable.html Accessed: 22 February 2011.

the Highlands were much more wooded than they are at present. The latter was not of much interest to the Romans because it did not produce the grain that they needed in order to feed the troops. Over all the direct occupation of the southern part of Scotland by the Romans did not last more than 40 years, spread out over three periods between the first and third centuries AD. But the empire successfully dominated the country beyond the fixed frontiers for most of this time, employing raids, bribery and the establishment of client states. The extent of the indirect Roman pressures on the woodlands is unknown but it is very likely that they bought wood from the beyond the established borders from areas under their influence.

The direct impact of Roman presence on the woodlands appears to have been limited to the close vicinity of their forts and other military installations, which required large quantities of wood.[30] For example, it is thought that the legionary fortress at Inchtuthil near Dunkeld required over 100 hectares of wood for its walling and other structures. Regrowth would have readily occurred after the Romans had left, provided that grazing pressures were low.[31]

The Medieval period to the 19th century

By the early Middle Ages there are indications that the amount of woodland on the east coast in Fife and further north in Aberdeenshire increased. It has been suggested that these localised increases are related to the Roman invasion and that local populations were either wiped out or compelled to abandon the area. However, in other parts of the country, for example in the Borders and the western Cheviots there are indications that from the early 5th century grassland increased in a partly wooded landscape, and has persisted ever since due to grazing pressures.[32]

By the end of the first millennium most wildwood had gone, except from the remoter parts of the Highlands. Forest cover had shrunk to perhaps as low as 20 per cent of the Scottish land surface. With the shrinking forests, habitats of many animals came under pressure and large mammals such as aurochs, beaver, boar or red deer were disappearing fast. Most remaining woodlands were small and probably intensively managed as coppice. Archaeological evidence suggests

30   William S. Hanson, 'The Roman Presence: Brief Interludes', in: Kevin J. Edwards & Ian B. M. Ralston, *Scotland: Environment and Archaeology, 8000 BC − AD 1000* (Chichester: John Wiley & Son, 1997), pp. 198, 201-202; William S. Hanson, 'Scotland and the Northern frontier: second to fourth cenuries AD', in: Malcolm Todd (ed.), *A Companion to Roman Britain* (Oxford: Blackwell Publishing, 2004), 136-161, p. 144.
31   Smout *et al.*, *The Native Woodlands*, p. 32.
32   Ibid., pp. 34-35.

that most rural houses and barns as well as town houses were constructed of turf, wattle, and thatch using wooden frames obtained from readily accessible coppice woods.[33]

On the other hand more prestigious buildings such as churches, castles and the houses of richer merchants in towns contained large oak and pine timbers. During the 12th century many nascent towns were granted burgh status and this was followed by a flurry of building activity that may have resulted from the prosperity that their new status brought. In many of these new buildings the burgesses used locally sourced oak from mature woodlands which suggests that there was not yet a severe timber shortage in Scotland at that time. However, this is deceptive because timber for such high status sites was often sourced from protected reserves to which the owners had access, either through ownership or royal grants.[34] These wood resources were limited and not accessible to most of the population and as a result major problems of supply already existed before 1200. Excavated evidence from Perth shows a gradual increase in the use of scrub and hedgerow species in domestic buildings during the 13th century,. This trend suggests that local sources of structural timber were increasingly exhausted due to overexploitation.[35] In response to these timber shortages the import of fuel-wood and building timber from outside the burgh's hinterland was encouraged by special protections granted by King William I (1165-1214) in 1205 to anyone bringing 'ligna vel materiem' (wood and timber) to Perth and that prohibited anyone to trouble people bringing those commodities to the burgh.[36]

Further evidence of a lack of wood in eastern Scotland is fact that wood was being moved over long distances. In 1178 King William failed to grant Arbroath Abbey any nearby woodland but granted instead Trustach Wood which is nearly 55 kilometres away near Banchory on Deeside as its closest source of building-timber.[37] The same story was repeated when Earl David, brother of King William, founded Lindores Abbey in 1195, and no local timber resources were granted. Instead the monks received grants for access to building-timber and firewood 30 kilometres to the west in Strathearn. In addition they were granted the right to collect 'dry' or 'dead' wood for fuel and broom, a hundred loads of hazel rods for making sleds, and one hundred long alder rods for

33 K.J. Kirby, R.C. Thomas, R.S. Key, I.F.G. McLean and N. Hodgetts, 'Pasture-woodland and its Conservation in Britain', *Biological Journal of the Linnean Society*, 56 (1995) 1 (Suppl), 135-153, p. 138.

34 Anne Crone and Coralie M. Mills, 'Seeing the Wood and the Trees: Dendrochronological Studies in Scotland', *Antiquity*, 76 (2002) 293, 788-794, p. 791.

35 A. Crone, and F. Watson, 'Sufficiency to Scarcity: Medieval Scotland, 500-1600', in: T.C. Smout, (ed.), *People and Woods in Scotland* (Edinburgh: Edinburgh University Press, 2003), 60-81, pp. 66-67.

36 G.W.S. Barrow (ed.), *Regesta Regum Scotorum, ii, The Acts of William I, 1165-1214* (Edinburgh: Edinburgh University Press, 1971), no. 467.

37 Cosmo Innes and Patrick Chalmers (eds.), *Liber S. Thome De Aberbrothoc; Registrorum Abbacie De Aberbrothoc* (Edinburgh: Bannatyne Club, 1848), nos. 65, 66, pp. 43-44.

making hoops, in the woods of 'Tulyhen' in Glen Garry in northern Atholl, 70 kilometres north-west of the abbey.[38] In the 1450s, Perth was able to get some wood for constructing carts from Birnam Wood 25 kilometres to the north on the bishop of Dunkeld's land, but by 1500 the bishop himself had no good timber source closer to Dunkeld than the Black Wood of Rannoch almost 50 kilometres away in the central Highlands.[39]

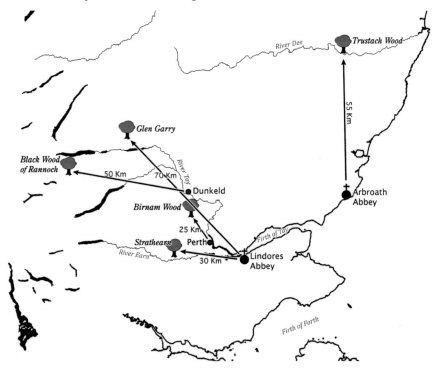

Map 1.5: Distances to wood resources of monasteries and towns in eastern Scotland during the Middle Ages (distances in kilometres).

Source: Author's research.

In the west of Scotland there is also evidence of the availability of wood resources throughout this period in contrast to eastern and central parts of Scotland. It is known that there was sufficient supply of timber for the construction of Highland galleys for the local chiefs and in particular the Lords of the Isles. The maintenance of the fleet on which their power was based presupposes the availability of mature local woodland resources.[40]

---

38   J. Dowden, (ed.), *The Chartulary of the Abbey of Lindores 1195-1479* (Edinburgh: Scottish History Society, 1903), XXIV, pp. 27-28; LXXIII, p. 79; CXI & CXII, pp. 133-137.
39   R.K.Hannay (ed.), *Rentale Dunkeldense* (Edinburgh: Scottish History Society, 1915), pp. 122, 129, 130, 139, 266.
40   Smout *et al.*, *The Native Woodlands*, pp. 41-42.

Despite the existence of these significant areas of oak and pine woodlands in the Highlands and the west, these were beyond the effective reach of most consumers in the lowlands, who became increasingly dependent on imports of foreign timber. Over much of the Lowlands large timber became an increasingly scarce resource during the course of the 14th and 15th centuries. Few buildings constructed after about 1450 contain oak identifiable as native and increasingly timber beams for the construction of churches and other large buildings were imported. From at least the 1330s Scottish burghs on the East Coast were increasingly obtaining their timber from the Baltic and so-called Estland Boards were being imported from Poland-Lithuania into Berwick and Dundee.[41]

The shortage of large construction timber affected royal construction projects most, such as the castle and palace at Stirling, where timber needs were met through imports. Ordinary people were much less affected by the lack of large timber because their needs were met with the products of the native woods which were managed through the sustainable practices of coppicing and pollarding. The local farmer and cottar only needed small wood for construction, tool making and fuel. The use of the woodlands for wood pasture, providing shelter and grazing for domestic stock was also extremely widespread. In some sense there was not a general shortage of wood, but just a lack of locally produced large straight timbers necessary for major construction projects or shipbuilding.[42] It is therefore not surprising that various attempts were made by the crown to improve timber production in Scotland by protecting the forests. For example, in 1503 the Scottish parliament exclaimed that 'the woods of Scotland are utterly destroyed'[43] and passed two Acts to deal with the problem. Felling and burning were outlawed and in the second Act landowners were instructed to plant at least one acre (0.4 hectares) 'where there are no large woods or forests'.[44] The twin measures of halting deforestation and encouraging reforestation were repeated in legislation in the next two centuries reflecting concern and problems familiar across Europe. In Scotland, as elsewhere, monarchs and their agents were nervous about being unable to get their hands on the timber supplies needed to build castles and forts and maintain navies, which were seen as essential for the national economy and security. Further measures followed at intervals, but none was successful in reversing the long history of forest contraction. The

41   John Stuart and George Burnett (eds.), *The Exchequer Rolls of Scotland (Rotuli scaccarii regum scotorum)*, Vol. 1, 1264-1359 (Edinburgh: H.M. Register House, 1878), p. 411; George Burnett (ed.), *The Exchequer Rolls of Scotland (Rotuli scaccarii regum scotorum)*, Vol. 7, 1460-1469 (Edinburgh: H.M. Register House, 1884), pp. 288, 370, 404.

42   T.C. Smout, 'The Pinewoods and Human Use, 1600-1900', *Forestry*, 79 (2006) 3, 341-349, p. 343; Smout *et al., The Native Woodlands*, p. 45.

43   *The Records of the Parliaments of Scotland to 1707*, K.M. Brown et al., eds. (St Andrews, 2007-2011) (hereafter RPS), 1504/3/33. Date accessed: 16 February 2011. www.rps.ac.uk/trans/1504/3/33

44   RPS, 1504/3/39. Date accessed: 16 February 2011. www.rps.ac.uk/trans/1504/3/39

problem lay in enforcement and in translating the aspiration of forest protection into action on the ground because local interests in traditional forest use made the enforcement of forest laws by local lairds almost impossible.[45]

The commercial exploitation of native woodlands

During the 17th and 18th centuries there was an intensification of exploitation of the native woodlands. This section will briefly discuss the management and exploitation of the oakwoods for charcoal production and leather tanning and the management of the native pinewoods. The chapter concludes with an assessment of the extent of the woodlands and forests in Scotland by the end of the 19th century.

The commercial exploitation of the oakwoods of western Scotland started in the early 17th century and was fuelled by an influx of external capital from the Lowlands, England and Ireland. In 1611, Sir George Hay from Perthshire, in partnership with capitalists from the Sussex Weald, were granted the right to construct iron works at Loch Maree, exploiting the local woods as a source of charcoal. This operation was short-lived and ceased in 1630 due to exhaustion of the local wood resources.[46]

---

45   Mather, 'Forest Transition Theory', p. 84.
46   T.C. Smout, 'Oak as a Commercial Crop in the Eighteenth and Nineteenth Centuries', *Botanical Journal of Scotland*, 57 (2005) 1, 107-114, p. 108.

Figure 1.2: The Lorn Furnace at Bonawe on the banks of Loch Etive.

Photo: Nigel Homer, www.geograph.org.uk with permission.

It took over a century before the oakwoods again attracted industrial scale iron making when a sophisticated blast furnace and forge was established at Glen Kinglass in 1725. This furnace operated only for a dozen years before it was closed down due to the commercial incompetence of its operators. This was a taste of things to come and in 1753 Richard Ford and Company of Furness in Lancashire opened the Lorn furnace at Bonawe on Loch Etive. A couple of years later in 1755 Craleckan furnace on Loch Fyne was established by Henry Kendal and Richard Latham and partners, also of Furness. Over time six blast furnaces operated in western Scotland, allof which had been attracted by a cheap and abundant supply of charcoal. The amount of wood needed to sustain the iron works was quite significant. Lorn furnace at Bonawe produced 700 tonnes of iron by the end of the 18th century and it has been estimated that at least 8,000-10,000 hectares of oakwood per annum were needed to supply the furnace with fuel. Wood was sourced from a remarkably wide area of the west coast and Islands; some woods were more than 60 kilometres away (Map 1.6).[47]

47   J.M. Lindsay, 'The Iron Industry in the Highlands', *The Scottish Historical Review*, 56 (1977) 161, part 1, 49-63, pp. 61-62; Smout, 'Oak as a commercial crop', pp. 109-110.

Under commercial pressures mixed semi-natural woods were turned into highly profitable oak coppice monocultures. During the 18th century the main estates in the region were organising woodland into haggs or felling coups, cropped on a 20-30-year rolling programme. Each hagg was fenced to keep cattle and sheep out, and the 'spring' from each coppice stool was reduced to a smaller number of shoots than would occur naturally, to give stronger growth. From an ecological point of view the oakwoods were artificially kept in a state of immaturity and structural uniformity and the later stages of stand development were eliminated. This management regime lasted through into the 1800s and played an important role in the survival of the Atlantic oakwoods.[48]

By the early 1800s iron making on the west coast was in decline and Craleckan blast furnace closed in 1813 while Bonawe continued at a lower level of production until 1876. Notwithstanding, this period is the high water mark of coppice management in the Atlantic oakwoods of western Scotland, fuelled by a demand for tanning bark by a growing shoe and leather industry. Landowners quickly switched to tanbark production because it was usually worth twice the value of charcoal in a coppice rotation. As a result many land owners considered a combination of tanbark and spoke wood (used for wheels) sufficient justification for managing their woods regardless of the demands of the iron industry. But this was not to last and after the 1860s it became clear that traditional coppice management would no longer be profitable. This was caused by foreign competition and the invention of cheaper chemical substitutes for oakbark tannin. By the beginning of the 20th century the commercial exploitation of the oakwoods of Western Scotland had all but ceased.[49]

48 Philip Sansum, 'Argyll Oakwoods: Use and Ecological Change, 1000 to 2000 AD - a Palynological-historical Investigation', *Botanical Journal of Scotland*, 57 (2005) 1, 83-97, pp. 91-92; Smout, 'Oak as a Commercial Crop', p. 111.
49 Smout, 'Oak as a Commercial Crop', pp. 110, 112-113.

Map 1.6: Sources of charcoal for the Lorn Furnace (black dots).

Source: Modified from J. M. Lindsay, 'Charcoal iron smelting and its fuel supply; the example of Lorn furnace, Argyllshire, 1753–1876', *Journal of Historical Geography*, 1 (1975) 3, 283-298, with permission from Elsevier.

During the 17th and 18th centuries interest in the commercial use of the native pinewoods of the Highlands also increased and wood from young native pine trees was increasingly used in buildings. This coincided with the creation of new plantations by Scottish landowners for profit and ornament. At the same time, the native pinewoods of the more remote parts of the Highlands were being exploited by outside speculators of which the York Building Company is the best known. One of the features of this activity appears to be the high rate of business failure, generally before much sustained felling had taken place. For example, the York Building Company went out of business before any substantial felling had taken place.[50] The company had purchased woodlands in the Cairngorm Mountains and as a result of its failure the pinewoods survived

---

50   Smout, 'The Pinewoods and Human Use', p. 344.

into the 20th century. Note that the failure of the York Building Company had little to do with the timber trade but the end result was good for the forests they had purchased.

In the first half of the 19th century, the impact of commercial exploitation of the native pinewoods increased when local lairds took the management of their estates over from outside speculators in order to increase the revenue from their estates. There was substantial felling in the native pinewoods of the Highlands driven by high timber prices, particularly during the Napoleonic wars. This episode of felling was partly replenished with the creation of non-native conifer plantations by lairds all over the Highlands, in the latter half of the 18th and early 19th centuries. The most extensive of these plantations were the woods created by the Dukes of Atholl, who planted millions of trees on their estate in Perthshire. However, by 1850 timber prices had dramatically fallen and lairds responded in three ways: most abandoned active forest management altogether and turned to sport (hunting) as the main source of income from their estates. In addition, large areas of land were cleared of old-established settled populations or abandoned to facilitate the introduction of large-scale sheep farming and millions of sheep were introduced in the Highlands, a process that had started in the last quarter of the 18th century. A minority of landowners concentrated on modern forestry plantations of pine and non-native conifer species, which became the core on which the Forestry Commission estate would be built in the 20th century. As a result of these developments, the felling of native semi-natural pines declined dramatically, which allowed natural regeneration of the pine stands where sheep grazing was not too intense.[51]

What was the extent of the woodlands by the early 19th century? By around 1800, the forest had probably contracted from a historical maximum of 50-60 per cent to as little as nine per cent of the Scottish land area. During the 17th and 18th centuries, the rate of decline may have been checked as better management was established in some of the remaining woods, but in any case it would have slowed as the forest area contracted and was increasingly concentrated in the remoter areas. Increased coppice management of oakwoods for charcoal and tan bark also contributed to the slowing of forest cover decline. There is even evidence that these woodlands expanded during the 18th and 19th centuries and that the survival of the Atlantic oakwoods can be attributed to its commercial management and exploitation. Nevertheless, during the 19th century the area of woodland in Scotland declined even further. Semi-natural woods were partly replaced by plantations but many ancient woods disappeared because of increased grazing pressure caused by the large number of sheep that were introduced in the Highlands during this period. In addition the rising popularity of deer and grouse shooting required an open landscape and

---

51   Smout *et al.*, *The Native Woodlands*, pp. 273-274; Smout, 'The Pinewoods and Human Use', pp. 345-346.

forestry was abandoned on many estates in favour of sport. As a consequence the woodland cover fell to a historic low of about six per cent by the beginning of the 20th century.[52]

---

52   Smout *et al.*, *The Native Woodlands*, pp. 67-69.

2. Scottish forestry in the 19th century

Scotland has been at the centre of forestry in Britain since at least the seventeenth century. While German forestry, in particular in Prussia in the late 18th century, shifted towards state intervention and a decline of the independent, privately owned estate, in Scotland the opposite happened and from the seventeenth century landowners started to experiment with new modes of forestry, without any form of centralised state intervention. From the early 1600s, tree planting on Scottish estates increased steadily, while 'improving' Scottish landowners began to introduce tree species from continental Europe such as sycamore maple, Norway spruce, larch and European silver fir, none of which was native to Scotland. The availability of considerable 'wastelands' in the Scottish Highlands facilitated these experiments with new species and planting methods.[1]

Scottish landowners were interested in using the forest resources on their estates more efficiently to increase revenue. This went hand in hand with the ideal of aesthetically improving their estates and of securing a sustainable yield to support future generations. This latter aspect shared similarities with the German ideal of *Nachhaltigkeit*, a system to secure forest resources for the future.[2] The difference with the German mode of thinking was that the Scottish ideal combined both aesthetic and profit-driven elements to create a kind of early multiple use forest resource.[3] Furthermore, the traditional woodland management system of coppicing was maintained in tandem with the new forestry plantations, catering to the needs of a wide range of traditional users, while preserving game and aesthetic values.[4] For example, John Murray (1755-1830), fourth Duke of Atholl, who was nicknamed 'Planter John', wrote that forestry operations should be carried out for 'beauty, effect and profit'.[5] The efforts of the Fourth Duke and other plantation schemes in Scotland during the late eighteenth century and early 19th century were the first attempts anywhere to establish major plantations of conifer trees *ab initio*, as opposed to the conversion of natural forests or coppices that took place in continental Europe.[6]

---

1   Syd House and Christopher Dingwall, 'A Nation of Planters: Introducing the New Trees, 1650-1900' in T.C. Smout (ed.), *People and Woods in Scotland: A History* (Edinburgh: Edinburgh University Press, 2003), 128-157, pp. 131-132; S. Ravi Rajan, *Modernizing Nature: Forestry and Imperial Eco-Development 1800-1950* (Oxford: Oxford University Press, 2006), p. 111.

2   Rajan, *Modernizing Nature*, p. 41.

3   Multiple use forestry became fashionable among forestry services in the western world during the 1950s and 1960s with the rise of the automobile and increasing numbers of visitors to the forests. This type of forestry aimed at combining recreational use and nature conservation with wood production.

4   Rajan, *Modernizing Nature*, p. 110.

5   Quoted in House and Dingwall, 'A Nation of Planters', p. 135.

6   Ibid., 139-40.

The most notable of these forest plantations emerged in Argyll, in Perthshire and on the Moray coast in the North East of Scotland. The earl of Moray, earl of Fife and the Dukes of Atholl and Argyll planted millions of trees to 'improve' their landholdings, and by the last quarter of the eighteenth century smaller landowners had begun to imitate their grander neighbours.

The extent of the planting can be deduced from the fact that by 1818 enough timber had been grown on the Atholl estates for the construction of a 170-ton brig at Perth. A 28-gun frigate ordered by the Admiralty followed the success of this first vessel, and the launching of this ship, the 'Atholl', in 1820 was a tribute to the Fourth 'Planting Duke' of Atholl.[7] It is estimated that by the time the 'Planting Duke' died in 1830 over fourteen million larches had been planted on the Atholl estates.

The forests of Atholl were not unique and trees were being planted and harvested in estates all over the Highlands. In her memoirs, Elizabeth Grant of Rothiemurchus (1797-1886), gave a vivid description of logging activities on the Rothiemurchus estate: 'It was a busy scene all through the forest, many rough little horses moving about in every direction, each dragging its load, attended by an active boy as guide …'.[8]

She went on to describe log floating in the Spey catchment. There was a sophisticated system of dams and sluices that regulated the flow of water that was needed to float the timber logs downstream. Gangs of specialised woodsmen who lived along the riverbanks gathered when the logging season started, and guided the floating timber rafts down the river.[9] This labour-intensive system of extracting timber, which involved numerous timber floaters, suggests that timber production was an important ingredient of the Highland economy in the Spey catchment during the first decades of the 19th century.

There was also forestry activity in other parts of the Highlands and Islands during the early decades of the 19th century. In the west, the MacGregors planted between 1804 and 1809 more than 24 hectares of mixed plantations on the Isle of Arran.[10] The species used included European larch, pines, silver firs, ash and oak. In the north, around Speyside, the Earls of Seafield planted some 18 000 hectares on their estates between 1811 and 1881. Over two thirds of this area was planted with newly introduced conifer species from North America.[11]

---

7   Ibid., p. 149.
8   Elizabeth Grant of Rothiemurchus, *Memoirs of a Highland Lady, 1797-1827* (London: John Murray, 1911), p. 219.
9   Ibid., p. 220.
10   Stirling Council Archives (hereafter SCA): PD60 Bundle 394, MacGregor Papers.
11   National Archives for Scotland (hereafter NAS): FC7/3 Working Plan Glenurquhart, 1950-1965.

Figure 2.1: Log Floaters on the River Spey, ca. 1900.

Source: Elizabeth Grant of Rothiemurchus, *Memoirs of a Highland Lady*, 1911 edition, p. 120.

The emergence of forestry plantations as a core aspect of Scottish estate management was associated with patriotism and good taste, as well as with making better and more profitable use of the land. By the end of the eighteenth century, tree planting was regarded as a respectable and progressive activity, and a shared vision of what constituted appropriate forest management was widely accepted throughout Scotland.[12]

Much of the knowledge acquired on the Scottish estates from these early experiments and planting activities was disseminated through the learned societies in Edinburgh, such as the Botanical Society of Scotland, as well as through botany and other courses at the university. Particularly important in the spread of modern forest management practice was the creation of the Physic Garden in Edinburgh in 1670, which is now known as the Royal Botanic Garden. In 1723 the Honourable Society of Improvers in the Knowledge of Agriculture in Scotland was established by a group of influential landowners whose aim was to improve the management of the land, including forestry.[13]

---

12   Judith Tsouvalis and Charles Watkins, 'Imagining and Creating Forests in Britain, 1890-1939', in: Mauro Agnoletti and Steven Anderson (eds), *Forest History: International Studies on Socioeconomic and Forest Ecosystem Change* (Wallingford: CABI, 2000), 371-386, pp. 374-5.
13   House and Dingwall, 'A Nation of Planters', p. 138. These landowners included the duke of Atholl and the earl of Breadalbane.

Encouraged by these developments Scottish seed collectors, of whom David Douglas (1799-1834) is the most famous, introduced many North American tree species to Europe. In the late 1820s Douglas introduced the Douglas fir and Sitka spruce, trees that were to form the backbone of Scottish forestry during the twentieth century. After Douglas' untimely death in 1834, other Scottish seed collectors continued to introduce new trees such as the lodgepole pine, western hemlock and western red cedar. Scottish landowners, driven by the usual desire to improve their plantations for profit and pleasure, enthusiastically embraced these trees.[14] This formed a breeding ground of practical foresters whose experience was disseminated, as stated above, through the publications by the learned societies and books.[15]

One of these books, entitled *The forester*, published by James Brown,[16] a professional forester on the Arniston estate in Midlothian, was of particular importance. Published in 1847, this book provided practical advise on how to create and manage a forest in the Scottish landscape based on scientific principles. It became a popular and influential book that marked the rise in the status and professionalisation of estate foresters in Scotland.[17] James Brown was also the first president of the Scottish Arboricultural Society which was established in 1854. The Arboricultural Society was established by a group of landowners and foresters who were determined to 'place Scottish forestry on a sounder basis as an important section of rural industry.'[18] This event signalled the emergence of a body of professional estate foresters in Scotland, from which the Indian Forest Department was to draw so many of the forest officers who ultimately populated its middle and higher echelons. These men brought with them a forestry tradition that was decentralised, open to experimentation, and which combined aesthetic planting and game management with commercial timber production.

The Indian connection

Before the creation of the Imperial Forestry Service, forestry regulation and legislation had been at best *ad hoc* in India. The East India Company had tried

---

14 Ibid., p. 150. A testament to the planting experiments by Scottish landowners are the Douglas firs of Craigvinean Forest near Dunkeld. Planted by the duke of Atholl in 1860, these are now among the tallest Douglas firs in the world.
15 Mark Louden Anderson, *A History of Scottish Forestry* (2 vols., London & Edinburgh: Thomas Nelson and Sons, 1967), II, pp. 308-312.
16 James Brown was the father of sylviculturist John Ednie Brown (1848-1899). John Croumbie Brown was a botanist at the Cape, South Africa, in the 1860s.
17 House and Dingwall, 'A Nation of Planters', p. 155.
18 Anderson, *A History of Scottish Forestry*, II, pp. 120, 314. The quotation is from Malcolm Dunn, 'Forestry in Scotland in the Reign of Her Most Gracious Majesty Queen Victoria', *Transactions of the Royal Scottish Arboricultural Society*, 15 (1898), 109-132, p. 129.

to control timber production and trade in India around the turn of the 19th century but they failed miserably. The colonial authorities were unable to control the indigenous trading structures. Instead, the British had to rely on the local timber market to meet their needs and by the late 1820s any attempt to regulate the trade and forestry has been abandoned. It was this private trade which led to over exploitation of certain forest areas in India and fears of the negative environmental impacts that this bought such problems as soil erosion, climate change and water shortages.[19]

In 1850, alarmed by these developments the British Association meeting in Edinburgh set up a committee to study the forest destruction and its impacts at the behest of Hugh Cleghorn (1820-1895), a medical doctor working in India. A year later the committee presented their report, which was based on testimonies of forest administrators in India who feared the potential long-term negative environmental effects of deforestation caused by indiscriminate logging. The committee advised to introduce tighter controls over the forests in India but they stopped short of proposing the creation of a central forestry authority.[20]

It was in this context that the Earl of Dalhousie (1812-1860),[21] the Governor-General of India issued a Memorandum of the Government of India on forestry, later dubbed the 'Charter of Indian Forestry', in 1855. This memorandum was based on reports submitted by John McClelland (1805-1875), who was Superintendent of Forests in Burma and formed the basis for the Forest Act of 1865, which established the Indian Forestry Department.[22]

When the Indian Forest Department was established in 1864, British officials possessed little knowledge of continental scientific forestry. Determined to organise the Forest Department along the same lines as forestry departments in Germany, they appointed a German forester, Dietrich Brandis (1824-1907), as the first Inspector-General of Forests to the Government of India. Brandis, in turn, recruited forestry officers from Germany to fill posts in the upper echelons of the Indian Forest Deaprtment. Among these appointees were William Schlich (1840-1925) and Berthold Ribbentrop (1843-1917), who were later to follow in Brandis' footsteps as Inspector-General of Forests in 1883-8 and 1888-1900 respectively.[23]

---

19   Michael Mann, 'Timber Trade on the Malabar Coast, c. 1780–1840', *Environment and History*, 7 (2001) 4, 403-425.

20   Hugh Cleghorn *et al*., 'Report of the Committee Appointed by the British Association to Consider the Probable Effects in an Oeconomical and Physical Point of View of the Destruction of Tropical Forests', *Report of the Twenty-first Meeting of the British Association for the Advancement of Science* (London: John Murray, 1852), pp. 78-102.

21   James Andrew Broun Ramsay. He was made an English marquess in 1849.

22   Gregory A. Barton, *Empire Forestry and the Origins of Environmentalism* (Cambridge: Cambridge University Press, 2002), p. 57.

23   Ulrike Kirchberger, 'German Scientists in the Indian Forest Service: A German Contribution to the Raj?', *The Journal of Imperial and Commonwealth History*, 29 (2001) 2, 1-26.

The management of forests in India proved challenging for these European continental foresters coming from the scientific forestry tradition developed in Germany and France. This tradition was reductionist in nature and did not take much notice of varying environmental and social conditions. This led continental foresters to believe that a direct transfer of forestry practice from the temperate zone to tropical forests would not be too problematic. It soon became apparent, however, that the significantly different and highly variable environmental conditions to be found in India required the development of new forest management regimes.[24] An infusion of Scottish knowledge and experience was to assist in their development.

During the nineteenth century Scotland lacked the capacity to absorb its well-educated workforce, a large number of who found employment in Britain's expanding colonial services. That Scots occupied many senior professional positions as engineers and doctors is well known, but their importance as foresters is much less widely appreciated. Indeed, just as the Scots dominated the operational, scientific and technological aspects of British activity in India, forestry was no exception.[25] In the preface to the Indian section of the catalogue for the 1884 International Forestry Exhibition in Edinburgh, Sir George Birdwood, a senior administrator in India, gave Scottish botanists the credit for 'having first called attention to the necessity for forest conservation in India'.[26] As mentioned earlier, many officers in the early Indian Forest Service were Scottish-trained surgeons and botanists who had been recruited from other parts of the colonial service.[27] During their education in Scotland they had been exposed to the Scottish Enlightenment traditions that connected medicine with knowledge about botany, climate and geology. This led them to adopt a holistic approach that advocated rigorous field observations and flexible tree-planting programmes that took into consideration local variations in soils, climate and vegetation. Colonial authorities drew upon the expertise of these naturalist surgeons to gain knowledge about India's natural and agricultural resources. Hugh Cleghorn (1820-1895), who held one of the top positions in the early Indian Forest Service, was a prime example of such a surgeon turned botanist, having

---

24 Marlene Buchy, 'Forestry: From a Colonial Discipline to a modern Vision', Keynote Paper, *Workshop on Changing Learning and Education in Forestry*, Sapa, Vietnam, 16-19 April 2000, http://www.mekonginfo. org/mrc_en/doclib.nsf/0/8223AC38A3BA7C6347256A0E002C9035/$FILE/FULLTEXT.html Accessed: 18 November 2009; William Somerville, 'Influences Affecting British forestry. Inaugural Lecture in the Course of Forestry, Edinburgh University, 23 October 1889', *Transactions of the Royal Scottish Arboricultural Society*, 12 (1890) 3, 403-417, p. 406.

25 Kapil Raj, 'Colonial Encounters and the Forging of New Knowledge and National Identities: Great Britain and India, 1760-1850', *Osiris*, 2nd Series, 15, 'Nature and Empire: Science and the Colonial Enterprise', (2000), 119-134, pp. 124-125.

26 'The International Forestry Exhibition', *The Scotsman*, 7 July 1884, 5.

27 Tentatively suggested by Grove in his work on South Africa and other parts of the Empire. See: Richard Grove, 'Scottish Missionaries, Evangelical Discourses and the Origins of Conservation Thinking in Southern Africa, 1820-1900', *Journal of Southern African Studies*, 15 (January 1989) 2, 163-187.

originally been appointed to the Indian Medical Service.[28] Cleghorn and other Scottish trained surgeons were likely to have been familiar with estate forestry practices in Scotland. The Indian colonial authorities, like their counterparts in Australia, also drew more directly on the experience of estate forestry in Scotland by recruiting foresters who had been trained on Scottish estates.[29]

Middle and higher ranking officers recruited for the Indian Forest Department had to pass a competitive exam in order to be admitted to the forester training programme. In first six years of the existence of the Forest Department recruits were sent to forestry schools in Germany and France, but after 1871 students ceased to be sent to Germany because it was cheaper and more convenient to concentrate all instruction in France.[30] In addition, forestry recruits were also required to train for several weeks under the supervision of an approved forester on a Scottish estate before they were sent out to India.[31] It must be noted that after the introduction of the competitive exam in 1855 the number of Oxbridge graduates in the ranks of the Indian Civil Service rose quickly resulting is a reduced dominance of Scotsmen in the Forestry Department.[32] Nevertheless, the fact that forestry recruits were trained in both Scotland and in France ensured that the ideas and principles of continental forestry were unquestionably inter-mixed with those of Scottish forest management.

The blending together of continental and Scottish forest management regimes, as well as adaptation to Indian environmental conditions, led to the creation of a distinctive Indian branch of scientific forestry. While rendering the forests profitable remained the primary goal, the conservation of existing forests was also undertaken in order to counter negative environmental effects such as desiccation, flooding and soil erosion. In addition it was observed that forestry knowledge had to be applied to 'entirely new conditions of climate, and deal with trees and plants not known [in Scotland]'.[33] The limited numbers of commercially useful trees in Indian forests was a particular concern, with teak trees, for instance, making up only about 10 per cent of the so-called teak forests. The diversity and mixed nature of the Indian forests therefore required a management regime that favoured 'valuable commercial species' while 'eliminating the less

---

28 For an in-depth discussion of Hugh Cleghorn and Scottish trained foresters see Pallavi Das, 'Hugh Cleghorn and Forest Conservancy in India', *Environment and History*, 11 (2005) 1, 55-82.
29 John Dargavel, 'Forestry', in: John Dargavel (ed.), *Australia and New Zealand Forest Histories: Short Overviews* (Kingston, Australian Forest History Society, 2005), 25-31, p. 27.
30 F. Bailey, 'The Indian Forest School', *Transactions of the Royal Scottish Arboricultural Society*, 11 (1887) 2, 155-164, pp. 155-6. Note that people like Cleghorn never worked on Scottish estates or were sent to forestry schools. Only new recruits after establishment of the Forest Department followed this route.
31 'Advertisement for Recruitment of Officers in the Indian Forest Service', *The Scotsman*, 15 November 1869.
32 C.J. Dewey, 'The Education of a Ruling Caste: The Indian Civil Service in the Era of Competitive Examination', *The English Historical Review*, 88 (1973) 347, 262-285, p. 276.
33 'India as a Field for Our Educated Youth', *The Scotsman*, 11 December 1869, p. 7.

valuable and those interfering with the growth of the former.'[34] The variety and density of Indian forests, as well as their extensiveness, also encouraged the use of natural regeneration. Ribbentrop concluded that the 'average cash revenue per acre is too insignificant' to justify clearance of the jungle and the creation of plantations.[35] The creation of forestry plantations was therefore less important than in Europe, although a considerable number of teak plantations, especially in Burma, were created in places where no forests had previously existed.[36]

The adaptation of German and French models of scientific forestry to the Indian environment was aided by the Scottish experience of decentralised estate forestry. The introduction of exotic tree species in the variable and often extreme environmental conditions of the Scottish highlands and islands had led Scottish foresters to develop an experimental approach to forestry, with a strong emphasis on observation. This resulted in an adjustment of planting and management practices in order to encourage these newly introduced trees to grow in different environments. To some extent they found a similar situation in the varied environments of the Indian subcontinent, ranging from tropical to semi-arid to alpine, though on a very much greater and more complex scale.

The success of the fusion of continental forestry and Scottish practice in India was recognised at the time. In 1891 it was noted in *The Scotsman* that 'Scottish ideas and Prussian experience have combined to produce [successful forestry] in India.'[37] The decentralised model of Scottish estate forestry was to some extent replicated in India, and applied on the much larger scale of the provincial forestry districts[38] which were essentially run as large estates. Here on the regional level Scottish estate and enlightenment forestry fused with continental European and local traditions to form (regional) hybrid practices that were continually and creatively adapted to varied political, economic and ecological circumstances of the different locales in India.[39] The central forestry policy, which provided general guidance on objectives and goals of forestry in India, did not prevent the development of local forest management practice because it did not prescribe how individual forests or districts were managed. A

34 E.P. Stebbing, *The Forests of India* (2 vols, London: The Bodley Head Ltd., 1922), II, p. 578.
35 Berthold Ribbentrop, *Forestry in British India* (Calcutta: Office of the Superintendent of Government Printing, 1900), p. 166.
36 Sir Richard Temple, 'Lecture on the Forests of India', *Transactions of the Scottish Arboricultural Society*, 10 (1881) 3, 1-20, p. 15; Indra Munshi Saldanha, 'Colonialism and Professionalism: a German Forester in India', *Environment and History*, 2 (1996) 2, 195-219, p. 204.
37 'The Indian Forest Service and its Founders', *The Scotsman*, 17 August 1891, 8.
38 Forestry Districts or Forest Circles were formed in each province in British India and each was run by a Conservator of Forests. See for further detail: R.S. Troup, *The work of the Forest Department in India* (Calcutta: Office of the Superintendent of Government Printing, 1917), p. 9.
39 On the development of hybrid forestry models in the colonial Empires of Asia see Peter Vandergeest and Nancy Lee Peluso, 'Empires of Forestry: Professional Forestry and State Power in Southeast Asia, Part 2', *Environment and History,* 12 (2006) 2, 359-393, pp. 359-93.

significant difference with Scotland was that India had this central overarching forest policy by 1865. Scotland, like the rest of the United Kingdom, had to wait until 1919 for such a development.

The influence of returning foresters

Following their service in India, the botanists and foresters who created these hybrid forestry practices returned to Britain to become teachers at the newly-created institutions designed to train forestry officers for India and other parts of the Empire, as well as Britain itself.[40] Foresters returning from India shared the desire of other Scottish foresters, as well as Scottish landowners, to make better use of the country's forest resources. They therefore lent their voices to growing calls for universities to establish lectureships and forestry courses for the education of professional, scientifically trained foresters who would help to increase the revenue from estates in Scotland. To promote formal forestry the Scottish Arboricultural Society invited prominent Indian forestry officials to give talks about forestry practice, policy and education on the Indian subcontinent. These men included Dietrich Brandis and Hugh Cleghorn as well as Colonel Frederick Bailey (1840-1912), the first director of the Indian Forestry School in Dehra Dun. They championed in their talks the creation of forestry schools in Scotland and England and even the creation of a central forestry service.[41] The return to Scotland of lesser-known foresters who had served in India likewise contributed to the dissemination of the new ideas of scientific forestry. In 1910 A.C. Forbes, Chief Forestry Inspector to the Department of Agriculture for Ireland, described this process in his book *The Development of British Forestry*:

> Since about 1860, when Cleghorn and Brandis inaugurated the Indian Forest Service, a small stream of continental trained youths has been going out to India, and an equally small stream of retired Indian foresters, on furlough or pension, has been returning from it. Whatever the exact practical results of this intermixture of British and Anglo-Indian ideas may have been, there is little doubt that fresh ideas were instilled into British foresters and proprietors, and a wider knowledge of forestry as an industry instead of a hobby resulted.[42]

---

40 These included the forestry course at the University of Edinburgh, and the course at the Engineering College at Coopers Hill, and later the Forestry Department in Oxford.

41 See for example Hugh Cleghorn, 'Address Delivered at the Nineteenth Annual Meeting', *Transactions of the Royal Scottish Arboricultural Society*, 7 (1875) 1, 1-9; Bailey, 'The Indian Forest School', 155-164; Dietrich Brandis, 'The Proposed School of Forestry', *Transactions of the Royal Scottish Arboricultural Society*, 12 (1890) 1, 65-77.

42 A.C. Forbes, *The Development of British Forestry* (London: E. Arnold, 1910), p. 252.

The calls for formal forestry education in Britain was bearing fruit and by the late nineteenth century, a forestry degree had been established at the University of Edinburgh with a curriculum that included the measuring and valuation of woods, forest utilisation and forest policy, silviculture, pathology and zoology.[43] Courses were often taught by foresters with a colonial background, such as the aforementioned Colonel Frederick Bailey, who occupied the first chair in forestry at the University of Edinburgh after his return from India in 1906. In 1892 a special course for forest workers was established at the Royal Botanic Gardens in Edinburgh. In the years that followed, the three Scottish Agricultural Colleges in Glasgow, Edinburgh and Aberdeen introduced both evening and day courses in forestry. These courses ceased when the Scottish Education Department stopped funding them in 1918 in anticipation of the Forestry Act of 1919, which established the Forestry Commission and conferred it with responsibility for educating forest workers below university level.[44]

Pressure for a formal forest policy

Foresters returning from their tour of duty in the India and other parts of the Empire were not the only people concerned about the state of Scotland's forests. Over the course of the Victorian period unease about the productiveness and extent of the forests had slowly developed. In many ways the middle of he 19th century was an age of optimism and witnessed the introduction of new technologies such as steam trains, the electrical telegraph and electricity. At the same time science made major discoveries and the geographic expansion of the British Empire accelerated. Many foresters and landowners shared this optimism with regard to the development of forestry in Scotland. In 1889 Stuart Dunn noted in an article published in the *Transactions of the Royal Scottish Arboricultural Society* that forest plantations had considerably expanded during this period:

> ...extensive planting operations have been carried on all through [the Victorian Age] with more or less continuity; and ... it is natural to believe that our forests are spreading in their extent, and yearly adding to their acreage.[45]

It was observed with approval that some of the big landowners in Scotland had planted thousands of hectares of trees. This was the continuation of a trend

---

43   Charles J. Taylor, *Forestry and Natural Resources in the University of Edinburgh: A History* (Edinburgh: Department of Forestry and Natural Resources, 1985), p. 5.
44   M.L. Anderson, 'Forestry Education in Scotland, 1854-1953', *Scottish Forestry*, 8 (1954) 3, 114-126, pp. 118-21.
45   Dunn, 'Forestry in Scotland', pp. 118-119.

that had begun in the second half of the 18th century. These developments were well described by Francis Innes in his article *A Century of Forestry-1806 to 1906-on the Estate of Learney, Aberdeenshire* that was published in 1907 by the Royal Arboricultural Society. The first plantations on the Learney estate, mainly consisting of larch, were created between 1806 and 1825. Up to 1844 there was little activity in the plantations while the trees were growing, followed by an active period 1844 and 1906 of thinning, clear cutting, planting and replanting was carried out. The extent of planting was considerable and between 1806 and 1844 the forest area increased with 550 hectares, and in the next 50 years 554 hectares were harvested. Of the cleared ground 267 hectares were replanted and 68 hectares of new ground were planted in addition. By the early 20th century, the total land area under trees on the Learney estate accounted 356 hectares compared to only 20 hectares at the start of the 19th century.[46] According to James Brown, wood manager to the Earl of Seafield, and Surveyor General of Woods, the Learney estate was fairly typical for a Highland estate. In 1861 he commented that 'after the year 1830 ... many proprietors, especially in Scotland commenced to plant largely.'[47] Three decades later Colonel Bailey, then lecturer in forestry at the University of Edinburgh, agreed with this observation when he wrote:

> Scotland can show numerous well-managed forest estates – such, for example, as those of the Duke of Atholl, of the Earls of Mansfield and Seafield, of Lord Lovat, and of other proprietors who might be mentioned; and it is universally admitted that the art of raising nursery plants, of establishing plantations ... is here carried out with a success unsurpassed by foresters of any other country.[48]

The expansion of forest plantations was fuelled by the rapid economic growth and related increase in industrial activity in Scotland. This was driven by the expansion of the British Empire and increasing globalisation of trade that connected the Scottish economy to a global market. The industrial activities related to this economic success also required large quantities of wood. The shipbuilding industry on the banks of the Clyde constructed about a quarter of all shipping tonnage in the early 20th century. The fishing industry also needed wooden barrels to export their catch and the expansion of the railways in Scotland needed large quantities of wood for railway sleepers. The impact of the railways on this development was considerable and by 1870, it was reported

---

46   Francis N. Innes, 'A Century of Forestry-1806 to 1906-on the Estate of Learney, Aberdeenshire', *Transactions of the Royal Scottish Arboricultural Society*, 20 (1907) 2, 168-175, pp. 168-169.
47   James Brown, *The Forester. A Practical Treatise on the Planting, Rearing, and General Management of Forest Trees* (Edinburgh: Blackwood, 1861), p. 5.
48   Frederic Bailey, 'Introduction to a Course of Forestry Lectures', p. 184.

that timber prices in Aberdeenshire and increased with a quarter since coming of the railways and in parts of the Northern Highlands they had doubled over a period of 20 years.[49]

However, the increase of the area of forest plantations had not been a linear affair and there are suggestions that the total area had fallen in the decades after the 1850s. Nairn, a naturalist and writer, observed in 1890 that forest surveys in the 1880s 'shewed that plantations in Scotland had again rapidly recovered lost ground, there being an increase of 95,000 acres in nine years.'[50] This total acreage planted sounds impressive but if we consider this as a per centage of Scotland's total land area it becomes less impressive: the area of new plantations covered only 0.5 per cent of the total Scottish landmass. If this increase of forest plantations was sustained at the same rate since the 1830s, the time that Brown claims the forests started to expand, the total acreage up to the 1880s should have increased by about 2.5 per cent. But because of the lack of reliable surveys it is doubtful if this were the case. There is no surprise then that during the last quarter of the 19th century the Scottish Arboricultural Society became alarmed about the condition of the forests in Scotland.

The perception of the bad state of Scotland's forests had not much to do with the destruction and decline of semi-natural woodlands, but with the way a large number of estate plantations were managed. It was this concern that made not all 19th century observers share the optimism of Dunn and Innes. In 1892 Nairn saw the development of Scottish forestry during the second half of the 19th century as a story of decline, and in doing so contradicted himself in the same article on forestry.[51] Why then, if plantations were actually expanding and actively managed, was there a growing feeling that the opposite happened? There are two explanations for this. First of all, the view of decline and neglect was fuelled by the development of the technological advances, industrial development and the related globalisation of commodity markets, including timber, during the 19th century.

The same processes of globalisation that spurred industrial and economic growth in Scotland acted as a double-edged sword because it not only opened up new markets for Scottish-produced timber but also brought foreign competition on a scale never seen before. The introduction of the ocean steamer and railways caused a transport revolution in the second half of the 19th century. The result was the opening up of huge timber producing areas in North America, Scandinavia and the expanding British Empire.

---

49   Smout *et al.*, *A History of the Native Woodlands*, pp. 271-272.
50   David Nairn, 'Notes on Highland Woods, Ancient and Modern', *Transactions of the Gaelic Society of Inverness*, 17 (1891), 170-221, p. 191.
51   Nairn, 'Notes on Highland Woods'.

The small scale of Scotland's forests could not compete successfully with these newly opened markets and the bubble really burst when the import tariff on timber was completely removed in 1866 and the price of imported timber fell further. By the second half of the 19th century the level of imports determined the price of Scottish-grown timber, and this was rarely high enough to encourage Scottish producers to grow more trees. As a result many Scottish landowners converted their woodlands into areas for deer or grouse shooting. Rent from sporting activities paid better than forestry so it made economic sense to scale down forestry or abandon it altogether.[52]

This convinced 19th century observers that domestic forests were neglected, and that there was hardly any replanting, and the total area of woodlands decreased. Oxford based forest Economist W.E. Hiley, observed in the late 1950s that the cause of forest decline in the 19th century was complex but that '… one important factor was the increase in timber imports and the improved facilities for distributing them through the country.'[53]

The second reason why many landowners and foresters felt uneasy about forestry in Scotland during the last decades of the 19th century was the realisation that the potential for forestry in Scotland was considerable and some landowners wondered why this had not been utilised by preceding generations. By the start of the 20th century a group of large landowners in Scotland believed that the expansion of the forests would have several advantages. Firstly, the land would be used more efficiently because previously unproductive land would be made productive. Secondly, the expansion of forestry would bring jobs to the Highlands and higher incomes to the landowners. Thus the economy of the Highlands could be improved and prevent depopulation of rural areas, a theme that would run right through the 20th century. Lastly, an increased production of home-grown timber would decrease the dependence on timber imports, which was regarded as a weakness in times of war.[54] These arguments were used to try to convince the government that state action was needed to increase the area of forests in Britain.

Prelude to a State forest policy

The story of British State forest policy did not start with its first formulation by the Forestry Sub-committee of the War Reconstruction Committee in 1918. It started around the turn of the 20th century with the activities of a small

---

52 Smout *et al.*, *A History of the Native Woodlands*, pp. 274-276.
53 W. E. Hiley, *Economics of Plantations* (London: Faber and Faber, 1956), p. 21.
54 Lord Simon Lovat, 'Afforestation', *Transactions of the Royal Scottish Arboricultural Society*, 22 (1909) 2, 156-167, pp. 157-161.

group of men, mainly Scottish landowners and foresters, who were to become the founders of the Forestry Commission. They were farsighted men who had become uneasy at the perceived lack of planting for timber production. Among the most important people were John Stirling Maxwell, Lord Lovat, Roy Robinson, and John Sutherland. They all contributed in different ways to the development of Scottish forestry but their ideas concerning the need for a State forestry authority were very similar.

As we have seen, their concern for the neglected state of Britain's forests was fuelled by the belief that from the mid-19th century until the 1890s the rate of planting for timber production had slowed down in Great Britain. This state of affairs was attributed to the fact that most of Britain's timber was imported cheaply from abroad. In addition, the low percentage of land used for growing trees in Britain caused alarm to those who made a study of the world's timber resources. They were convinced that a world-wide 'timber famine' was imminent and that Britain could not depend indefinitely on imports from abroad.[55] Royal Commissions and Parliamentary Committees held several enquiries, but little was done. One of the most important of these committees was the Royal Commission on Coast Erosion that reported in 1909. This report advised to establish a national scheme of afforestation with the aim of planting 3.6 million hectares by the state over sixty years and to be overseen by a state forestry department. In reaction to the report the Royal Scottish Arboricultural Society sent a deputation to the Chancellor of the Exchequer to urge for its adoption. However, the report was greatly ignored and no action was taken to establish a state forestry organisation.[56] This was partly due to the fact that the proposed extent of the plantations frightened most stakeholders, including the Royal Scottish Arboricultural Society, which suggested instead a survey of Scotland to see which areas could and could not be afforested.[57]

In a reaction to the report of the Royal Commission on Coastal Erosion, Lord Lovat (1871-1933), an influential landowner in northern Scotland and future chairman of the Forestry Commission, wrote in the *Transactions of Royal Scottish Arboricultural Society* that the State had to play an indispensable part in forestry. He proposed the creation of a central forestry board in Britain that would oversee the creation and management of a timber reserve. Its mission would include the establishment of experimental and demonstration areas; the creation of schools for foresters; a survey of mountain and moorland areas suitable for forestry; acquisition of areas suitable for afforestation and subsequent planting; and finally encouragement of co-operation between private landowners and

---

55 Glasgow City Archives (hereafter GCA): T-PM 122/4/7/2 BBC forestry talk no. 2, 29 March 1928; See also: *Final Report of the Forestry Sub-committee of the Reconstruction Committee* (Cmd. 8881) (London: HMSO, 1918), p. 5.

56 John Davies, *The Scottish Forester* (Edinburgh: Blackwood, 1979), p. 21.

57 Smout *et al.*, *A History of the Native Woodlands*, p. 279.

the state. These tasks of the proposed forestry board anticipated the mission of the Forestry Commission after its creation in 1919. Lovat's article and his speeches in the House of Lords reveal that he associated the question of forestry with the issue of depopulation and economy in the Highlands.[58] Lord Lovat and other Scottish landowners believed that any forestry scheme had to maintain in decent comfort a larger number of people on the land and afforestation offered the only large-scale solution to the difficulty of enabling the smallholder to supplement his living from the land. According to Lovat, afforestation would turn much unproductive land into productive areas that would be able to sustain a considerable number of families in the Highlands.[59]

But Lord Lovat and others were conscious of the fact that many landowners were wary of a large afforestation programme by the state:

> … the colossal schemes advocated in the Report have roused the fears of public bodies whose source of revenue, and of individuals whose means of living, were bound up in the present uses of the land indicated for wholesale afforestation.[60]

Instead Lovat, together with John Stirling Maxwell urged the government to conduct a survey of the country to determine what could and could not be used for afforestation. This proposal was not taken up by the Government but instead the Royal Scottish Arboricultural Society took up the challenge and sponsored a much more limited survey of the Great Glen.[61]

The survey was carried out by Lord Lovat, Captain Archibald Stirling of Keir (1867-1931),[62] and Colonel Frederick Bailey, the first director of the Indian Forestry School in Dehra Dun, who was editor of the Arboricultural Society's *Transactions*. The area chosen for the survey, the Great Glen, also known as Glen More, is the glen in which Loch Ness is situated and runs from Inverness in the east all the way to Fort William in the west. The reason why the Great Glen was selected for the survey was that it represented both east and west coast climate and soil conditions and contained all the typical social and physical elements of the Highlands such as crofters, extensive sheep farming, soil and climate, deer forests, grouse moor and old estate forests.[63] The survey concluded that Scotland had a large area of under utilised land suitable for forestry and that

58   See for example: House of Lords (hereafter HL) Debate 15 July 1909, vol. 2, Column 530, *Crofting Parishes (Scotland) Bill*.
59   Francis Lindley, *Lord Lovat. A Biography* (London: Hutchinson, 1935), pp. 154-158; Davies, *The Scottish Forester*, p. 23.
60   Lord Lovat and A. Stirling of Keir, 'Afforesation in Scotland. Forest Survey of Glen Mor and a Consideration of Certain Problems Arising Therefrom', *Transaction of Royal Arboricultural Society*, 25 (1911) 1, p. 2.
61   Lord Lovat and Stirling of Keir, 'Afforesation in Scotland', pp. 156-169; John Sirling-Maxwell, 'Report of the Royal Commission on Afforestation', *Transactions of the Royal Scottish Arboricultural Society*, 22 (1909) 2, pp. 86-87. Loch Ness is located in the Great Glen.
62   Brother of John Stirling Maxwell, a future Chairman of the Forestry Commission.
63   Lord Lovat and Stirling of Keir, 'Afforesation in Scotland', p. 6.

this land could be quickly and successfully afforested under direction of a state programme. A single Central Forest Authority for Scotland was thought to be necessary to carry out a 'well-framed scheme' of forestry. The duties of the Forest Authority would include the provision of forestry education and creation of demonstration areas; the organisation of research and the undertaking of surveys; the creation and management of forests; marketing of forest products and lastly the encouragement of private forestry. The survey further concluded that afforestation would eventually bring a considerable financial return to the state as well as creating extra employment in the Highlands. To accommodate the forest workers it was suggested that 'in all cases the building of the dwelling house should be financed by the Forest Authority'.[64] It was envisaged that these 'dwelling houses' would be set up as smallholdings with farmland that could supplement the forest worker's income. The idea was that the small holders worked a guaranteed number of weeks in the forests and used the remainder of the year to work their own land.[65] Forestry and the smallholdings were seen as a means to stop the decline of the rural population in Scotland.

The Great Glen survey was published in a special edition of the *Transactions of the Royal Scottish Arboricultural Society* in July 1911 and was a model of what a woodland survey of the Highlands should be. The report of the survey brought together all the elements that were to determine Scottish forestry during the 20th century together for the first time. It was a blueprint for the organisation, functions and policies of the Forestry Commission. The Board of the Society heralded the survey as 'The first serious attempt to grapple with the economic difficulties which confront afforestation in that part of Great Britain where the largest extent of plantable land – that is to say, land sufficiently cheap – is to be found.'[66] This statement determined the future status of upland Scotland as the most important area for afforestation in Britain as well as the nature of the future forests.

In the same year that the Great Glen survey was undertaken the Department of Agriculture appointed a Committee on Forestry in Scotland. The chairman of this committee was another influential landowner: John Stirling-Maxwell of Pollok (1866-1956). Maxwell took a particular interest in forestry and devoted a large part of his life to the work of the Forestry Commission, becoming the chairman in 1929. The Secretary to the Committee was John Sutherland (1868-1952) of the Board of Agriculture for Scotland, who later became the first

---

64   Ibid., p. 34.
65   Ibid., pp. 37-38.
66   Lovat, and Stirling of Keir, 'Afforestation in Scotland', p. i.

Assistant Commissioner of forestry for Scotland.[67] The Report of the Committee on Forestry in Scotland was published in the autumn of 1911 and the objective of the report were formulated as follows:

> ... to report as to the selection of a suitable location for a Demonstration Forest area in Scotland; the uses present and prospective, to which such area may be put (including the use that may be made of it by the various Forestry teaching centres in Scotland); the staff and equipment required for successful working; the probable cost; and the most suitable form of management.[68]

The Report summarised the purpose of the demonstration forest and the state of forestry education in Scotland and advised on its development. It laid the blueprint for forestry education and research in the United Kingdom after 1919. Most of the areas under consideration as demonstration areas were later incorporated in the forest estates owned by the Forestry Commission and played an important role as examples of forestry practice and organisation used by the Forestry Commission.[69]

It was not by accident that Stirling Maxwell chaired a committee that advised on forestry in Scotland. He was an expert on forestry in the Highlands and in the early 20th century he had experimented with new forestry techniques on his Corrour estate near Loch Ossian with methods of afforestation on elevated and peaty grounds. His most important contribution to Scottish forestry was the introduction of a new system of turf planting from Belgium and the adaptation for the Scottish environment.[70] During the First World War Stirling-Maxwell was appointed Assistant Controller of Timber Supplies and worked in France together with Lovat.

Although most planting experiments were undertaken on private estates, of which Corrour was probably the most important, the state started some experimental work in the early 20th century. In 1907 the Office of Woods, which managed the crown woods, acquired Inverliever Forest in Argyll[71] as an experiment in large-scale afforestation. Planting started in 1909 but was not supervised by an academically trained forester and therefore not managed according to the latest ideas in forest science. This changed three years later when Roy Lister Robinson (1883-1952), a young forester from Australia, was placed in charge of the experimental plantation. Robinson was a graduate from the Oxford School

---

67   John Sutherland was the son of Mr. John Sutherland, County Assessor of Ross-shire. 'Scots Expert on Forestry: Death of Sir John Sutherland', *The Glasgow Herald*, 7 August 1952, p. 8, Col. 1.
68   *Report of the Committee on Forestry in Scotland*, (London: HMSO, 1911), p. i.
69   Highland Council Archives (hereafter HCA): 538/37 Munro of Novar Papers, 1882-1948. Scottish Forestry Committee. Confidential memorandum on estates visited by the Committee.
70   NAS: FC7/6 Working plan Inverliever Forest, 1907-1951.
71   Inverliever Forest is situated on the north bank of Loch Awe in Argyll, western Scotland.

of Forestry and had studied with Professor William Schlich. After graduation, he was employed by the Board of Agriculture and later transferred to the Office of Woods to report on the effectiveness of the management of the Crown Forests. When Robinson was put in charge of Inverliever Forest he laid down fifty experiments dealing with planting on difficult soils and wet and windy climatic west coast conditions. The experience gained at Inverliever helped the Forestry Commission with the successful creation of new plantations after 1919. Robinson continued his work at Inverliever until he was appointed as the first Technical Officer of the Forestry Commission.[72]

By 1914 a small group of men together with the Royal Scottish Arboricutural Society and the Office of woods had laid down the main features on which Britain's forest policy would be based for most of the 20th century. They believed that the British Government should set up a state forest agency with the task of creating large forests to ease the difficulties of a possible world-wide timber shortage. At the same time the afforestation programme would stimulate the economies of remote rural areas in the Highlands, provide jobs and help to stabalise a declining rural population. The development of better silvicultural techniques that had started just before the First World War made the possibility of reforesting exposed upland areas seem more feasible, but there lay still a long road of experimentation and technical development ahead before large-scale afforestation of the uplands would be successful.

Besides technical problems of planting the uplands, the political climate was not ready for the adoption of a state forest policy and the creation of a national forest agency in the years before the First World War. The formation of a formal forest policy in Britain was delayed because of the belief in laissez-faire economic policies and an attitude of what can be described as the 'arrogance of the centre'. Although the continental and Indian models of a central forestry service had been around for a long time, it was deemed unnecessary to establish such a service in Britain. It was believed that Britain could rely indefinitely on a secure timber supply from Northern Europe, Canada and the Empire. But the First World War changed all that and more than fifty years after the creation of the Forest Department in India, centralised scientific forestry was about to make a breakthrough in Britain. It needed the combination of the mounting pressure from influential landowners plus a national emergency to convince the government to introduce a formal forestry policy and to create a state run forestry service.

---

72   G.B. Ryle, *Forest Service. The First Forty-five Years of the Forestry Commission of Great Britain* (New Abbot: David and Charles, 1969), p. 21-22; NAS: FC7/6 *Forest History Inverliever Forest*.

3. The upland question

At the outbreak of the First World War, hardly anyone in Britain had foreseen the devastating consequences of the German submarine campaign for the wood supply of the country. Before the war 92 per cent of timber was imported occupying 12 per cent of total shipping space entering British ports.[1] In addition modern warfare required immense quantities of wood for huts, hospitals, roads, barges, trenches, ammunition cases, provision boxes and a whole host of other purposes. Even more important was the use of wood in mining operations and a shortage of pit props meant no mining, no coal, no heating, and no transportation and thus hampering a modern war effort. Indeed, importation of such a bulky material as timber naturally created difficulty when tonnage became scarce due to the activities of the German U-boats. The Prime Minister, David Lloyd George, speaking to the House of Commons in January 1917 on the limitations of imports by the submarine menace, placed timber first as absorbing most of the tonnage. He concluded, 'if tonnage is to be saved [wood production] is the first problem to be attacked'.[2] It is here that the men who had lobbied for the creation of a state forestry authority before the war saw their chance. This time they were successful in the light of the emergency of looming timber shortages and because of the fact that the leading figures in forestry of the day, such as Lord Lovat, had contacts high up in the government hierarchy.[3] As a result, a forestry sub-committee was added to the Government Reconstruction Committee with the mission to 'consider and report upon the best means of conserving and developing the woodland resources of the United Kingdom, having regard to the experience gained during the war'.[4] The forestry sub-committee was headed by Francis D. Acland (1874-1939), and became subsequently known as the 'Acland Committee'. Roy Robinson of His Majesty's Office of Woods, and future chairman of the Forestry Commission, assisted Acland as secretary of the Committee. The Committee included most of the people who had played an important role in Scottish forestry before the war and who were destined to play major roles in the future Forestry Commission. Other committee members included Lord Lovat, who was to become the Forestry Commission's first chairman, T.H. Middleton of the Board of Agriculture and Fisheries; Professor William Schlich from the Oxford School of Forestry; John Sutherland of the

---

1   *First Annual Report of the Forestry Commission* (London: His Majesty's Stationery Office, 1920), p. 11; Robert Miller, *State Forestry for the Axe: A Study of the Forestry Commission and De-nationalisation by the Market* (London: Institute of Economic Affairs, 1981), p. 42

2   House of Commons (hereafter HC) Debate, 23 February 1917, vol. 90, col. 1595, *Speech on Limitation of Imports*.

3   Glasgow City Archives (hereafter GCA): T-PM 122/4/7/2 BBC forestry talk no. 2, 29 March 1928.

4   Final Report of the Forestry Sub-committee of the Reconstruction Committee (Cmd. 8881) (London: HMSO, 1918), p. 3.

Board of Agriculture for Scotland and who became the Forestry Commission's first Technical Commissioner; and John Stirling Maxwell, who went on to become a Commissioner and third Chairman of the Forestry Commission.[5]

The work of the Committee was not easy because of the lack of information on the extent and quality of the country's wood reserves. In his history of the Forestry Commission George Ryle,[6] commented that 'the sub-committee examined in great detail the available, if rather unreliable, statistics in regard to the acreage of woodlands ... and land suitable for expansion'.[7] It is almost certain that the Committee relied heavily on Lovat's knowledge of the extent of woodland and land suitable for forestry in upland Scotland that he had gained during the Great Glen survey of 1911. Notwithstanding the lack of reliable statistics, the Acland Committee was not prevented from producing a report that recommended the introduction of an adequate nation wide forest policy. The timber shortage caused by the First World War did not need hard statistics to prove the need for such a policy.

After a description of British forestry before the war, the Acland report next looked at the depredations on the forests in Britain as a result of the war. It concluded that dependence on imported timber had proven a source of strategic weakness in time of war and had caused a serious shortage of timber. The forestry sub-committee believed that a timber famine would be inevitable not only in a future war but also in peacetime because of the escalating world demand for timber. In this context, the sub-committee showed a deep concern about the over-exploitation of Canada's natural forests.[8] The Acland report also emphasised the social and economic benefits of afforestation such as rural employment and a strengthened Highland economy. The Acland Committee regarded the creation of smallholdings by a new State forestry agency as one of the cornerstones of forestry policy. In their view forestry was a means to repopulate upland rural areas and to create a secure supply of labour to carry out the massive planting programme. They envisaged that 'the small holdings will be grouped together on the best land within or near the forests so as to economise labour in the working of the holdings, ... and to provide an ample supply of ... labour for [forestry] work. Families settled on new holdings in forest areas will be a net addition to the resident rural population'.[9]

The final conclusions of the Acland report formulated three objectives for a British forest policy: firstly maintaining an adequate reserve of standing timber in case of any emergency, secondly the desire to make better use of uncultivated

5 Ibid.
6 G.B. Ryle was deputy director of the Forestry Commission from 1963 to 1965.
7 Ryle, *Forest Service*, p. 26.
8 Ibid., p. 5,14, 27.
9 *Report of the Sub-Committee on Forestry*, p. 28.

and derelict land and thirdly, the general well-being of rural Britain, including rural employment. These three objectives remained the justification for British forest policy for almost 40 years.

The Acland Committee concluded that in order to meet these objectives the woods of Great Britain should be gradually increased from 1.2 million hectares to 3.12 million hectares. It suggested further that in the first ten years 61,000 hectares should be planted by the state and 20,000 hectares by private landowners receiving state assistance. The planting had to be supervised and conducted by a state forest authority 'equipped with funds and powers to survey, purchase, lease and plant land and generally to administer the areas acquired'.[10] The Committee advised the Government to create a forest authority with the responsibility to co-ordinate and carry out forest policy in Britain, and that it should be called the Forestry Commission.

It is must be borne in mind that the Acland Committee considered forests as the source of a commodity: timber. The main purpose of the forestry programme was the economic wellbeing and security of the country: 'the true justification for national afforestation is the wellbeing of the country. Wood is one of the prime necessities of life'. Wood was placed here on the same footing as grain and other agricultural products and the report concluded that 'next to food, [timber] is the article of which an abundant supply is most essential to the nation'.[11] Considerations such as amenity, wildlife and nature conservation were not mentioned in the report because this was not within the merits of the Acland Committee and the Forestry Commission was simply not envisaged as a nature conservation organisation.

The Government implemented the recommendations of the Acland Report almost to the letter and in the summer of 1919 the Forestry Bill was smoothly rushed through parliament and received Royal assent in August of that year. The discussions in parliament focussed on issues such as the organisation of the Commission, employment in rural areas and finance.[12] Again, environmental issues were not raised because they were not an issue in the context of the aims and objectives of the proposed national forestry policy. The Forestry Act of 1919 established the Forestry Commission and charged it with the responsibility for 'promoting the interests of forestry, the development of afforestation, and the production and supply of timber, in the United Kingdom'.[13]

The main goal of the Forestry Commission was to establish strategic wood reserves in order to decrease reliance on imports in case of another war. The

---

10   Ibid., p. 5.
11   Ibid., p. 76.
12   HC Debate, 5 August 1919, vol. 119, col. 217, *Forestry Bill second reading*.
13   Forestry Act 1919, 3-1.

Commission had two main roles: it was to function as a 'forestry enterprise', which would acquire, plant and manage forested lands. Its second function was to serve as a 'forestry authority' that would administer licenses for felling and grants for planting.[14] The Forestry Commission was given public authority over all of Great Britain (including Ireland) and the legal status of a government department. It was the first state-controlled production industry in Britain.[15]

Practical problems

The Forestry Act that established the Forestry Commission came into force in September 1919. The first Forestry Commissioners were appointed on 29 November of the same year and on 7 December they held their first meeting in London. After the meeting, chairman Lovat and commissioner Clinton decided on a wager and a little competition to see who could plant the Commission's first trees. When Lovat arrived at Elgin in Scotland he was handed a telegramme from Clinton informing him that the Commission's first trees, all broadleaves, were planted at Eggesford forest in Devon. The Forestry Commission's planting programme in England had started a few hours ahead of Scotland.[16]

These first trees, a number of beech and larch, were only the beginning of the large planting programme the Commission was embarking on. However, these first trees were planted on fertile and accessible land unlike the majority of the millions of trees that followed. The creation of large new forests was difficult because the majority of land available for forestry was on poor soils in the upland and exposed to severe climatic conditions. It was realised from the early days of the Forestry Commission that the best grounds had to be reserved for agriculture to secure food production. After the two World Wars food production was perceived as more important than the production of timber because it helped to reduce imports of agricultural products, saving money, and provided a strategic advantage in time of war. A quote from a little booklet on afforestation written by John Boyd, head forester of Corrour estate,[17] just after the First World War illustrates this concern:

---

14   Alexander S. Mather , *Afforestation in Britain, Afforestation: Policy Planning and Progress* (Boca Raton, Fla.: Belhaven Press, 1993), pp. 13-33.
15   Steve Tompkins, *Forestry in Crisis: The Battle for the Hills* (London: Christopher Helm, 1989), pp. 11-37.
16   Douglas Pringle, *The First 75 Years. A brief Account of Commission* (Edinburgh: Forestry Commission, 1994), pp. 7-8.
17   John Boyd was forester on the Corrour estate, owned by John Stirling Maxwell. He oversaw planting experiments conducted here and contributed considerably to the knowledge of planting on elevated peat.

...it must be borne in mind that all land suitable for cultivation, excepting such small areas as are required for nursery purposes, will be excluded from planting in any well-considered planting scheme.[18]

Furthermore, as the Forestry Commission began to acquire land, it could only afford to purchase cheap, marginal, upland areas that were mainly used as grazing lands. In order to reduce the costs of forestry, the Commission also had to carry out land acquisition on a large-scale, and the only place where inexpensive land was held in large unit ownership was in the Scottish uplands and, to a lesser extent, in northern England. In addition, it was still widely believed that these marginal upland areas were economically wasted and had generally degenerated from a more fertile turning into a '...wide desert where no life is found'. This was blamed on a combination of a wet climate and agricultural mal-practices: 'Selective grazing by sheep or deer, and, in this region of high rainfall, the tragic practice of moor burning, have hastened the process of regression into utter wasteland'.[19] This perception of the Scottish uplands as a 'wet desert' was made popular by the famous Scottish ecologist Frank Fraser Darling a decade later.[20]

In general, the upland areas available for forestry were characterised by high elevation, the presence of peat and heather, low soil fertility, high rainfall and high wind exposure, which meant that these grounds were not particularly suitable for forestry. When the Forestry Commission started its work, it included some old woodland areas, such as Eggesford Forest in the south of England, where the ground was fertile and which were within existing forestry science experience. However, for the reasons explained above, it was necessary to push beyond the limits of traditional estate forestry into the poorer upland grazing, heathland and moorland. It was here that the Commission was confronted with the problem that large-scale planting of upland peat lands far outstripped contemporary experience, as was observed by Henry M. Steven (1893-1969), Professor of Forestry at Aberdeen University: 'This raised many technical difficulties because ... their successful afforestation was a battle with nature'.[21] The Forestry Commission faced four interlinked problems: which species grow best on upland soils; how to cultivate wet and peaty soils on a large scale; how to deal with extreme varying climatic and soil conditions and how to deal with wind exposure.

---

18   John Boyd, *Afforestation* (London/Edinburgh, 1918), p. 17.
19   J. Alan B. Macdonald, 'The Lon Mor: Twenty Years of Research into Wasteland Peat Afforestation in Scotland', *Forestry*, 19 (1945) 1, 67-73, p 67.
20   Frank Fraser Darling, *West Highland Survey: An Essay in Human Ecology* (Oxford: Oxford University Press, 1955), p. 353.
21   H. M. Steven, 'The Forests and Forestry of Scotland', *Scottish Geographical Journal*, 67 (1951) 2, 110-123, p. 118.

Choice of tree species

During the 18th and 19th centuries Scottish forestry was centred on the counties on the east side of Scotland between the Firth of Tay and Moray coast. These included the counties of Inverness, Nairn, Moray, Banff, Aberdeen and Angus and further south Fife and the Lothians. As a result of the work of the Forestry Commission, there was a striking shift of forest cover to the counties in the west, north and south of Scotland, most notably Argyll, Ayrshire, Kirkcudbrightshire and Ross and Cromarty.[22] This break with tradition, as Anderson calls it, was most visible in the shift of tree species planted. During the 19th century tree planters had favoured European larch, Scots pine and Norway spruce and to a lesser extent various broadleaves, in particular oak. In 1889 the vice-president of the Royal Scottish Aboricultural Society observed in his opening address at the thirty-sixth annual meeting of the Society that oak was no longer worth cultivating, while the replacement of oak timber by iron for shipbuilding had made oak forests unprofitable. On the other hand he doubted if plantations of conifers would succeed in replacing broadleaves and he warned: 'the newer coniferous trees are not to be recommended as plantation trees'.[23] It seems that by the late 19th century broadleaved trees and the native Scots pine were still preferred over the newly imported North American conifers.

With the creation of the Forestry Commission in 1919 the situation changed dramatically because it required the afforestation of large areas of treeless and less fertile uplands. In addition the Ackland report had called for the greatest possible production from the land, which required the planting of high yielding species, in particular conifers. It was these developments that caused the break with tradition and brought non-native conifers into the prominent place that they came to occupy in the Scottish forests and woodlands of the 20th century.

When the Forestry Commission was established in 1919 all non-native conifers that we see today in Britain had already been grown successfully in Scotland. From the second half of the 19th century Douglas fir was increasingly planted and around the turn of the 20th century Sitka spruce, Japanese larch and Corsican pine appeared increasingly in the landscape.[24] The question remained which tree would be most suited for the harsh conditions of the Scottish uplands that were available to the Forestry Commission. In addition no one had planted any of these non-native conifers on a large scale in these areas and for this reason much research was devoted to the selection of suitable tree species.

---

22   *National Inventory of Woodland and Trees, Scotland* (Edinburgh: Forestry Commission, 2001), p. 48.
23   William M'Corquodale, 'Address Delivered at the Thirty-sixth Annual Meeting, 6th August, 1889', *Transactions of the Royal Arboricultural Society*, 12 (1890) 3, 375-378, pp. 377-78.
24   James Macdonald, R.F. Wood, M.V. Edwards and J.R. Aldhous, 'Exotic Trees in Great Britain', *Forestry Commission Bulletin*, no. 30 (London: HM Stationery Office, 1957), p. 3.

Initially much effort was put into the selection of tree species with the objective of matching tree species to the right soil conditions, or, to put it another way, to find the trees that grow best on a certain soil. Some trees demand fertile soils to grow well and these trees are called exacting species, for example beech, ash, elm, oak and silver fir. At the other extreme are a few trees that will accommodate themselves to poor soils and they are called accommodating species and include pines, spruces, birch and willow. This distinction has huge consequences. Because broadleaf trees are more demanding than conifers, it is for this reason that conifers came to dominate plantations on poor upland soils.[25]

Tree species	Pre-1901	1901-1920	1921-1940	1941-1960	1961-1980	1981-1995	Total
Conifers							
Corsican Pine	0.1	0.0	1.0	0.4	0.1	0.1	0.2
Douglas Fir	0.3	1.1	1.2	1.5	0.6	1.1	0.9
European Larch	1.3	3.1	3.9	1.3	0.3	0.2	0.8
Jap/hybrid Larch	0.2	1.2	3.3	9.9	4.1	4.3	5.0
Lodgepole Pine	0.5	0.0	0.5	5.1	16.2	11.4	10.8
Norway spruce	0.2	1.6	5.3	6.8	3.0	0.7	3.1
Scots pine	18.3	25.1	25.0	24.9	8.4	4.7	12.5
Sitka spruce	0.2	0.4	7.2	24.6	58.3	67.5	47.0
Other conifers	0.4	0.1	1.0	0.6	0.5	0.4	0.5
Mixed conifers	2.3	1.1	1.3	1.3	0.4	0.4	0.7
Total conifers	**23.8**	**33.7**	**49.8**	**76.6**	**91.8**	**90.8**	**81.6**
Broadleaves							
Ash	2.1	1.7	1.1	0.5	0.1	0.3	0.4
Beech	10.9	4.2	1.6	0.5	0.1	0.2	0.9
Birch	7.3	28.7	27.1	11.7	3.8	2.2	6.9
Elm	0.7	0.2	0.3	0.1	0.0	0.1	0.1
Oak	25.4	6.6	3.7	0.3	0.1	0.8	1.9
Poplar	0.0	0.2	0.1	0.1	0.0	0.0	0.0
Sweet Chestnut	0.1	0.0	0.0	0.0	0.0	0.0	0.0
Sycamore	3.6	2.2	2.4	1.6	0.6	0.2	1.0
Other broadleaves	3.0	3.9	2.9	2.3	1.0	1.3	1.6
Mixed broadleaves	23.0	18.6	11.2	6.4	2.5	4.1	5.5
Total broadleaves	**76.2**	**66.3**	**50.2**	**23.4**	**8.2**	**9.2**	**18.4**

Table 3.1: Percentage of forest area by principal species and planting year classes,1995.

Source: The Scottish Government/Forestry Commission.[26]

---

25   W.H. Rowe, *Our Forests* (London: Faber & Faber, 1947), pp. 66-67.
26   www.scotland.gov.uk/stats/envonline/_data/FORESTRYpercentageareahighforest.xls accessed: 1 June 2011.

The shift in the composition of the Scottish woodlands can be observed in the change in the area of principle species in planting year classes from latter half of the 19th century up to 1995 (table 3.1). In 1995 the remaining areas of productive forest planted before 1921 are predominantly broadleaves, such as oak and birch, because these trees were more popular in the pre-Forestry Commission era. However, it is important to keep in mind that these figures do not provide the full picture of the composition of pre-1919 woodlands due to the fact that most of the conifers planted in that period had been harvested by the 1990s. From the 1920s onwards, conifers are more abundant in younger forests, with conifers contributing over 90 per cent of trees planted after 1960.

Figure 3.1: Scots pine in Glen Affric.

Photo: Justine Kemp.

Over time, the range of conifers narrowed to a few species, in particular the Sitka spruce. As can be seen from table 3.1, the total land area planted with Scots pine came second only to Sitka spruce. However, the data gives a false impression of the levels of planting of this tree during the period 1919-1970. During the first decade of its existence, almost half of the trees planted by the Forestry Commission were Scots pine, but by the 1970s the planting of this tree was almost negligible.[27] Scots pine was initially the most planted tree because it was believed that this species, being the only native pine in Britain, grew well under most conditions in Scotland.[28] It is true that Scots pine will grow under a wide variety of conditions but even by the early 1920s Henry Steven, then Forestry Commission research officer for Scotland, recognised that Scots pine would not do well on poorly drained peat soils. If planted on wet moorland, Scots pine will survive but grows too slowly to be of any commercial value. For this reason plantations of Scots pine were mainly located on the dryer soils of the east of Scotland. For the poor upland moors Steven observed '…[that] it will be necessary to seek for some more productive species for conditions which previous forestry experience has considered suitable for Scots pine'.[29]

By 1933, the experiments at Inverliever had shown that only a few conifers were suitable for planting on wet peat soils. Scots pine thrives in areas where Sitka spruce, lodgepole pine and other spruces are likely to fail because the soil is too sandy and dry. Scots pine does well on well-drained sands, gravels and other well-drained sites. As a result Scots pine was dismissed as a useful tree on wet peat and confined to the drier sandy soils in the east of Scotland and to drier heath lands. On the wetter sites Sitka and Norway spruce overtook Scots pine as the most planted trees from the 1930s onwards. Norway spruce was planted on moist waterlogged sites of medium to high fertility, including the less acid peats, but because Norway spruce is less accommodating the proportion of planting fell in comparison with Stika spruce and lodgepole pine from the 1940s onwards.[30] Lodgepole pine resembles Scots pine and, like the latter, is tolerant of poor soils and can tolerate wet conditions much better than Scots pine. It is therefore widely planted at high elevations on the poorest soils of western Scotland and will grow well with only low inputs of fertiliser. Its hollow roots bring air into the ground which helps to dry out water logged peat. Lodgepole pine is widely planted as a nurse to provide shelter for other trees, usually in mixtures of Sitka spruce. This practice almost ceased by the 1960s in favour of Sitka spruce because it was cheaper to concentrate on only one species.[31]

The use of Sitka spruce had a profound impact on the shape of British forestry. Early in the 20th century J.D. Crozier had suggested that it was the best tree for producing timber on elevated land with wet soils, echoing the prophetic words of the famous tree seed collector David Douglas that Sitka spruce 'would

27   Mark Avery and Roderick Leslie, *Birds and Forestry* (London: Poyser, 1990), pp. 7-8.
28   Ibid., p. 69.
29   H.M. Steven, 'Coniferous Forest Trees in Great Britain', *Transaction of the Royal Scottish Arboriculural Society*, 34 (1920) 1, 61-82, p. 63.
30   Steven, 'Coniferous Forest Trees in Great Britain', pp. 8, 49-50; Peter S. Savill, *The Silviculture of Trees Used in British Forestry* (Oxford: CAB International, 1991), pp. 59-60, 76-77.
31   Savill, *The Silviculture of Trees*, pp. 65-66; Joy Tivy (ed.), *The Organic Resources of Scotland, Their Nature and Evaluation* (Edinburgh: Oliver Boyd, 1973), pp. 176-177.

thrive in such places in Britain where even *P. sylvestris* finds no shelter'.[32] The ascent of Sitka spruce to become the most prominent plantation tree in Scotland began in the 1920s when Henry Steven wrote that he did not know 'a species, … , which gives greater promise than Sitka spruce'. As head of the Scottish research branch he recommended that 'its various problems should be investigated without delay'.[33] It was in conjunction with research into new planting techniques for marginal grounds that Sitka spruce began to assume its dominant position on difficult sites. Because of its suitability for planting on the upland peat areas of Scotland, more research has been devoted to Sitka spruce in Scotland than to any other tree species during the 20th century.[34]

Figure 3.2: Sitka spruce plantation.

Photo: Steve Partridge, from www.geograph.org.uk with permission.

32   J.D. Crozier, 'The Sitka Spruce as a Tree for Hill Planting and General Afforestation', *Transaction of the Royal Scottish Arboriculural Society*, 23 (1910) 1,   7-16; David Douglas, *Journal Kept by David Douglas During his Travels in North America 1823-1827 Together with a Particular Description of Thirty-three Species of American Oaks and Eighteen Species of Pinus* (London: W. Wesley & Son, 1914), p. 341.
33   Steven, 'Coniferous Forest Trees in Great Britain', p. 77.
34   F. K. Fraser, 'Studies of Scottish Moorlands in Relation to Tree Growth', *Forestry Commission Bulletin*, 15 (London: HMSO, 1933), p. 100; R.F. Wood, 'Fifty Years of Forestry Research', *Forestry Commission Bulletin No. 50* (London: HMSO, 1974), pp. 17-19; Zehetmayr, 'Afforestation of Upland Heaths', *Forestry Commission Bulletin No. 32* (London: HMSO, 1960), p. 80.

By the late 1920s many foresters had determined that Sitka spruce was the more suitable tree for wet and windy upland sites in Scotland. Although Sitka appears very well adapted to the conditions of the Scottish uplands, it has a few problems that prevented it from becoming the dominant tree in the interwar period. Sitka spruce thrives in a wet climate, but it does not grow in waterlogged conditions, and it hardly grows in competition with heather unless the heather is killed or enough fertiliser is added to enable it to outgrow the heather. It needed the development of the Cuthbertson plough in the 1940s and 1950s that could cultivate deep peat and suppress the heather, the aerial application of fertiliser and mechanical drainage that would fully unlock the potential of Sitka spruce in Scotland.[35] For this reason, ground preparation became one of the major research areas for the Forestry Commission during the inter-war years.

Ground preparation

Fortunately, the Forestry Commission did not have to invent everything from scratch. In previous centuries, Scottish foresters had created a corpus of technical knowledge unrivalled in Britain. This experience was mainly gained during the hundred years between 1750 and 1850, when landowners in Scotland planted for pleasure but also started to create commercial forests, although their main aim was to enhance the amenity of the estates and not timber production. The arrival of exotic conifers from all parts of the world, but especially North America, helped to increase the interest in forestry among estate owners. Around 1890 most of the exotic conifers planted in Scotland were between 35 and 60 years old and the majority of these trees had been planted on fertile and sheltered sites where they thrived.[36] Hardly any attempt had been made to grow these trees on more difficult sites and it was only around the turn of the 20th century that experiments were initiated and the work done by John Stirling Maxwell at Corrour and by the Office of Woods at Inverliever was breaking new ground.

The Corrour estate is situated on Rannoch Moor in the middle of the Highlands around Loch Ossian in Inverness-shire, just east of the West Highland Railway line to Fort William. John Stirling Maxwell bought the estate in 1892 and he began the forestry plantations to improve the landscape and to create shelter for deer, but also to find out 'whether it is possible to convert bad moorland soil into forest at this altitude in Scotland'.[37] The conditions around Loch Ossian are not very well suited for forestry; the site being situated above 380 metres

---

35   Smout *et al.*, *The Native Woodlands*, p. 285.
36   John D. Matthews, 'Forestry', *Proceedings of the Royal Society of Edinburgh*, 84B (1983), p. 145, 159.
37   John Stirling Maxwell, *Loch Ossian Plantations* (Glasgow, 1913), p. 5.

(1250 feet)[38] with poor, water logged peaty soils and very exposed slopes. In order to prove that such upland sites could be successfully planted Stirling Maxwell, with the help of his foresters Simon Cameron and John Boyd, tried several experiments involving planting on peat soils in the early years of the 20th century.

Figure 3.3: Loch Ossian and the Corrour plantations.

Photo: Jan Oosthoek.

The idea of forestry trail plantations on high peat lands was first proposed by botanist Professor Augustine Henry, who occupied a chair in forestry at the Royal College of Science in Dublin. He suggested to John Stirling Maxwell that he visit Belgium to see the planting experiments on peat in the Hertogenwald near the German border. This visit was made in 1906 and the Belgium planting method was soon after introduced on Stirling Maxwell's Corrour estate.[39]

---

38   Because of its location in the North Atlantic, 350 meters of altitude corresponds with a sub-alpine climate in Scotland.

39   J.A.B. MacDonald, 'John Stirling Maxwell: an Appreciation', *Forestry*, 30 (1957) 1, 46.

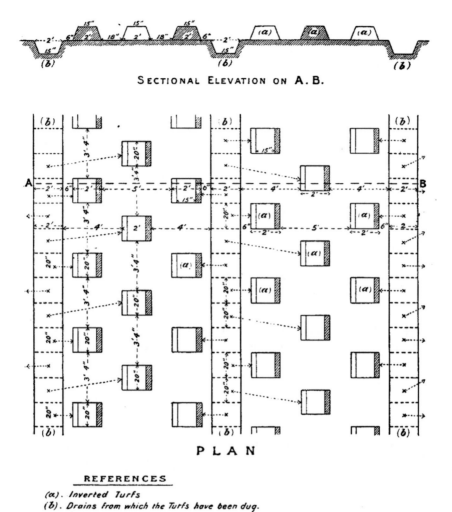

SECTIONAL ELEVATION ON A.B.

PLAN

REFERENCES

(α). *Inverted Turfs*
(b). *Drains from which the Turfs have been dug.*
Note:— *The Arrows indicate the manner of distribution of the Turfs.*

Figure 3.4: Belgium system for planting on peat.

Source: From John Stirling Maxwell, 'The Planting of High Moorlands', *TRSAS*, 20 (1907) 1, 1-7, reproduced with permission.

The Belgium Forest Service had developed a method by which a network of ditches was created to drain the peat. The surface material that came out of the drains, referred to as turf, was dragged out of the drain and turned upside down in rows several feet apart and left to dry. By planting time the turf would have settled and dried sufficiently to be easily slit open to insert a tree, spreading out the roots under the turf. With the original Belgium method a circular plug was cut from the centre of the turf, creating a hole in which the young plant was placed and the hole filled with a mix of sand, gravel and manure. However, the Corrour experiments showed that spreading the roots under the turf provided the young tree with a better nutrient supply and more stability. A tree planted according to the Corrour method stands in the centre of the turf with its roots sandwiched between the two layers of rotting vegetation, which release nutrients, provide aeration, and keep roots away from the peat soil which may still be too wet and cold.[40]

The experiments showed that the conifers planted in the turfs thrived, proving that it was possible to plant trees successfully in deep peat at higher elevations. One of the most important innovations at Corrour was the use of phosphatic fertilisers to give the young trees a growth boost.[41] The general value of the Loch Ossian plantations for Scottish forestry was that it demonstrated the benefits of both a raised planting position in turfs and the use of phosphate fertiliser. The experiments at Corrour laid the foundation for modern ploughing techniques on peat land that were developed in subsequent decades based on the pioneering work done by Stirling Maxwell.

Another important demonstration forest was created by the Office of Woods at Inverliever on the shores of Loch Awe in Argyll. The experiments at Inverliever were focussed on trying different tree species and planting methods on different soils. The work at Inverliever differed from that at Loch Ossian in some important ways. Whereas the latter was designed as an experiment in peat without a strong commercial objective, the former was laid out as the first large-scale planting of conifers on land with hugely differing soil and environmental conditions as if it were a commercial undertaking. Inverliever Forest, being situated on the north side of Loch Awe, was thought to be reasonably representative of large areas of plantable land in the west of Scotland. In 1912 Roy Robinson (1883–1952), a future chairman of the Forestry Commission, was put in charge of Inverliever and together with the local forester, John Boyd, started a scheme that was meant as a model for large-scale afforestation of upland areas. They set out to develop a standard procedure for selecting land for afforestation. The land was

---

40   John Stirling Maxwell, 'The Planting of High Moorlands', *Transaction of the Royal Scottish Arboricultural Society*, 20 (1907) 1, 1-7, pp. 3-4; John Stirling Maxwell, 'Belgian System of Planting on Turfs', *Transaction of the Royal Scottish Arboricultural Society*, 23 (1910) 2, 153-157, pp. 153, 155; T.A. Robbie, *Teach Yourself Forestry* (London: English Universities Press 1955), pp. 92-93.
41   Stirling Maxwell, *Loch Ossian Plantations*, p. 46.

first surveyed in advance of planting to find out which parts were expected to produce good timber. From these surveys it became clear that soil conditions and exposure to wind were factors that played a major part in limiting tree growth, while existing vegetation also affected the growth of young trees. Robinson and Boyd also classified types of vegetation as an indicator of the character and condition of the soil and as a measure for the productivity of the site. The second group of experiments was related to large-scale planting of spruces on poor sites. Unlike the trails at Loch Ossian most of the trees were directly planted in the peat soil and no fertilisers were applied.[42]

In 1920 Inverliever Forest was taken over by the Forestry Commission from the Office of Woods and, because the forest was a decade ahead of the first plantations of the Commission, it was carefully monitored. The examination of its development, silviculture and management provided the Commission with invaluable information on the problems of afforestation and silviculture of fast growing conifers on difficult sites.[43] Unfortunately, the manual planting of trees at Inverliever and Corrour was a slow process and the scale of forest expansion envisaged over the whole country required solutions that would make mass cultivation of the uplands efficient, fast and affordable.

The Forestry Commission picked up the work done at Corrour and Inverliever in the early 1920s. In the autumn of 1919 the Commission appointed Henry Steven as research officer for Scotland and a year later in 1920 a Research Branch was set up. One of the first problems the Research Branch faced was the question of how to establish quickly and efficiently large-scale plantations in the uplands peat areas of Scotland, Northern England and Wales that had not been under forest vegetation before.[44] The work at Corrour and Inverliever had proved that the development of forests on peat was possible, but the costs were very high and growth slow. The Research Branch continued the research and concentrated on testing different tree species, improving the turf planting methods and the use of fertilisers, and on drainage work and later ploughing.

Between 1925 and 1928 the well-known Scottish forester Mark Anderson (1895-1961) designed a series of experiments to improve the turf planting method that was carried out on the Lon Mor, which means 'Great Damp' in Gaelic. This upland area is part of Inchnacardoch Forest and is situated just northwest of Fort Augustus above the Great Glen. Anderson's experiments confirmed the findings of the Corrour planting trails and by 1929, turf planting had been adopted in every district on the peat soils suitable for forestry.[45] Unfortunately, there was still no immediate hope of turning out the required turfs by mechanical means on

---

42   NAS: FC7/6 Notes on Inverliever Forest by Roy L. Robinson, 1923, 195.

43   Matthews, 'Forestry', p. 148.

44   *First Annual Report of the Forestry Commission*(London: HMSO, 1920), p 42.

45   J.A.B. MacDonald, *The Forestry. An Autobiography* (Unpublished, 1997), pp. 15-16.

a large scale, but the new method was making the best use yet of manual labour and ordinary, non-mechanical draining tools. Additional problems related to turf planting were the fact that it did not improve drainage sufficiently, and it did not break through podzolic iron pans to enable roots to penetrate deeper into the soil and thus achieving better stability.[46] Equally importantly, it was simply not practical to dig drainage ditches and create turf ridges by hand on the thousands of square kilometres that had to be planted.

Figure 3.5: Experimental ploughing on the Lon Mor, ca. 1927. Man viewed from the back standing on the plough is Mark Anderson.

Photo: Forestry Commission, with permission.

In 1925 when Mark Anderson took the Scottish research over from Steven, he realised that, if the land could be ploughed, it would solve all these problems and make it possible to cultivate upland moors and plant them economically on a large scale.[47] In 1927 a horse drawn agricultural plough was tested by Anderson on the Lon Mor. These trials were only moderately successful but it showed that shallow drainage ditches could be produced with the turfs inverted beside them. A year later the experiment was repeated at Glen Righ, just south of Fort William, with three horses instead of two. Both experiments showed that it was difficult to plough at depth and to keep the plough at one level and the horses

---

46   Personal comment Jim Atterson, 13 August 1999.
47   Davies, *The Scottish Forester*, p. 33.

were not able to drag the plough through hard knolls. This was the last attempt of deep pleat ploughing by the Research Branch until 1939 but it showed that ploughing had potential.[48]

According to the first edition of the Forestry Commission's Handbook, *Forestry Practice*, published in 1933 only dry heath areas was considered ploughable.[49] The obstacle to plough deep peat was their low bearing pressure which excluded the use of wheeled tractors. On shallow peat, for example, in Castleton Forest in Liddesdale in the Scottish Borders, tractors were used for ploughing by the mid-1930s. Around 1937 the advantages of crawler type tractors to deal with deep peat became obvious and the first trials were initiated. The first full-scale experiments with crawler tractor ploughing and turfing was carried out at Borgie in Naver Forest in the far north of Sutherland in 1939. These experiments were quite successful but the immediate adoption of large-scale ploughing was delayed because of the outbreak of war. The use of ploughs was further delayed by the fact that the wetter sites demanded more powerful tractors than the drier heathlands, but when these machines became available by the end of the Second World War the development of ploughs for the cultivation of the wet peatlands accelerated. Davie Ross, a Forestry Commission employee stationed at Minard in Argyll, western Scotland, designed one of the first specialised forest ploughs for use on wet sites. But it was James Cuthbertson, an engineer of plough manufacturer Biggar, who further developed Ross' ideas. The result was the famous Cuthbertson Plough that combined with more powerful crawler tractors, made large-scale mechanical cultivation economically feasible by the late 1940s.[50] A few years later ploughing for drainage and cultivation was an established practice and by 1970 the Forestry Commission ploughed at least 70 per cent of the annual afforested area.[51]

Another important development in ground preparation for planting of peaty upland soils was the use of fertiliser. In the early phase of afforestation in Britain, much attention was given to matching species to site. But when forestry was pushed into poorer areas it became clear that fertiliser was needed to kick start trees to outgrow competing heather and other vegetation. The success of Sitka spruce in upland areas led foresters to plant this species on a wide range of sites of varying fertility. The value of adding phosphatic fertilisers at planting on the poorest sites was soon established, following the early fertilising trials carried out by John Stirling-Maxwell on the Corrour estates

48   S.A. Neustein, 'A History of Plough Development in British Forestry. II. Historical Review of Ploughing on Wet Soils', *Scottish Forestry*, 30 (1976) 2, 89-111, p. 90.
49   S.A. Neustein, 'A History of Plough Development in British Forestry. I. Introduction and Early Developments', *Scottish Forestry*, 30 (1976) 1, 2-15, p. 7.
50   Davies, *The Scottish Forester*, p. 34.; Avery and Leslie, *Birds and Forestry*, pp. 50-51. Wood, *Forestry Research*, pp. 17-18; S.A. Neustein, S.A., 'A History of Plough Development in British Forestry. II.', pp. 90-91.
51   Wood, *Forestry Research*, p. 68.

and in subsequent trials at Lon Mor by the Forestry Commission during the 1920s. As the plantations progressed, however, it became apparent that on some sites, subsequent applications of phosphates would be necessary. By the 1960s, afforestation was increasingly pushed into the least fertile sites, as land for afforestation became scarcer, and this contributed greatly to the increased use of fertilisers in forestry during the 1960s. From being considered as purely an aid to create new plantations, the application of fertilisers was also extended to topdressings of established stands showing nutrient deficiencies. By the late 1960s aerial fertilising using helicopters became a routine practice which made it possible to extend forestry into even poorer land.[52]

By the end of the1960s most problems related to the cultivation of the Scottish uplands for forestry had been solved. The result was the ability to successfully establish plantations of coniferous species on a wide range of sites, from the sands of the Moray Coast to the deep peat in the north and west of Scotland and the uplands heaths of the south and east. The emergence of ploughing, aerial fertilising and Sitka spruce as the dominant species made the large-scale afforestation of the post-war decades possible.

Figure 3.6: Mechanical ploughing at Glenbranter in the early 1970s.

Photo: Norman Davidson, from http://forestry-memories.org.uk with permission.

52 E.J.M. Davies, 'Silviculture of the Spruces in West Scotland', *Forestry*, 40 (1967) 1, 37-46, p. 46; R. McIntosh, 'Fertiliser Treatment of Sitka Spruce in the Establishment Phase in Upland Britain', *Scottish Forestry*, 35 (1981), 3-13, p. 3.

Figure 3.7: Aerial fertilising by helicopter.

Photo: Norman Davidson, from http://forestry-memories.org.uk with permission.

4. Post-war policy: The end of the strategic reserve

The massive felling during the Second World War justified the strategic underpinning of the British forestry programme as it had been formulated in 1919. When the war broke out in 1939, almost all of the plantations created by the Forestry Commission were less than 20 years old. This resulted in the felling and depletion of many of the older forests in Britain in general and in Scotland in particular. In response, the Government asked the Forestry Commission to produce a review of forestry policy and to advise on how to deal with the loss of woodlands due to the war effort once hostilities had ceased. In 1943 the Commission published the *Report on Post-War Forestry Policy*, which was modelled on the Acland Report; its findings carried a strong resemblance to its 1918 predecessor.

The combination of a wartime context and a review body with a vested interest produced a predictable appeal to confirm and intensify the policy laid down in 1919. The report restated the importance of wood as a raw material and the unfavourable balance of trade as far as Britain was concerned and concluded that a renewed effort was needed to create an adequate timber reserve for 'national safety and ... also provide a reasonable insurance against future stringency in world supplies'.[1] The military argument was reinforced by the review but, surprisingly, no financial analysis of the necessary investment was offered. The report proposed that over two million hectares should be devoted to forestry to create a sufficiently large timber reserve and suggested, like its 1918 predecessor, that most of the ground for planting was to be found on the bare, 'unproductive' upland areas of Scotland. The report also emphasised the social advantages of the afforestation programme for rural communities in the uplands of Scotland (and Wales) when it stated 'there are valuable contingent advantages associated with forests, such as the development and settlement of rural Britain'.[2] A new element that was introduced by the report was the idea of forestry as a valid form of business investment, included in order to attract investors to finance the proposed planting programme. The incentive for the private sector to collaborate was the introduction of a dedication scheme under which landowners could dedicate woodland for the purposes of timber production under a management plan agreed with the Forestry Commission. The Commission would provide landowners with practical advice and a subsidy for woodland management. Since the Forestry Commission would oversee the dedication scheme, this forestry incentive programme extended the norms of

---

1 Forestry Commission, *Post-war Forest Policy* (Cmd. 6647) (London: HMSO, 1943), p. 8.
2 Ibid.

state afforestation to the private sector.[3] This was to have serious consequences for both forest policy and the shape and nature of the forests decades later, in the last quarter of the 20th century, as will be discussed in detail in subsequent chapters.

The 1943 forestry review also highlighted amenity and recreational advantages. It was proposed to reserve 400,000 hectares for recreation, amenity and conservation. This was in recognition of the mounting demand for access and recreational facilities, which led to the Forestry Commission's belief that it had to formalise its policy with regard to amenity where the National Forestry Parks were concerned. The review therefore laid the foundations for the development of formalised environmental and conservation policies within the Forestry Commission in the decades ahead.[4]

The Report on *Post-War Forest Policy* was the blueprint for the Forestry Act of 1945, and it was implemented to the letter, just as the Acland Report had been before it. The new Act referred to the 1919 Act in repeating that the Commission was charged with the creation and maintenance of adequate reserves of timber grown in plantations. The 1945 Act also reformed the organisational structure of the Forestry Commission, in that the Commissioners became responsible to the Minister of Agriculture and the Secretary of State for Scotland. Although it had been mentioned in the 1943 review, the 1945 Act did not include a clause on amenity, recreation or nature conservation. These were still unofficial objectives of the Forestry Commission, although the Government stated that it 'would continue to establish and extend National Forest Parks as and when suitable opportunities occur'.[5] However, National Forest Parks were only a sideshow and the Commission had more important problems to deal with. In the first place, it had to cultivate land for forestry that no one had attempted to cultivate before. Before and during the war, research into cultivation techniques, complemented by improved cultivation machinery, had provided foresters with a robust set of silvicultural techniques for establishing conifer plantations on a range of sites that had been off-limits to forestry at the beginning of the 20th century. It was now possible to put these new techniques into practice, to make up for the massive war fellings, and to push large-scale monoculture forestry plantations high into the uplands.

Until 1957, the Commission's focus was on the expansion of the forest area and to secure a large reserve of timber. It was also part of the post war aim to make Britain as self-sufficient as possible in the interests of limiting imports and the outflow of hard currency needed to recover from the war. The Forestry

---

3 H.M. Steven, 'The Forests and Forestry of Scotland', *Scottish Geographical Journal*, 67 (1951) 2, 110-123, p. 120.
4 *Post-war Forest Policy*, section 5.
5 HC Debate, 30 November 1945, vol. 416, col. 1781, *Forest Policy (Government Programme)*.

Commission felt very confident that it would be able to successfully carry out its ambitious planting programme because it felt that its policy was 'in line with the Government's own policy for developing native resources under state initiative'.[6]

In 1952 the Chancellor of the Exchequer called for the need to reduce national expenditure in order to safe Britain from bankruptcy.[7] In addition, wages of forest workers had increased over the previous year, putting a strain on the Commission's finances. In response, the Commission reviewed its finances and the various ways in which their budget was spent. It was decided to curtail the construction of new buildings, houses and roads, and to limit the employment of new staff. However, the Commissioners were very clear that there could not be a reduction in the proposed planting programme. In 1952 the Commission stated that a reduction of the planting operations or abandonment of the goal of creating a timber reserve would be a waste of public money and labour.[8] This plea for not reducing Treasury funding for forestry was successful and the planting effort continued to intensify. However, the commissioners expected a future downward trend in the planting programme, caused not by financial problems but by a shortage of land available for planting. This had already been a problem before the war but in the post-war years became more serious. The problem was that the Commission had to compete with agriculture for land because a national policy for the expansion of home food production was being pursued with even greater vigour than the forestry policy, a repeat of the situation after the First World War. As a result, officials of the Department of Agriculture exercised 'a *de facto* veto over the release even of land in the possession of the Forestry Commission' for afforestation.[9] The Forestry Commission itself did not have the power to override the Department of Agriculture if the latter thought that certain areas could be better used for the production of food. This forced the Forestry Commission to advance up hill, making use of poorer land for forestry, a development that was made possible by the introduction of new planting techniques, fertilisers and the use of hardy tree species. This had considerable consequences for the appearance of the landscape and biodiversity in large areas of Scotland.

---

6   TNA: PRO T224/234 General policy. Draft joint memorandum by Minister of Agriculture and Secretary of State for Scotland to the Treasury, 1947, p. 2.

7   '"Solvency, Security, Incentive" in "Save the Pound Budget"', *The Canberra Times*, Thursday 13 March 1952, p. 1.

8   Forestry Commission, *Annual Report 1952*, p. 7-8; *Annual Report 1953*, p. 7.

9   Donald Mackay, *Scotland's Rural Land use Agencies. The History and Effectiveness in Scotland of the Forestry Commission, Nature Conservancy Council and Countryside Commission* (Aberdeen: Scottish Cultural Press, 1995), p. 32.

The Zuckerman Report

In the 1943 report on *Post-War Forest Policy* it was stated that 'the post-war position will demand speedy and large-scale action'.[10] The coincidence of the need for timber during the reconstruction period following the Second World War, and the desire to restore strategic timber reserves, created a fertile environment for the development of the ideas of the Oxford-based forestry economist W.E. Hiley on the forestry economics of shorter tree crop rotations. William Mutch, a retired lecturer in forestry at the University of Edinburgh, noted that Hiley's ideas were very influential 'among some of the younger people in the Forestry Commission [and] there emerged a concept of big scale forestry'.[11] But Roger Bradley, an economist involved in these developments within the Forestry Commission, felt that the emergence of large-scale forestry in Scotland was not due to changes in the attitudes of foresters. Rather, he felt it to be the result of increased opportunities for land acquisition in the uplands.[12]

Figure 4.1: Even-aged high forest Scots pine plantation.

Photo: Jan Oosthoek.

In the late 1940s and early 1950s forestry on an ecological basis, a practice that took local environmental and biological conditions into consideration, was still popular among foresters, as will be explained in more detail in chapter eight. However, at this point the official silvicultural practice of the Forestry

---

10   Forestry Commission, *Post-War Forest Policy*, p. 7.
11   Personal comment William E.S. Mutch.
12   Written comments by Roger Bradley.

Commission was that of even-aged monoculture high forestry on long rotations of clear felling and restocking, which was regarded as the 'only practical means of exploiting the large even-aged plantations made by our ancestors'.[13]

In 1957, the *Report of an Enquiry into Forestry, Agriculture and Marginal Lands*, better known as the Zuckerman Report, was published and its conclusions undermined completely the basis for the existing forest policy. The Zuckerman Report suggested that it was 'less meaningful to consider our forest policy in relation to war-time needs than in a primarily economic and social light'.[14] The more influential conclusions were that end-users for forest products had to be actively sought and that the strategic need for a three-year self-sufficiency of timber had disappeared with the advent of nuclear warfare; any future war was expected to be short. A further recommendation was that forestry and agriculture should be integrated and planned together, and that more attention should be devoted to the amenity and recreational aspects of forestry.[15]

The Commissioners welcomed the Zuckerman report, feeling that its findings were, on the whole, supportive. Although it removed the main justification for forestry as it currently existed, the report reflected on the fact that the commercial and social functions of forestry were becoming increasingly important. In recognition of this, the Forestry Commission acknowledged publicly that there was 'evidence of a growing public demand for the recreational facilities provided by the Commission'.[16] The response of the Commissioners was the publication of new expanded editions of forestry park guides and pamphlets about camping and facilities in the parks.

After the Zuckerman Report had removed the main justification for the existence of the Forestry Commission, an inter-departmental working party was established to review forest policy and to formulate new aims for British state forestry. The report of the working party, made public in early 1958, can be roughly divided into two sections: a section on forestry economics and a section on the social aspects of forestry including amenity and nature conservation. The opening pages of the working party report made a clear statement about the type of trees and timber deemed necessary for the future:

> The growing of hardwoods on a large scale is commercially unattractive
> in the United Kingdom because the main species mature slowly and yield

13 'How Should we Grow Conifers? Forestry Meeting at Dartington Hall, Devon, June 1958', *Scottish Forestry*, 12 (1958) 1, 19-29, p. 24.

14 Quoted in: 'Forest Policy Review', *Scottish Forestry*, 12 (1958) 2, 92-94, p. 92.

15 Pringle, *The First 75 Years*, pp. 44-45; Mackay, *Rural Land Use Agencies*, p. 33.

16 Forestry Commission, *Annual Report 1957* (London: HMSO, 1957), p. 56.

very little revenue in the early years. Home production of hardwoods is therefore likely to decline and need not be taken into account as a factor of major importance in the future.[17]

It was expected that the demand for softwood would rise dramatically in the following decades. In 1956, 6.6 million cubic metres of softwoods were imported. Since 226,500 cubic metres were produced in Britain, imports made up 97 per cent of all softwoods and thus the question was whether timber should be produced in Britain at all. The problem was that so much had been invested in new plantations that abandoning the forestry schemes would have been seen to be a waste of money and effort. It was acknowledged that Britain's forests were reaching maturity and that it was to be expected that the output of timber would increase. An additional concern was the question of whether the existing wood processing industry had the capacity to deal with an increased supply of home-grown timber. The working party advised creating new manufacturing capacity by means of further investment in, and the subsidisation of, pulp and chipboard mills, particularly in the remoter areas of Britain such as northern Scotland. It was expected that these domestic mills would meet heavy foreign competition for the wood resources needed to sustain them. To counter this effectively, the success of the wood processing industry would depend on further expansion of the forest area in order to create a softwood surplus that would make the mills independent of wood imports.[18]

Changing attitudes towards forestry also reflected the global economic and political shifts that took place during the 1950s. In similar fashion as the Zuckerman report, the working party concluded that the division of the world into two political blocs and the introduction of the atomic bomb had undermined the objectives of forest policy in Britain. In addition, the working party believed that the economies of the western world, including Britain, were becoming more integrated. It was thought that the liberalisation of trade would have a self-regulating effect and that import restrictions would have to be abolished and government subsidies limited. The working party advised therefore:

> ...although a measure of subsidy may be justified on social grounds it would not be to our general advantage, or accord with our policy of increasing liberalisation of trade, to foster the production of raw materials for British industry at anything other than truly competitive prices... .[19]

It was further recommended that direct investment by the State, by means of the subsidisation of forestry through the Forestry Commission, could no longer

---

17 TNA: PRO F18/815 Cabinet Working Party on Forest Policy, Draft Report, p. 4.

18 Ibid., p. 7-8.

19 Ibid., p. 8.

be justified. Forestry, according to the working party, needed to become as profitable as agriculture, requiring only loans from the State. However, it was recognised that the repayment of loans would be problematic, even when the first forests started to become productive, given the long period needed for trees to mature.[20]

The conclusions of the working party were the opening the Treasury had been looking for to cut expenditure on forestry. Before the war the Treasury had already been pressing for the adjustment of the 'planting programme to the most economic figure'.[21] In 1958, the minimum return of any government investment that was applied by the Treasury was 6.25 per cent, which also applied to forestry. Estimates by the working party forecasted a return of between 3 and 3.5 per cent on new planting by the Forestry Commission, which meant that state forestry did not meet the criteria set by the Treasury, which was problematic if state-funded forestry was to survive. The working party realised that a solution had to be found to this problem. The solution was to make use of a proven strategy from the past, by pointing out that economic criteria 'are not the only grounds on which the State forestry programme must be determined'.[22] These non-economic criteria amounted to the social benefits of forestry, which were more difficult to quantify.

The working party recognised two important social aspects of forestry: the amenity aspect and the economic and demographic problems experienced by the inhabitants of the remote upland areas of Scotland. Although the amenity section was the shortest of the report, this was the first time that amenity was explicitly mentioned in a government policy document on forestry. However, the significance of this first reference should not be overstated; according to the working party, amenity was not to be considered more than 'a make-weight in the determining of policy'.[23]

Nevertheless, around 1960 the issue of amenity was becoming increasingly important. Since the 1930s the Commission had opened up their plantations to walkers and established National Forest Parks. By the second half of the 1950s, the Commission had adopted as one of its objectives the need for attention to be given to the aesthetic and conservation role of the forest, calling for due regard to be paid to recreation and sporting interests, and flora and fauna. These objectives were not included in the statutory aims of the Commission but the working party thought that it was time to correct this. In doing so, it was by no means a lone voice. The National Parks Commission and the Nature Conservancy had also recommended expanding the Forestry Commission's statutory aims in

20 Ibid., p. 14.
21 TNA: PRO F18/142 Forest policy. Forestry Commission memo no 128/36, 2nd November 1937, p 1.
22 TNA: PRO F18/815 Interdepartmental Working Party on Forest Policy 1958, Draft Report, p. 14a.
23 Ibid., p. 15.

order to enable them 'to take account of the contribution which forestry can make to the conservation of soil, water, protection from exposure and erosion, nature conservation, sport and recreation and the development of a more balanced rural landscape'.[24] However, this argument could not be justified by itself, with the result that the working party looked for ways to embed the amenity issue within the wider context of forestry. It did this by connecting amenity with the social objectives of forestry in upland areas.

Like the founding fathers of the Forestry Commission, the working party was convinced that forestry would be able to stop the decline the rural populations. It believed that 'great weight must clearly be given to the social factor in determining forestry policy'.[25] These social objectives, such as the provision of rural employment and the creation of new rural communities, especially in the remote parts of Britain, were copied from the 1919 Acland Report, but the rural population situation in 1958 was very different from that of 1919. Contrary to popular belief, census data relating to rural Scotland shows that the population was in slow decline prior to the Second World War. Only in the very remote north did the population decline quite rapidly between 1881 and 1921. However, following the Second World War the population in many rural areas of Scotland started to decline rapidly.[26] Contemporary commentators warned that this would leave behind an ageing population, abandoned homesteads and villages, and a decline in the availability of social services such as schools and shops. This in turn would accelerate the drift of people away from the land, meaning that the countryside would slip into a vicious cycle of depopulation and economic decline.[27] By the end of the 1950s, there was a much stronger case for promoting forestry in remote rural areas in the interests of economy and society then there had been during the inter-war period. In fact, by the 1960s it had become one of the main objectives to justify public money spent on forestry. In the process, the issues of amenity, recreation and nature conservation became linked to the social issue because it was believed that these would stimulate rural economies.

The Government largely accepted the findings of the Zuckerman report and the working party. A ministerial statement removed the emphasis on creating reserves of standing timber and gave greater weight to economic considerations and to the social benefits of tree planting through the diversification of employment, particularly in the upland areas of Scotland and Wales. The Government endorsed a curtailed planting programme and also announced that

24 Ibid.
25 Ibid., p. 18.
26 Michael Flinn (ed.), *Scottish Population History from the 17th Century to the 1930s* (Cambridge: Cambridge University Press, 1977), pp. 306-307.
27 J.D. Matthews, M.S. Phillip and D.G. Cumming, 'Forestry and the Forest Industries', In: J. Ashton and W.H. Long (eds), *The Remoter Rural Areas of Britain* (Edinburgh: Oliver and Boyd, 1972), pp. 39-41.

the planting programmes of the Forestry Commission would be fixed for periods of ten years and that the programme would be reviewed every five years. The first review was to be conducted in 1963, which was clearly an effort to keep the Treasury happy. With regards to the private sector, the Government moved in the opposite direction of the Working Party. A dedication scheme[28] had been introduced after the war to encourage private landowners to dedicate their land to the production of timber. While the working party had advised the abolishment of the dedication scheme, the Government, under pressure from the landowners lobby, instead increased the grants for dedicated woodlands. The system of felling licences continued, but a new statutory instrument meant that felling in dedicated woodlands no longer required a licence. The abolition of felling quotas made it possible for private landowners to control their own woodlands with a view to the most economic management of their estates. It was also announced that future planting would be further concentrated in the upland areas, particularly in Scotland and Wales, where the expansion of forestry would provide a source of employment.[29] With all this in hand the Forestry Commission had the go-ahead to continue for another five years before having its work scrutinised again.

---

28   The dedication scheme was a de facto subsidy to landowners to plant trees. Many landowners used this to make money out of land that was not suitable for agriculture. As a result these forests were not the most productive.

29   HC Debate, 24 July 1958, vol. 592, cols. 684-90, *Forestry Policy*; Forestry Commission, *Annual Report, 1958*, pp. 7-8.

5. Contradictions in the forests: Economics versus conservation

By the early 1960s the Forestry Commission was in search for a new justification to underpin forestry policy. The problem was that the Zuckerman Report and the working party set up in its wake recommended a two strand forestry policy that was on the one hand based on amenity and social objectives and on the other economics. During the 1960s the Commission struggled to come to terms with these two seemingly contradictory directions in forest policy and this chapter will chart the evolution of this struggle, which ended in favour of hard economics. This outcome laid the foundation for the troubles with environmentalists and momentous changes in forest policy and practice during the last two decades of the 20th century.

The 1963 forest policy review

In July 1962 another working party, also known as the Dew Committee, was appointed to review the progress made since the working party of 1958. The report was finished by the summer of 1963 and confirmed and reinforced the findings of the 1958 government statement. The profitability of forestry came once more under scrutiny and the working party believed that the likely return on investment in new planting might be better than was previously thought. It estimated that the rate of return could rise to 4.5 or 5 per cent, but that was still half the rate the Treasury preferred at that time.[1] In the years between the Zuckerman report and the first five year forestry review, the Treasury had put up its borrowing rate considerably and the minimum return on any new investment was now between 8 and 10 per cent. The working party realised there was a problem and tried to find a way out to secure the financial future of the Forestry Commission by continuing to justify any planting programme with social considerations. The 1962 working party put even more emphasis on the social aspects than its 1958 predecessor had, however, it was not enough because it was observed that 'planting may, by itself, be adequate to stop or at least retard the depopulation of an area... [but] the full benefit will result only when wood becomes to be extracted and used in enterprises ranging from small rural industries to large pulp mills ...'.[2]

---

1   TNA: PRO F18/755 Forestry Policy. Report by a Working Party of Officials, July 1963, p. 3.
2   Ibid., p. 4.

The working party also observed the increasing importance of forests for recreation and leisure activities: 'recreational value of the forests is increasing every year'. Hard figures backed this up and between 1951 and 1963 the number of campers on Forestry Commission sites increased five fold to 250,000.[3] Although the Forestry Act did not give the Forestry Commission specific powers to spend money on access or recreation, the Commission applied a broad interpretation of the 1919 Act to provide recreational facilities such as footpath and car parks. By the early 1960s the Forestry Commission declared a policy of so-called 'open forests', which was a deliberate attempt to attract the public. The working party supported this development and was of the opinion that the 'commission should now broaden its approach'. Options under consideration included providing scenic routes and harmonising buildings, bridges and forests with the landscape. This last aspect was by no means new, as it had been attempted since the 1930s in the Forest Parks. It was thought that providing recreational facilities 'would cost little money and would not require special legislation'.[4]

With respect to landscape preservation and nature conservation, the working party thought that the extent of the future planting programme should not be influenced by this factor. On the other hand, the working party welcomed the proposed employment of a landscape consultant by the Forestry Commission, and advised:

> Ministers should direct the Commission to take public access for recreation and the appearance of the landscape positively into account when they draw up their programme for the planting and acquisition of land.[5]

It was not thought necessary to formalise this objective in a new Forestry Act because there was '… now sufficient awareness of the importance of preserving the landscape to make any special legislation unnecessary'.[6]

The Minister of Agriculture presented the working party's findings to the House of Commons in July 1963, exactly five years after the Government's statement following the Zuckerman Report. The most important feature of the new statement was that the Commission's planting programme was determined for a period of ten years between 1964 and 1973. Unlike the programme outlined in the statement of 1958, the planting programme was not meant to fall off towards the end of the period but instead to increase. Most of this planting was to take place in the uplands of Scotland and the Government once more confirmed the

---

3   Ibid., p. 10.
4   Ibid., p. 9.
5   NAS: AF79/191 Cabinet Working Party on Forest Policy 1963, draft report.
6   Ibid.

importance of forestry for the rural economy and communities in the upland areas of Scotland and Wales. Secondly, the government and the Forestry Commission were confident that private forestry, with the aid of grants administered by the Commission, would increasingly play a large part in forestry.

Thirdly, the Commission was encouraged to pay more attention to the beauty that well planned forestry could bring to the landscape, and to continue its policy of providing access and recreational facilities. Finally the Government recognised the benefits that increased home production of wood could bring to the national economy. Mounting supply of raw materials from forests necessitated expansion in timber processing, which deserved the support of the Government through the agency of the Forestry Commission.[7]

By 1964 the future of the Forestry Commission depended upon three factors: firstly, the success of reinforcing the rural economy in upland Scotland and Wales; secondly, success in the production and supply of raw materials for an emerging domestic wood processing industry; and, finally, provision of recreational facilities and landscape preservation.

Search for a new purpose

By the close of the 1950s the Forestry Commission found itself in a reflective mood and in its 1959 *Annual Report* the Commission was redefining forestry policy objectives. The removal of the strategic underpinning of British forestry policy created a lot of uncertainty among foresters. Questions about the aim of British forestry had become paramount. For decades foresters were accustomed to the practice of planting trees, growing them and leaving the crop as long as possible in the forests as a timber reserve. They did not bother much with the needs of the market, economics or marketing. By the 1960s foresters were forced to take these things into consideration; it was felt that the former policy was not very economical and locked up an excess of capital in the woods.[8] In 1958, Sir Henry Beresford-Peirse, deputy director general of the Forestry Commission, defended this state of affairs during a meeting of foresters at the Forestry Training Centre at Dartington, in Devon. Beresford-Peirse questioned:

> Whether one could say we were growing conifers badly in the absence of certain knowledge of what we were growing conifers for. In a period of building up stocks, economics tended to be pushed in the background.[9]

---

7   HC Deb., 24 July 1963, vol. 681. Cols. 1467-72, *Forestry Policy*.
8   G. B. Ryle, 'New Trends in Silviculture of Conifers Consequent upon Manufacturing Requirements', *Scottish Forestry* 15 (1961) 2, 72-79, p. 72.
9   'How Should we Grow Conifers? Forestry Meeting at Dartington Hall', p. 20.

However, as we have seen above, the findings of the two working parties had put economics centre stage together with social, recreational and conservation concerns. The development of a wood-processing industry would meet both the social and economic objectives of the post-1958 forest policy by providing an outlet for forest products and it also encouraged the planting of more trees to secure future supply. The Forestry Commission rationalised its operations by increasingly applying short rotation forestry and mechanisation. In this way, forests were turned into 'wood factories'.

This mood was reflected at a symposium on natural resources held at the Royal Society of Edinburgh in October 1960, where James Macdonald, deputy director general of the Forestry Commission, recognised the need for a domestic wood processing industry to absorb forest products. The Government understood that the Forestry Commission needed an outlet for its products to ensure forestry would be profitable. Although the Government was convinced of the value of forestry for the rural economy in Britain, the Treasury was clearly sceptical about the proposed forestry programme. As discussed above, the return of forestry was about half the rate of return prescribed by the Treasury for investment of public money. That was why the Forestry Commission wrote a memorandum to the Treasury arguing that forestry could make a profit if two conditions were met: firstly, if better soils could be planted to produce quicker and better timber; and, secondly, if a significant domestic wood processing industry were to develop to buy the timber. Growing timber faster would mean that interest paid on the investment would be lower and, as a result, forestry would become more profitable. The problem was that the best land was needed for agriculture and remained unavailable to forestry. As a result the creation of densely packed plantations of fast growing conifers on heath and moorland had to be expanded even further. But the Commission was aware that if this did not work another justification would be needed. To counter any future criticism the memorandum included a statement emphasising the non-economic benefits:

> It should be recognised ... that the returns to capital vary widely from one form of public investment to another, and that there is no one rate of interest that can be regarded as the minimum acceptable return from all forms of public expenditure in view of the diversity of non-monetary benefits.[10]

The memorandum was written in 1963, a year after the Government decided to subsidise construction of a large paper and pulp mill at Fort William in Scotland.[11] This bizarre example of economic engineering was clearly aimed at maintaining

---

10   TNA: PRO T224/618 Factors influencing investment in forestry, Memorandum of the Planning & Economics Branch of the FC to the Treasury, September 1964.
11   See: Forestry Commission, *Annual Report*, 1964, 1965, 1966, 1967-69.

forestry's image as a financially viable industry, but it is surprising that the Treasury did not see through this ploy. The most important problem facing any pulp mill is that of access and transport and the locations of the plantations were spread across mountainous country. It was found that transporting wood from Sweden to Fort William was cheaper than sourcing it directly from the Highlands on the mill's doorstep.[12] An additional problem applying to most pulp mills is that continual increase in production capacity is needed for them to be economic. This became apparent in the early 1980s when the Fort William Paper Mill closed, after profitable subsidised contracts ended and realistic high price contracts had to be negotiated. On top of that no help was forthcoming from the government to modernise the mill's equipment or to increase capacity.[13]

Notwithstanding these potential problems, subsidised construction of the Fort William pulp mill and the creation of mills in other parts of the United Kingdom went ahead during the 1960s. The emergence of a subsidised domestic forest products processing industry reinforced the need for large-scale single-species plantations, since manufacturers did not like to vary their chemical formulae, and they needed a cast-iron guarantee of supply.[14] This required a highly rationalised and mechanised forestry practice that would make it possible to grow large quantities of timber in short rotations.

This type of forestry was made possible with the development of mechanical site preparation and aerial application of fertiliser, allowing afforestation on the poorest sites. In 1961, Ryle noted in an article in *Scottish Forestry* that 'mass production in the factory needs to be fed by raw materials mass produced in the forests'.[15] The silvicultural system that was thought to answer the needs of the market was that of short rotations and an even-aged, one-species crop. This silvicultural system was regarded as the easiest to manage, to harvest and to market, and therefore the most economic. Sites could now be adapted to the species, rather than species to the site. Ryle concluded that

> there must be a very sound reason for any divergence from the silvicultural system which will be the cheapest to manage: the selection forest or the forest changing in age or constitution by tiny cellules, though delightful aesthetically and of unending interest to the silviculturist, must be discounted ... as a commercial investment.[16]

These developments gave rise to a new type of plantation, with a particularly hard-edged commercial aim to produce cheap timber in the fastest possible way.

---

12   Walter Reid, 'Transport of Timber Too Costly', *Scottish Forestry* 22 (1968) 1, 60-63.
13   Roy Douglas, 'A View of Forestry with Special Reference to Mull', *Scottish Forestry*, 40 (1986) 1, 87-106, p. 96.
14   Mackay, *Scotlands Rural Land Use Agencies*, p. 35.
15   Ryle, 'Trends in Silviculture of Conifers', p. 79.
16   Ibid.

This new kind of forestry was at loggerheads with the newfound emphasis on landscape conservation and the provision of recreation. Despite this, a rudimentary environmental and recreation policy developed within the Forestry Commission during the 1960s.

Recreation and conservation

The 1959 *Annual Report* of the Forestry Commission made for some interesting reading, since for the first time a section was devoted to environmental issues. The Commission admitted that its planting policy had irretrievably ruined many square miles of unspoiled upland by imposing large blocks of commercially managed conifers on land where the semi-natural cover is heather, bracken, moorgrass and scrub. It is interesting to note the perception of this landscape by the Forestry Commission as natural, given that moorland and scrub were the result of a long history of sheep and cattle grazing. Surprisingly the Commission agreed that in some areas large-scale conifer plantations were not acceptable, although these were, according to the Commission, only exceptional areas. They tried to make single-species conifer plantations acceptable by stating that 'intelligent managed conifer plantations ..., can be a positive enhancement to the scenery as soon as they have passed out of the thicket stage, when no plantation ... is beautiful'.[17] Finally the Commission defended itself against accusations that it had a prejudice against hardwoods and replied that 'where hardwoods will make a worthwhile crop the Commission will continue to plant them'. If conifers grow better then hardwoods, these should be used instead to make 'best use of the land available to them'.[18]

The Commission seemed to anticipate in which direction the tide of forestry was moving and that environmental issues and landscape utilisation were becoming more important. In doing so the Forestry Commission saw hardly any contradiction with its new emerging policy of forest expansion and efficient timber production on a large-scale to cater for the wood processing industry. It would create forests that could be used for recreation and other purposes, which was part of the emergence of the new management philosophy of multiple use forestry. Many of these developments drew upon the Forestry Commission's experience with the National Forestry Parks and the conflicts over the impact of forestry on the landscape, for example in the Lake District. It might be considered a sign of the times that an entire paragraph in the forestry policy statement of the Minister of Agriculture in July 1963 was devoted to

17 Forestry Commission, *Annual Report 1959*, p. 8.
18 Ibid.

recreation, and paying attention to the beauty of the landscape.[19] For the first time, a government minister included themes of forest recreation and amenity in a policy statement.

The first theme, recreation was one of the discussion topics during a meeting of the Scottish Forest Parks Advisory Committee in December 1963. The chairman, Lord Waldegrave, referred at this meeting to the Ministerial forestry statement of July 1963 in which it had been stated that the Commission 'will bear in mind the need, whenever possible, to provide public access and recreation ...'.[20] In pursuance of this policy the commissioners were prepared to spend a certain amount of money on the improvement of facilities in the existing Forest Parks, although the Treasury did not look favourable on this. It was also agreed that the creation of one or two new forest parks in Scotland in addition to those already in existence would be considered. To make these forests more attractive to the public the Commission was aware it had to make them less monotonous. It was for this purpose that in 1963 the Commission stated that it was 'clearly directed to give more attention to the beauty that well planned forestry can bring to the countryside'.[21]

To achieve this goal of integrating forestry with aesthetic considerations and the provision of recreational facilities the Commission appointed two landscape consultants. The first was Betty Moira, a landscape architect from Edinburgh, appointed to make a plan for the Glen More Forest Park in the Cairngorms. Her task was described as follows:

> ...to investigate and report in the best way to develop the facilities afforded to the public in [the Glen More] Forest Park so as to co-ordinate the demands of the various amenity and holiday bodies into an integrated plan.[22]

That same year Sylvia Crowe, a former president of the Institute of Landscape Architects, was appointed to assist the Commission in making its forests as attractive in appearance as possible without interfering with wood production. For the first time attention to the aesthetic and recreational functions of the forests were included as an active part of the Commission's objectives. Crowe's work will be reviewed in chapter seven.

These beginnings developed slowly but steadily during the 1960s. In 1964 it was noted that nature conservation in the countryside had been added to the policy objectives of attention to amenity and recreation. It is no coincidence

---

19   Forestry Commission, *Annual Report 1963*, pp. 6-7.
20   PRO F18/596 Glenmore: correspondence. Notes of meeting, 4 December 1963.
21   Ibid., p. 7.
22   TNA: PRO F18/596 Letter from R.I. Affleck to D.R. Collinson of the Treasury, considering the appointment of Mrs. Moira,18 December 1964.

that during that same year the communal interest in land use of the Forestry Commission, the National Parks Commission and Nature Conservancy was given special recognition, with the establishment of quarterly meetings of their chairmen. This initiative was taken to ensure cohesion between the development of forestry, the preservation of amenity and the conservation of nature. These arrangements had their counterpart in Scotland, where the chairmen of the Scottish National Committee of the Forestry Commission, the Nature Conservancy and the National Trust for Scotland were engaged in quarterly meetings.[23]

In 1965, two years after the official adoption of conservation elements as policy objectives, the Commissioners recognised that they were custodians of 'magnificent scenery and great variety of wildlife'.[24] The Commission also recognised the importance of timber production as well as conservation and recreation as important functions of its forests when it wrote in reaction to the Government's 1965 white paper on leisure in the countryside:

> While the Commission's primary function is to produce timber to help to meet the steadily increasing demands of industry, there is growing recognition both inside and outside the Commission of the part which the forests can and should play in improving the landscape and in improving opportunities for open-air recreation... .[25]

Landscape conservation and recreation were regarded as closely linked and almost treated as the same problem. This was made possible with the emergence of the concept of the multi-purpose use of forests, which was introduced from the United States in the 1950s. In this concept the forests are managed for production of timber, the protection of water and other resources, to preserve landscape beauty and attractiveness for recreational purposes, and to maintain a favourable habitat for wildlife. All these resources had to be co-ordinated under a 'multiple use' plan aimed at managing and sustaining the production of a variety of services as wide ranging as commercial timber production and recreation.[26] The concept of multiple land use fitted perfectly with the Commission's aim of producing timber for a growing wood processing industry and increased demand for recreation and nature conservation. The Commission regarded the integration of forestry, recreation, visual amenity and nature conservation as 'a practical demonstration of multiple land use'.[27]

---

23   Forestry Commission, *Annual Report 1964*, p. 10-11.
24   Forestry Commission, *Annual Report 1965*, p. 10.
25   Ibid., p. 9.
26   TNA: PRO F18/617 Memorandum of evidence by the Nature Conservancy, pp. 3-4.
27   Forestry Commission, *Annual Report 1965*, p. 10.

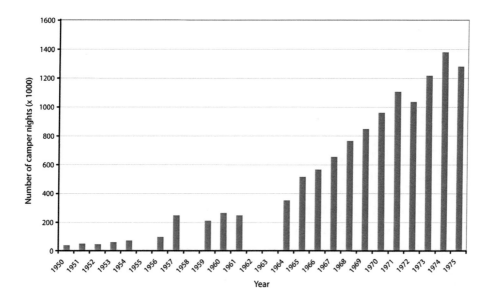

Figure 5.1: Number of camper nights on Forestry Commission campsites, 1950–1975.

Source: Forestry Commission Annual Reports.

By 1970, pressures on the Forestry Commission to protect landscapes of outstanding beauty and to provide and recreational facilities were mounting because public demand for countryside recreation was increasing rapidly (Figure 5.1). As the largest landowner in Scotland, the Forestry Commission realised it was in a unique position to meet that demand, since its forests were situated in some of the most scenic parts of the country. The size and the wide distribution of these estates also meant it had a considerable capacity for absorbing visitors without putting too much pressure on the environment.

In response to increasing recreational use of its forests, the Commission established a recreation and conservation branch in 1969. A year later the chairman of the Forestry Commission, Lord Taylor of Gryfe, called a press conference to explain its newly formulated recreation policy. During this press conference Lord Taylor pointed out that it was the Commission's aim 'to develop the unique features and potential of its forests [for recreational purposes]'.[28] He further explained that the Commission was to allow the public to enter all its forests on foot without charge and that plans were in the making for the expansion of car parks, campsites and other facilities. Finally the Chairman explained that special attention would be given to the use of the forests for educational purposes and the study of natural history. Because conservation

---

28 Forestry Commission, *Annual Report, 1970-71*, p. 40.

and recreation were so closely linked, emphasis was put on the protection and preservation of the forest environment and its wildlife. These were some of the most important attractions for visitors, which meant the Commission could not afford to neglect them.

Cost-benefit review of 1972

By the start of the 1970s everything seemed to be progressing smoothly and forestry had found its new aims: producing commercial timber for a growing domestic wood industry, playing its part in sustaining the rural economy, providing recreational facilities and the protection of the beauty of the landscape. However, this sense of optimism was soon put under pressure thanks to another major review of forestry policy in 1972. For the first time an attempt was made to evaluate a range of environmental and economic impacts, such as those on recreation, labour provision and import saving. The review attempted to estimate forestry's cost to the nation, of devoting land and labour to forestry.[29] The assessment's conculsion was that when viewed purely as a financial investment forestry offered low yields, with a return of about three per cent on capital. For this reason, it was concluded that the case for new planting, whether by the Forestry Commission or with financial aid from the private sector, rested mainly on social benefits, notably improved employment and landscape and recreational use.

Publicly, the Forestry Commissioners welcomed the review and felt it was supportive but the reality proved quite different. In the Commission's *Annual Report* of 1972 they concluded that the 'main justification for Forestry Commission planting is to be found in the part which it can play in sustaining the rural economy'.[30] The report continued with the happy message that the Forestry Commission was encouraged to further increase forest acreage and that there should be a 'marked increase on emphasis both on visual amenity and on realising their potential for recreation'.[31] The commissioners deliberately left out mention that the government's cost benefit analysis had concluded that the creation of state forests was simply uneconomic. The review's overall conclusion was that forestry fell far short of achieving the government's ten per cent target rate for return on investment. With regard to the role of forestry in sustaining the rural economy it became clear that the cost of providing jobs in state forestry was very high and that if cheaper means of job creation could be found, it

29   C. Price, 'Twenty-five Years of Forestry Cost-benefit Analysis in Britain', *Forestry*, 70 (1997) 3, 171-189, p. 172.
30   Forestry Commission, *Annual Report, 1971-72*, p. 7.
31   Ibid.

would surely move resources away from forestry.[32] It seemed that forestry was facing hard financial times but luckily for the Commission the forestry policy review also provided an answer, by putting emphasis on the value of recreation and amenity. This resulted in a remarkable greening of state forestry policy. In its 1971-72 *Annual Report* the Commission showed an acute insight into the nature of its own plantations:

> From the beginning the Commission was automatically oriented towards conifers; and the uplands of Scotland, England and Wales provided the widest and most natural scope for them on a large scale.[33]

This policy was initially designed to create a strategic timber reserve as quickly as possible, but by the 1960s this was no longer necessary and the Commission put increasing emphasis on the need for the best economic return form taxpayers' money. Broadleaves were attractive trees but were growing too slowly to be of any economic value to the newly emerging wood processing industry. Now that the government had removed the basis for the existence of even conifer plantations the question of what was left for the Forestry Commission to prioritise became paramount. The answer to this question was broadleaves. The Commission realised that even without a clear economic or employment function, its forests were still attractive to the rising number of urban dwellers visiting the forests. However, criticism could no longer be countered by the argument that young commercial plantations were not particularly attractive but were necessary for efficient wood production and the provision of employment in upland areas. The task of making forest plantations more attractive became paramount and for this reason the Commission began to put more emphasis on landscape values than ever before:

> More recently the Commissioners have, however, recognised that greater emphasis should be given to maintaining the woodland character of the countryside particularly in the south of England. They have recognised that to this end in certain of their woodlands the maintenance of hardwoods, where silviculturally this is possible, is an essential part of the landscape. The objective of the Commissioners is to perpetuate by active management the living character of the woodland landscape for future generations to enjoy.[34]

In 1972 the Forestry Commission 'discovered' broadleaves and in doing so it showed itself to be remarkable enlightened and ahead of its time. However, this development must not be overrated because from this statement it is clear that the new broadleaf policy mainly applied to the English countryside. North

---

32   Price, 'Twenty-five Years of Forestry Cost-benefit Analysis in Britain', p. 172.
33   Forestry Commission, *Annual Report 1971-72*, p. 10.
34   Ibid., p. 11.

of the border, the new policy aim was hardly noticeable and the planting of conifers continued, especially in the far north of Scotland. It continued because these regions, especially Caithness and Sutherland, were not regarded as important tourist destinations. A second and probably more important reason is that the Forestry Commission had invested in infrastructure to cultivate these areas for forestry and did not want to loose the money it had invested. Official statistics of the Forestry Commission showed no slowing down of the planting rate of conifers during the first half of the 1970s and the number of hectares of broadleaf trees planted was far from impressive. For example, between 1969 and 1975 only 120 hectares were planted with broadleaf trees while 91,120 hectares of conifers were planted during the same period (table 5.1).

	1969–70	1970–71	1971–72	1972–73	1974–75
Conifers	15,566	19,763	19,630	17,739	18,422
Broadleaf	19	15	12	25	49
Total	15,585	19,751	19,642	17,764	18,471

Table 5.1: Hectares of conifers and broadleaf trees planted in Scotland, 1969–1975.

Source: Forestry Commission Annual Reports.

The Forestry Commission paid lip service to broadleaves and environmental issues in general, but little value was assigned to the concept in practice. In the early 1970s the Commission stated that it was planting substantial areas with larch and other conifers 'in order to bring a variety of shades of green' to the forests.[35] What was not specified in the 1971 *Annual Report* or in reports of the following years was the area of 'other conifers' planted and their geographical distribution. We can only speculate as to why the Commission ceased to publish such details, but it was probably because the proportion of Sitka spruce was embarrassingly high in comparison with other species, especially broadleaves. Although the Countryside Acts of 1967 and 1968 had conferred new powers on the Forestry Commission with regard to recreation and conservation, no new resources were assigned to implement them.

---

35   Forestry Commission, *Annual Report 1970-71*, p. 11.

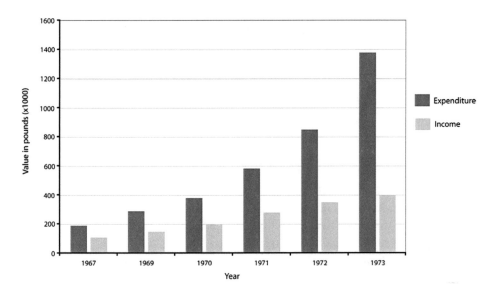

Figure 5.2: Expenditure and income for recreational facilities, 1967–1973.

Source: Forestry Commission Annual Report, 1972-73.

A glance at the expenditure on and income from recreational facilities explains why the Forestry Commission was more interested in conifer plantations that could possibly make a profit in the long run than plunging wholeheartedly into a policy with an emphasis on recreation and conservation. Between 1967 and 1973 money spent on recreational facilities rose by more than five times from about £200,000 to over £1,300,000, while recreational income increased only to about £400,000 (figure 5.2). Providing recreational facilities did not pay for itself and certainly not for a conservation and amenity programme. There was a recreation and open woods policy because taxpayers were granted access to the forests they had paid for. This harsh reality created a policy of double standards. On the one hand the Forestry Commission adopted, under public pressure, a new management policy for the New Forest in Hampshire, in which a priority was given to conservation of 'the ancient and ornamental woodlands [...] without regard to timber production objectives'.[36] On the other hand, planting of conifers was going strongly ahead on the 'bare grounds' of the Scottish uplands without much consideration for visible impacts. In 1977 this attitude of double standards was confirmed in the *Wood Production Outlook* which claimed that recreation was not an important issue, since areas of forest expansion lay far from population centres.[37]

---

36   Ibid., p. 9.
37   *The Wood Production Outlook in Britain. A Review* (Edinburgh: Forestry Commission, 1977), p. 63.

Although the emphasis of forest policy had changed, production and supply of timber remained a major objective of management in state and private forests in Scotland. In most cases it was still believed that this would combine well with social objectives, but there was awareness that conflicts could arise and that forests designed and managed for timber production, were not always well suited to recreation. In the view of George Holmes, director general of the Commission from 1976 to 1987, wood production required simplicity and uniformity while the needs of amenity and recreation were best met by a diversity of landscape, environmental and forestry conditions.[38] This gave rise to a schizophrenic forest policy and practice in which forest expansion led to the rise of commercial monoculture plantations, or forests of production, alongside forests of leisure and sites of conservation, which can be described as forests of consumption.[39] The development of this two strand forestry policy did not originate entirely with the policy reviews in the years between 1957 and the 1970s but started during the inter-war period when the Forestry Commission encountered its first serious popular opposition to planting policies. This will be explored in the next chapter. These developments would eventually feed into post-war forestry reviews and the creation of the two strand forestry policy, which put conservationists and foresters on a collision course in the last two decades of the 20th century.

---

38   G.D. Holmes, 'History of Forestry and Forest Management', *Philosophical Transactions of the Royal Society of London. Series B, Biological Sciences*, 271 (1975) 911, 69-80, pp. 77-78.
39   Paul Robbins and Alistair Fraser, 'A Forest of Contradictions: Producing the Landscapes of the Scottish Highlands', *Antipode*, 35 (2003) 1, 95-118.

6. Landscape aesthetics, conservation and public access before 1940

The story of Scottish forestry during the twentieth century is not only one of forest expansion and timber production, but also one of tourism, recreation and landscape conservation. This is a significant aspect of the interaction between the Forestry Commission, the general public and other stakeholders such as local landowners and conservation organisations[1] and its influence on forestry policy. The story begins during the Romantic period in the late 18th and early 19th centuries when poets, travellers and naturalists discovered both pleasure and scientific interest in British woods long before ecologists and conservationists in the middle of the twentieth century. This nineteenth century 'delight' in woods and forests led inexorably to the development of tourism and recreation in wooded parts of Britain such as the Scottish Highlands, the Lake District and the Forest of Dean.[2] It is therefore surprising that provisions for amenity and improvement and maintenance of the beauty of the landscape were initially not included in the objectives of forest policy. The Forestry Commission did not regard this aspect as necessary and they believed that afforestation in itself would improve the beauty and amenity value of the landscape, and therefore it was an explicit part of forestry that did not need any mention. The term amenity was used in a broad sense to describe the aesthetic and recreational aspects of the landscape as well as conservation of wildlife and natural beauty.[3]

Although amenity was not initially an explicit part of forest policy, an amenity stipulation was formulated soon after the creation of the Commission. During a meeting of the Commissioners in 1921, the Assistant Commissioner for Scotland, John Sutherland, mentioned that the amenity stipulation of the commission was used to keep scenic hilltops free from planting.[4] Because the amenity stipulation was voluntary and not compulsory, it was not sufficient to deal effectively with the problems that the Forestry Commission was about to experience in the Lake District in England. The following case study of the clash between conservationists and the Forestry Commission in the Lake District in the 1930s was the first time that the Commission encountered serious opposition to their

---

1 In the context of this book the use of 'organisation' refers to NGOs and 'body' refers to government organisations.
2 T.C. Smout, *Nature Contested. Environmental History in Scotland and Northern England since 1600* (Edinburgh: Edinburgh University Press, 2000), Ch. 1.
3 TNA: PRO F18/817 Amenity aspects 1956-1968, NC memorandum of Evidence, 11 February 1958; Working Party on Forestry Policy, Amenity and Forestry, 12 March 1958.
4 TNA: PRO F1/2 Minutes meeting 5 April 1921.

planting policies. In addition the conflict in the Lake District instilled an idea in the popular perception of the general public about the harmful visual effects of forestry on the landscape in Britain. This perception would inform and shape opposition to forestry in Scotland in the last three decades of the 20th century.

During the 1920s the Forestry Commission purchased considerable areas of land in the central Lake District for the purpose of creating plantation forests. The creation of these forestry plantations alarmed conservationists, visitors and some local people when they saw the impact on the landscape. The resistance to conifers in the Lake District was not new and dates back to the time of William Wordsworth in the early 19th century. Wordsworth's *A Guide Through the District of the Lakes in the North of England* struck a chord with the English upper and middle classes and attracted a growing number of people to the Lake District. Wordsworth's guide put the landscape and natural beauty of the Lake District in the national consciousness of the English and by doing so the region became a national asset. Wordsworth first formulated this notion almost 200 years ago:

> Persons of pure taste throughout the whole island . . ., testify that they deem the district a sort of national property, in which every man has a right and interest.[5]

Although Wordsworth valued the open landscape of the Lake District, he correctly believed that the landscape had been more wooded in the past:

> Formerly the whole country must have been covered with woods to a great height up the mountains.[6]

Wordsworth concluded that this was a long time ago and he did not regret that the forests had disappeared. In his opinion the woodlands were replaced by a more diverse and attractive landscape:

> The plough of the first settlers having followed naturally the veins of richer, drier, or less stony soil; and thus it has shaped out an intermixture of wood and lawn, with a grace and wilderness which it would have been impossible for the land of studied art to produce.[7]

Wordsworth voiced concern about any development that could damage or disrupt his beloved Lakes landscape. Among the threats he saw was the planting of non-native tree species in the Lake District. He wrote on this subject that:

---

5 Wordsworth, William, *A Guide Through the District of the Lakes in the North of England, With a Description of the Scenery, &c. for the use of Tourists and Residents* (Fifth Edition, Kendall, 1835), p.92.
6 Wordsworth, *A Guide Through the District of the Lakes*, p. 43.
7 Ibid., p. 44.

Other trees have been introduced within these fifty years, such as beeches, larches, limes &c., and plantations of firs, seldom with advantage, and often with great injury to the appearance of the country.[8]

He was one of the first public figures to object to this development, and he would not be the last.

It was the acquisition of land in Upper Eskdale by the Forestry Commission that triggered the mounting concern about forestry in 1933. The direct result was the establishment of the Friends of the Lake District in 1934. The founders of this organisation believed that the essence of 'Englishness' was to be found in the landscape: its fields, hedgerows, hills and lakes. They found their inspiration in Wordsworth's vivid descriptions of the landscape and the beauty of the lakes and the rugged mountains surrounding them.[9] They also asserted the belief that the ideal landscape of the Lake District was not heavily wooded but a mix of pasture, light shrub and herbaceous cover intermixed with broadleaf trees. In order to preserve this landscape, the Friends of the Lake District, with help of the National Trust, tried to persuade the Forestry Commission to limit the creation of conifer plantations in the Lake District, to plant hardwoods where possible and to safeguard rights of way.[10] The widespread nature of the controversy is illustrated by the flurry of correspondence that appeared in *The Times* newspaper, for example a letter by novelist Hugh Walpole, who lived in the Lake District, protesting against the planting of spruces and larches in Eskdale.[11] Member of Parliament for Hexam, Colonel Douglas Clifton Brown, summarised the basic objections against plantation forestry in the Lake District, in a speech which he prepared for a parliamentary debate about afforestion:

> There is the danger of grave damage to the peculiar beauty of the Lake District by monotonous planting of conifers; there is the danger to the organic life of a historic part of England by displacement of its native sheep-farming and traditions; there are dangers to free access in a holiday area of great renown.[12]

In addition to these objections it was felt that the non-native species were out of place and that broadleaves were more suitable for planting in the Lake District. It was further argued that the erection of deer fences around the forests prevented public access to land that had been open to the public by courtesy of farmers and landowners. Finally, forestry displaced the sheep and forced farmers

---

8   Ibid.
9   Adrian Phillips, 'Conservation' , in: Howard Newby (ed.), *The National Trust. The Next Hundred Years* (London, The National Trust, 1995), p. 32.
10 Geoffrey Berry, *The Lake District: A Century of Conservation* (Edinburgh: John Bartholomew, 1980), p. 14.
11 Ibid., p. 15.
12 Cumbria Record Office: WDSO 117/2/6/1/1/5, Parliamentary letters on afforestation in the Lake District, Amendment by Col. D. Clifton, final draft sent to the FLD, 24 January 1938.

to abandon farms that had been in their families for generations.[13] Clifton's statement suggests that sheep farming and its way of life was an integral part of the Lake District.

In 1935 the Forestry Commission purchased an additional 2800 hectares in Eskdale and Dunnerdale. To protect the area the Friends of the Lake District offered to buy back the land in question, but the Forestry Commission did not accept this because they were committed to meeting their planting targets. Frustrated by this failure the Executive Committee of the Friends of the Lake District decided to organise a petition against the proposed afforestation scheme.[14]

Early in 1935 a Joint Informal Committee of the Forestry Commission and the Council for the Preservation of Rural England (hereafter CPRE) was set up. The Commission was willing to join such a committee because planting in the Lake District had become a political issue and could no longer be ignored. The purpose of the Joint Committee was to consider how the interests of timber production and amenity could, as far as possible, be reconciled. In its final report the Joint Committee recognised that large-scale afforestation and the preservation of areas of natural beauty were both important for the nation. It was further stated that at some locations preservation should be the primary consideration.[15] In the summer of 1935 an agreement was reached between the CPRE and the Forestry Commission. The Commission agreed to refrain from planting 178 hectares of upper Eskdale provided that the CPRE and other conservation organisations paid £2 per 0.4 hectare (1 acre) in compensation for not planting that area. The friends of the Lake District were not satisfied with this result, as they considered that the agreement would do little to safeguard the amenity of the valley in question. They decided therefore to carry on with the petition to convince the Forestry Commission to refrain from planting any of the purchased area.[16]

Between 18 July and 3 September 1935, 13,000 signatures were received, of which 2,500 were persons resident in Cumberland and the Lake District. It was indicative of the widespread feeling that the Lake District afforestation scheme had aroused that the signatories included people from all over the United Kingdom. However, the number of signatures from Scotland was low: out of the 334 influential public figures mentioned in the petition, admittedly a sample of only 2.6 per cent of the total number of signatures, only two were from Scotland.[17] Although a small and sketchy sample the lack of signatures of public figures from Scotland is an indication that the issue of tree planting hardly

13   Friends of the Lake District, *Annual Report 1936*, p.6.
14   Ibid., p. 5.
15   Forestry Commission, *Afforestation in the Lake District. Report by the Joint Informal Committee of the Forestry Commission of the FC and the CPRE* (London: HMSO, 1936), p. 3.
16   CPRE, *Annual Report 1936*, p. 6.
17   H.H. Symonds, *Afforestation in the Lake District. A Reply to the Forestry Commission's White Paper of 26th August 1936* (London, 1936), pp. 79-92.

stirred the upper classes north of the Border during the 1930s. Furthermore, there was no similar organised opposition to the creation of conifer plantations by the Forestry Commission in Scotland until more than three decades later.

In June 1936, following the petition, the Friends of the Lake District sent a deputation to the Forestry Commission to underline their demands. The deputation was composed of prominent signatories of the petition that was received by the Forestry Commissioners in the autumn of 1935. The deputation was headed by the Archbishop of York, chairman of the Friends of the Lake Ditrict, and included the Vice-Chancellor of Oxford University (Rev. F.J. Lys), the Bishop of Peterborough, and a number of MPs. Also included were Rev. H.H. Symonds, who was to become Treasurer of the Friends of the Lake District, and John Dower, a member of the Friends of the Lake District Committee, and author of an influential report that led to the creation of National Parks in England after the Second World War.[18] Dower prepared a map showing areas that should be protected from planting and was used as the basis of an uneasy new agreement that was finally reached by the informal Joint Committee in July 1936. It was agreed that the Commission should not acquire any land for afforestation in the central 777 square kilometres (300 square miles) of the Lake District.[19] Although the Forestry Commission had tried to avoid any outside interference with its planting programme they finally had to give in to public pressure.

The legacy of the conflict over afforestation in the Lake District was considerable. It instilled a general dislike for non-native conifers and a preference for native broadleaf trees in the general public and conservationists in particular. The Lake District conflict made clear that beauty of the landscape would become an important issue for state forestry in the decades to come. In the late 20th century it gave also rise to the perception among nature conservation interests, such as the Nature Conservancy Council, and the Royal Society for the Protection of Birds, that the issue of visual impact of forestry plantations was also an early feature north of the border.[20] However, the cultural appreciation and attitudes to forestry and forests in Scotland were quite different from those south of the Scottish border and, like in England, the origins go back to the Enlightenment period and are embodied in the writings of Sir Walter Scott. To understand the initial lack of resistance to monoculture forestry plantations we must now consider the origins of the different perceptions of nature, landscape and land use in Scotland by examining the writings of Sir Walter Scott and comparing it to the Wordsworthian view of nature. In addition, Sir Walter Scott's writings

---

18   Friends of the Lake District, *Newsletter*, Dec. 1936, p. 1.
19   Forestry Commission, *Joint Report*, p. 4.
20   Michael McCarty, 'Planting Forests is a Good Thing, Right?', *The Independent*, 24 June 2006; George F. Peterken, *Natural Woodland: Ecology and Conservation in Northern Temperate Regions* (Cambridge: Cambridge University Press, 1996), p. 447.

on forestry set the tone for debates surrounding Scottish forestry for the next 150 years as he contended that commercial enterprise and stewardship of the landscape could co-exist.

Sir Walter Scott's woodlands

Like the Lake District, Scotland is a country of lakes and mountains but that is where the resemblance ends. One reason of the significant differences is the scale of the Scottish landscape which is so much bigger than the Lake District. While the Lake District is roughly 2000 square kilometres in area, Scotland covers 78,780 square kilometres, of which more than 50 per cent is situated in the Highlands and Islands. There are 277 mountains in Scotland that rise above 915 metres (3000 ft) compared with the Lake District, which has only four. The Scottish lakes are also much larger than in England and Wales with Loch Lomond and Loch Ness at the top of the list, which are the largest freshwater lakes in Britain. Wordsworth also observed this difference in scale when he wrote that the Lake District is so special because the landscape differs so much over short distances, distances so short that they are easily accessible for walkers. On the other hand he noted that:

> In Scotland and Wales are found, undoubtedly, individual scenes, which, in their several kinds, cannot be excelled. But, in Scotland, particularly, what long tracts of desolate country intervene! So that the traveller, when he reaches a spot deservedly of great celebrity, would find it difficult to determine how much pleasure is owing to excellence inherent in the landscape itself. And how much to an instantaneous recovery from an oppression left upon his spirits by the barrenness and desolation through which he has passed.[21]

Scotland was, in his opinion, a country with some beautiful mountain scenery separated by large tracts of 'barrenness' and 'desolation'. In this situation what can be better than planting the barren land with trees to make it more beautiful? However, this was not what Wordsworth meant by 'barrenness' and 'desolation'. In Wordsworth's view, that was necessary to create the remote spots of beauty and loneliness where the tired urban dweller sought to escape in the safe tranquillity of a non-human landscape. Wordsworth regarded nature as quite different, and often even opposite to, the cultivated world humans had created for themselves. The only connection of nature with the human world was that of a spiritual and moral source for those busy urban dwellers visiting these areas. Wordsworth did not claim to speak for the common urban

---

21 Wordsworth, *Guide to the Lakes*, p. 26.

dweller but for members of the cultured and well-educated middle and upper classes who, in his view, had the sensitivity to appreciate natural beauty. In his poems Wordsworth translated nature and natural landscape into moralising and spiritual symbols. In this way the landscape become something transcendental and far removed from the more utilitarian outlook of the countryman who lived from the land.[22]

Sir Walter Scott's view of landscapes as well as the natural world was rather different from the Wordsworthian view in that it was more utilitarian. Being a landowner himself, Scott saw the landscape through the eyes of a countryman, a farmer, a hunter and a forester. On the other hand there is Scott the storyteller, the historian who views the landscape as the product of past human action. In Scott's view a landscape becomes an interesting place only through human action, which invests the landscape with a meaning. Scott admires the landscape in which heroes like Rob Roy and others had lived and acted such that just seeing the landscape with all its historical elements stimulated his imagination. This attitude made it possible for him to accept changes in the natural landscape made by humans. To him, features created in the landscape in the past, such as castles, mills and farmsteads, represented a tradition and historical continuity. Nature in this view was not a trancedental world in which humans were visitors, but part of the human world itself.

In the Scottish context Sir Walter Scott's view of nature does not seem to be an isolated case but is part of an older tradition. In the centuries preceding Scott, the people living in the Scottish countryside, especially the Highlands, did not attribute any aesthetic or scenic value in the modern sense to their landscape, because they were not particularly keen on the idea of wilderness for its own sake. On the other hand, neither were they intimidated by the Scottish landscape. According to Smout most of the Scottish landscape in the 17th and 18th centuries was perceived by local people as a delightful place 'rich in natural resources for use, with excellent hunting grounds' but at the same time had no scruple 'to describe it as beautiful'.[23] The landscape was delightful because it was useful for human purposes. In this respect this attitude preceded the improvement movement that developed during the Enlightenment period. The Improvers regarded nature as a resource that was waiting to be exploited and in this view nature was 'untamed' and 'wasted'. But nature could be altered so that

---

22   Keith Thomas, *Man and the Natural World: Changing attitudes in England, 1500-1800* (London: Penguin Books, 1983), pp. 266-268; David Peter del Mar, *Environmentalism* (Harlow: Pearson Education, 2006), pp. 14-20.
23   Smout, T.C., 'Use and delight: Attitudes to Nature Since 1600', in: Smout, T.C., *Nature Contested. Environmental History in Scotland and Northern England Since 1600* (Edinburgh, 2000), p. 13. For a detailed discussion of Scottish attitudes to nature see chapter one of Smout's book.

it would serve human purposes better. A landscape that was not improved was in this view regarded as a 'waste land', a waste of opportunity to make better use of its resources.[24]

With this knowledge in mind we are better able to understand the context in which Sir Walter Scott wrote an unpublished treatise on forestry, *Sylva Abbotdiensis*, in which he described the forests of his estate and his ideas about how to improve them. The improvement movement was largely a movement of landowners, of which Scott was one. According to David Daiches, planting trees was for Walter Scott 'an absolute passion ... all his life'.[25] This passion reflects the delight side of the improvement movement.

Another of Sir Walter Scott's works on forestry includes his October 1827 review of Robert Monteath's *The Forester's Guide and Profitable Planter* for the *Quarterly Review*. This was not a book review in the modern sense and, with most reviews of the time, this piece is *de facto* an essay on Scott's ideas, in this case on forestry, that cites Monteath's book in support of his own views. The essay included all elements of the inconsistent forest policy and practice that developed during the 20th century. This essay clearly reflects Scott's utilitarian attitude to forestry and the landscape in general and Scott proposed to plant the upland moors of the Scottish hills to make better use of them. In his view forestry was not spoiling an untouched landscape, but improving, in good improvers' fashion, wasteland, turning it into a source of income and pleasure for future generations. Scott asserted that upland areas of wasteland 'may be converted into highly profitable woodland, without taking from agriculture the value of a sheaf of corn, or even greatly interfering with pastoral occupation'.[26] Scott was aware that food production took precedence over forestry and thought that forest expansion should be limited to the uplands.

Scott's attitude towards the newly imported trees from North America was surprising and out of step with most of his contemporaries. He doubted the viability of growing non-native conifers on a large scale in Scotland and believed that North American conifers were inferior to the local Scots Pine because, in his opinion, native trees were better adapted to the local climate and soil. For this reason Scott concluded that Scots pine should be planted wherever possible.[27] Scott was also concerned that use of the native Scots Pine in plantations would

---

24   Ibid., p. 20.

25   David Daiches, *Sir Walter Scott and His World* (London: Thames and Hudson, 1971), p. 86.

26   Sir Walter Scott, 'Review of The Forester's Guide and Profitable Planter. By Robert Monteath. (With Plates.)' Second Edition. Edinburgh, 1824. *The Quarterly Review*, 36 (October 1827), 558–600, p. 561.

27   Susan Oliver, 'Planting the Nation's "Waste Lands": Walter Scott, Forestry and the Cultivation of Scotland's Wilderness', *Literature Compass*, 6 (2009) 3, 585–598, p. 591.

decline because the imported tree offered a quicker financial return. As a result he believed that the use of monoculture plantations of North American conifers would change the appearance of the Scottish landscape and Scott observed:

> Other plantations [. . .] in order that they might not trespass upon some edible portion of grass land, have come to resemble uncle Toby's bowling-green trans- ported to a northern hill side. Here you shall see a solitary mountain with a great black patch stuck on its side, like a plaster of Burgundy pitch, and there another, where the plantation, instead of gracefully sweeping down to its feet, is broken short off in mid-air, like a country wench's gown tucked through her pocket-holes... These abortions have been the consequence of a resolution to occupy with trees only those parts of the hill where nothing else will grow . . . with 'up and down and snip and slash', whatever unnatural and fantastic forms may be thereby assigned to their boundaries.[28]

This concern of 'a great black patch stuck' to the hillsides precedes similar 20th century concerns by more than a century. In his essay Scott draws attention to the need to reconcile aesthetic concerns with the ideals of optimised commercial timber production. He insists that the only way to successfully plant the uplands is by adopting an overall programme that connects upland plantations to existing woodlands on more fertile grounds by planting continuous sweeping tracts of woodland and forest that follow the shape of the landscape.[29]

He concluded his essay with the practical advice to landowners:

> ...that improvement by plantation is at once the easiest, the cheapest, and the least precarious mode of increasing the immediate value, as well as the future income of their estates, and that therefore it is we exhort them to take heart the exhortations of the dying Scotch laird to his son: 'be aye sticking in a tree, Jock - it will be growing whilst you are sleeping'.[30]

The latter is a paraphrased quote from Scott's novel *The Heart of Midlothian* and it is perhaps no surprise that the forerunner of the Royal Scottish Forestry Society was strongly influenced by it, and adopted it as its motto in 1852. They took Scott's advice to improve the land by plantation of forests very seriously and promoted the expansion of the forests in the Highlands to improve the economic use of the land, a policy that would later be adapted by the Forestry

---

28 'Review of The Forester's Guide', p. 567.
29 'Planting the Nation's 'Waste Lands'', 592-93.
30 'Review of The Forester's Guide', p. 600.

Commission. Unfortunately, the call to pay attention to the aesthetic aspect of forestry by Sir Walter Scott was largely ignored by the Royal Scottish Forestry Society and the Forestry Commission.

Scott's influence on the founders of the Forestry Commission was slight, but it is not difficult to see the impact of his work on the popular perception of the Scottish landscape. With the publication of *Lady of the Lake* in 1810, Scott did for the Trossachs in Stirlingshire what Wordsworth had done for the Lake District in England. Robert Cadell, an Edinburgh based bookseller and publisher closely associated with Sir Walter Scott, observed that the publication of the *Lady of the Lake* inspired many to visit the Trossachs:

> … crowds set off to the scenery of Loch Katerine, till then comparatively unknown; and as the book came out just before the season for excursions, every house and inn in that neighbourhood was crammed with constant succession of visitors.[31]

Although Sir Walter Scott was critical of the use of non-native conifers, dislike of conifer plantations amongst visitors to the Trossachs is not evident, despite the creation of large conifer plantations in the last 150 years.[32] These visitors were in search of the landscape that Scott had created in his poem and later novels, and which became the archetypal Scottish landscape with rough mountains, and tranquil lakes surrounded by trees. Because trees were an integral part of Scott's landscape visitors expected trees to be there and it did not matter much what kind of trees these were. Scott appears to have remained a lone voice with his concerns about the visual impacts of non-native conifer plantations on the Scottish landscape. Serious opposition to the development of forestry plantations in the Scottish Highlands only emerged in the second half of the 20th century. In the meantime discussions about the visual effects of forestry on the landscape remained confined to internal discussions within the Forestry Commission and amongst the conservation organisations in the inter-war period.

Public access

Demand for access to forests was another aspect of forestry that was not considered as a part of modern forestry when the Forestry Commission was created. In spite of that, during the 1920s the number of people visiting the forests increased, and it was in recognition of this fact that the Forestry Commissioners obtained

---

31 Quoted in: David Daiches & John Flower, *Literary Landscapes of the British Isles. A Narrative Atlas* (New York and London: Paddington Press, 1979), p. 201.

32 Nick Hanley, Richard Ready, Sergio Colombo, Fiona Watson, Mairi Stewart, E. Ariel Bergmann, 'The Impacts of Knowledge of the Past on Preferences for Future Landscape Change', *Journal of Environmental Management*, 90 (2009) 3, 1404-1412, p. 1406.

powers in the Forestry Act of 1927 to make regulations governing the admission of people to State Forests. A few years later the Government appointed a National Parks and its task was 'to consider and report if it is desirable and feasible to establish one or more national parks in Britain'. The two main objectives of the parks were to be 'the preservation of natural characteristics, including flora and fauna, and the improvement of recreational facilities'.[33] The Forestry Commission, as an important landowner in rural areas, was represented on the National Parks Committee and was 'quite friendly to the idea' of creating a national park for recreational purposes.[34] It was a means for the Commission to sell off unplantable land or to turn it into useful areas for recreation, and in the process making some money from tourism. The Commissioners stated in a preliminary comment to the National Parks Committee Report that 'the Forestry Commission might be prepared to hand over some 3,237 hectares of Glen More Forest in the Cairngorms under provision that the plantations of the Forestry Commission may not be endangered through admission of the public'.[35] The Commission did not allow any interference with the creation and maintenance of its forests, in order to safeguard the standing timber reserve. It also wanted to protect the forests from fire or other damage caused by visitors. The National Parks Committee accepted this, probably to appease the Commission keep it involved with the national park movement, because it was the largest land-use agency in Britain at that time.

In April 1931 the Report of the National Parks Committee was presented to Parliament and concluded that a system of small parks and reserves should be created in Britain. The objective to be achieved by these parks would be to safeguard areas of outstanding natural beauty and to improve the means of access for tourists to these beauty spots. Finally, a national park system could be used as an instrument to introduce measures for the protection of vulnerable flora and fauna.[36]

Because of the economic difficulties at the start of the 1930s, caused by the deep international recession, no action was undertaken to implement any of the recommendations of the report. In the meantime the first large-scale conservation conflict over the planting activities of the Forestry Commission in the Lake District reached a climax. The whole Lake District episode had damaged the reputation of the Forestry Commission, which it attempted to restore by setting up its own National Forest Park Committee, with the task 'to advise

---

33   TNA: PRO F18/817, Amenity aspects 1956-1968, National Parks - Brief history of the present movement, June 11th 1936, p. 1.

34   John Stirling Maxwell, 'A Decade of State Forestry and its Lessons', *The Scottish Forestry Journal*, 44 (1930), p. 6.

35   TNA: PRO F19/9, National Forest Parks, correspondence and papers, 1925-1931, Preliminary comments, 17 Sept. 1929.

36   TNA: PRO F18/817, Amenity aspects 1956-1968, National Parks – Brief history, p. 2.

how the surplus and unplantable land in the forests [...] may be put to a use of public character'.[37] The Committee, headed by John Stirling Maxwell, who served as chairman of the Forestry Commission between 1929-1932, advised the Forestry Commission to create National Forest Parks for the purpose of outdoor recreation. It was recommended that the parks should be established mainly on unsuitable land for forestry, but production forests would be included in the lower parts of the parks. The report did not mention nature conservation because the Forest Park Committee did not regard this as part of the duty of the Forestry Commission. The Forest Park Committee referred to the report of the National Park Committee:

> ...we feel that it is desirable to indicate that this term, [National Forest Parks], is deliberately intended to denote something different from a National Park as described in the Report of the National Park Committee'.[38]

In fact the Forest Park Committee did not adopt any of the recommendations of the National Park Committee's report, except for the objective of improving recreational facilities and access for hikers. This attitude is not surprising considering the fact that the Forestry Commission was only set up to create a forest resource and not to act as a nature conservation body or national parks agency.

As soon as the forest park report was published the Forestry Commissioners took action and implemented the findings of the National Forest Park Committee immediately by creating the first National Forest Park in Argyll in 1935. This park is located on the west coast of Scotland on the banks of Loch Long and contains some spectacular mountain scenery and it contained some facilities like campsites. The Argyll Forest Park was and immediate success and during the first year over 13,000 overnight stays were recorded. The next year the number of visitors exceeded 20,000 and it continued to rise in subsequent years climbing to over 32,000 in 1941.[39] With the creation of the National Forest Parks the Commission realised that it had created a powerful tool to improve its popularity. During a general discussion on forestry policy in 1938 it was stated that the National Forest Parks were 'a good bid for popularity' and that it aroused interest 'in all grades of society'.[40]

---

37 Forestry Commission, *Report of the National Forest Park Committee 1935* (London, HMSO, 1935), p. 2.
38 Ibid.
39 TNA: PRO F18/817, National Parks, Preliminary draft section of Post War Reconstruction Report, p. 2.
40 TNA: PRO F18/142, General Discussion on forest Policy, 1 December 1938, p. 5, 7.

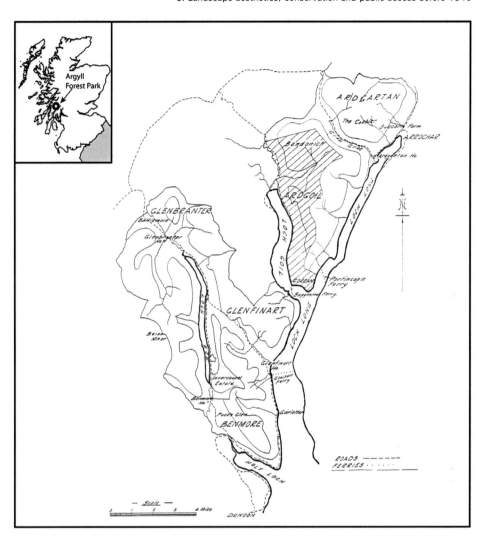

**Map 6.1: A 1935 map of the proposed Argyll National Forest Park.
The shaded area was not owned by the Forestry Commission.**

Source: Modified from Forestry Commission, *Report of the National Forest Park Committee 1935* (London, HMSO, 1935), p 7.

Encouraged by the success of the first forest park the Forestry Commission felt confident enough to state in the Post-war Forest Policy report in 1943 that a minimum of 'one new Park might be established every year for the next ten years'.[41] This rate was somewhat optimistic and by the early 1960s only eight forest parks were in existence in Britain, of which four were located in Scotland. On the other hand the Forestry Commission was so impressed with the public demand for access to their forests that they decided to provide better access to many more of their forests. But in an internal memo of 1967 the Forestry Commissioners reminded all forest site managers that although public recreation was now regarded as important, it would always be secondary to the primary aim of growing timber.[42] This left the Forestry Commission open to criticism in respect to the appearance of their plantations, the geometric blocs of conifers, from increasing numbers of visitors during the 1960s and 1970s. Visitors of the state forests expected more diverse forests than the boring monotony of dense conifer plantations, which often obscured pleasant views.[43] But this criticism from the general public was preceded by concerns within the Scottish conservation organisations that came into being in the inter-war period.

The Scottish conservation organisations

The formation of the Scottish conservation organisations in the inter-war period must be seen in the wider context of developments that took place in society as a whole. Firstly there was a growing national awareness in Scotland and a feeling that the natural and historical heritage of the country had long been neglected. It was felt that something had to be done to correct this and to safeguard 'the valuable natural and historical features of this country'.[44] Secondly the number of visitors in Scotland was growing due to an increase in car ownership. A survey of the number of cars passing through the town of Stirling in the 1920s illustrates this. At the beginning of the decade in 1921 there was an average of 375 cars passing through Stirling each weekday, but four years later this figure had trebled.[45]

In the spring of 1930 a series of articles appeared in the *Callander Advertiser* under the title 'Scotland's Glory' describing attractive day tours through the scenic landscape of the Trossachs and the Loch Lomond area. The author of the

---

41   Quoted by John Sheail, 'The Concept of National Parks in Great Britain 1900-1950', *Transactions of the Institute of British Geographers*, 66 (Nov., 1975), 41-56, p. 46.
42   Robert Lambert, '"Therapy of the Green Leaf": Public Responses to the Provision of Forest and Woodland Recreation in Twentieth Century Britain', *Journal of Sustainable Tourism*, 16 (2008) 4, 408-427, p. 415.
43   Christopher Hall, 'The Forestry Club', *Ecos*, 3 (1982) 1, pp. 10-13.
44   Robert Hurd, *Scotland Under Trust. The Story of the National Trust for Scotland and its Properties* (Edinburgh: NTS, 1939), p. xii.
45   'Motor Traffic Passing Trough Stirling', *Callander Advertiser*, August 29, 1925.

series, Richard Williamson, recommended a visit to the Trossachs as 'one of the most charming day's outings'.[46] He regarded Perthshire's mountains, lochs and moors not only as a Mecca for tourists, lovers of nature and rambles, but also for the motor enthusiast.

Another factor that helps to explain the emergence of organisations promoting outdoor activities and landscape conservation in the 1930s is an ideological one. In the first decades of the 20th century rural life became increasingly linked with physical and moral welfare. This ideology developed fully in the 1920s when back-to-the-land ideologies sprang up all over Europe. Illustrative in this respect is the growth of the Scout movement of Sir Baden Powell during this period, the creation of the Scottish Youth Hostel Association and the Ramblers Association. The idea common to all these organisations was to create a better society that avoided the evils of urban life and industrialisation such as pollution, overcrowding and crime. The emerging outdoor organisations were vehicles of reform with the mission to bring the countryside closer to urban people.[47] But many of the emerging conservation organisations of the inter-war period were not as egalitarian as these recreational organisations mentioned above and were mainly an affair of the upper classes.

The connections between the founders of the Scottish conservation organisations and the Forestry Commission were very close. Influential landowners were involved in the creation of all these organisations and a considerable number of them had also been key players in the efforts to establish the Forestry Commission. The first and initially most prominent of the amenity and nature conservation organisations to be established in Scotland was the Association for the Preservation of Rural Scotland (hereafter APRS). The APRS was the brainchild of the Royal Incorporation of Architects in Scotland and conceived by the Edinburgh Architectural Association. The driving force behind the idea was Frank Mears, one of Britain's leading planners at the time, who was to become the Association's first secretary. In 1926, the year that the Council for the Preservation of Rural England was established, Mears wrote a letter to the *Scotsman* suggesting the formation of a similar organisation in Scotland. The reactions were overwhelmingly positive and the Association was formally constituted on 4 July 1927.[48] The APRS was a federation of Scottish societies and private individuals interested in safeguarding the countryside from despoliation. This 'protection of rural scenery and amenities of country towns and villages' was mainly focussed on built structures and roads.[49] It called for

---

46   Richard, Williamson, 'Scotland's Glory', *Callander Advertiser*, 10 April 1930.

47   Bramwell, *Anna, Ecology in the 20th Century. A History*, (New Haven & London: Yale University Press, 1989), pp. 104-105.

48   Russell, *The National Trust for Scotland. The Formative Years*, Unpublished paper. Archives APRS, Edinburgh 1989.

49   APRS, *Association for the Protection of Rural Scotland*, Edinburgh 1928.

a harmonious blending of houses, bridges and roads into the rural landscape. It is not surprising that an organisation that was first conceived by a group of architects would focus on buildings and roads, but soon the concerns of the APRS expanded to include the pollution of water and air and the impact of forestry on the landscape.

When the APRS was founded it had some prestigious board members and among these were a considerable number of influential landowners (Table 6.1). The honorary president was the Earl of Crawford and Balcarres, who was also a founding member of the National Trust for Scotland. The president of the APRS was the Earl of Haddington, and John Stirling Maxwell, the third chairman of the Forestry Commission, became vice president. From 1931 Stirling Maxwell was the representative for the National Trust at the APRS council and he was also involved in the Glasgow Tree Lovers Society.[50] Another Forestry Commissioner involved in the APRS was Major Strang Steel, who was member of the APRS council for a period of two years during the mid-1930s.

Other landowners involved in the Association for the Preservation of Rural Scotland included the Duke of Atholl and Sir Ian Colquhoun, Baronet of Luss. The latter was chairman of the APRS during the early years and played an important role in the formation of the National Trust for Scotland, of which he became the first chairman in 1931, a post he held until 1946.[51]

	Association for the Preservation of Rural Scotland	National Trust for Scotland	Glasgow Tree Lovers Society	Forestry Commission
Earl of Crawford & Balcarres	Honorary President	Founding member		
Earl of Haddington	President			
John Stirling Maxwell	Vice President	Representative NTS at APRS Council	Member, Honorary President 1951	Chairman 1929-1932
Samuel Strang Steel	Member APRS Council			Commissioner 1931-1949
Ian Colquhuoun, Bart of Luss	First Chairman 1927-1931	First Chairman 1931-1946		
Duke of Atholl	Founding member			

Table 6.1: Founding members of the Scottish conservation organisations.

Source: Author's research.

50   A letter exchange in the *Glasgow Herald* in April 1932 drew together a number of people whose common link was to make Glasgow 'greener'. This group formed a Tree Planting Committee, under the aegis of the existing Civic Society. In the autumn of 1933 the Committee reformed itself into an independent organisation: the Glasgow Tree Lovers Society. John Stirling Maxwell, was made Honorary President in 1951. See: *Twenty Second Annual Report Glasgow Tree Lovers' Society, 1953-54,* 'Coming of Age Report, 1933-1954'.
51   Russel, *Formative Years*, p. 2.

From the start of its existence the Forestry Commission regarded the APRS as an important stakeholder, and formal contacts were soon established. The APRS became the cradle for the National Trust for Scotland and its creation was a direct result of attempts by the English National Trust to become the principal conservation organisation in Scotland. In 1929, the owner of the Loch Dee Estate in the Galloway hills offered his estate to the APRS, but the Association was not constituted to hold or manage land and the matter was discussed with the secretary of the National Trust (England).[52] Although the Trust was entitled to hold land in Scotland, there was a strong feeling in the APRS Council that Scotland should not be 'invaded' by the National Trust. It was this incident that gave birth to the National Trust for Scotland.

By mid 1929, the APRS realised that it was high time that Scotland formed its own National Trust. In particular John Stirling Maxwell was vehemently opposed to the National Trust extending its influence into Scotland, and is thought to have been the principal spokesman for the movement to create a Scottish National Trust. In his position as Vice President of the APRS and Chairman of the Forestry Commission he was able to influence the stance on this matter in both organisations. When it became clear that the English National Trust was trying to extend its work to Scotland he took action in support of the APRS. In the autumn of 1929 Stirling Maxwell organised a meeting with the APRS council to discuss the use of Glenmore Forest, near Aviemore, as a possible national park. The Assistant Commissioner for Scotland, John Sutherland, attended this meeting and recorded that the Commission appeared to be sympathetic towards the idea to co-operate with the APRS. It was during this meeting that Stirling Maxwell recommended forming a National Trust for Scotland based upon the same principles as the existing Trust in England and with powers to hold land.[53]

However, the Government was resistant to a National Trust being established in Scotland because there was a view that the creation of another Trust would take energy and money away from the effort to establish national parks. But the Government lost the initiative in Scotland where the idea of a National Trust was spreading. The National Trust for Scotland was established on 10 November 1930 and was incorporated in May 1931.

During the 1930s there were occasional informal contacts between the Forestry Commission and the APRS on issues of amenity planting. In general, the APRS was moderately critical of the lack of interest in landscape and amenity issues on part of the Forestry Commission. During the annual meeting of the APRS in 1934, John Stirling Maxwell said that the Commission 'paid little attention

---

52   Leaflet, *The First 70 Years of the APRS*, Edinburgh 1999; Russell, *Formative Years*.
53   TNA: PRO F18/596, Glen More correspondence, 1929–1966, Minute by the AC for Scotland, John Sutherland, meeting with APRS, 16 October 1929.

to the amenity side of its work'. He added that when he was a Commissioner 'amenity had never been discussed at any meeting' and Stirling suggested that the time had come that the Forestry Commission paid some attention to the amenity side of their work.[54]

The APSR turned their words into deeds and inspected some of the work of the Forestry Commission, mainly focussing on minor elements in the landscape. These elements included fences erected by the Forestry Commission and trees planted along roadsides and whether these fitted aesthetically into the landscape. On the whole, their criticisms did not affect the planting programme of the Forestry Commission in any significant way. Illustrative is the case of tree planting along the road between the Trossachs and Aberfoyle in Perthshire. The Forestry Commission had planned to plant trees on either side of the road and fence these off to protect them from deer, and the APRS offered to inspect the fences and to comment on the tree species used. This led to agreements that kept viewpoints (not official lookouts) from the road free of trees and to refrain from the use of certain exotic tree varieties in these locations. During the same year concern was also expressed that forestry operations around the village of Strathyre in Perhshire would cause the destruction of attractive stands of timber and obscure the landscape from some viewpoints. A party of APRS members was invited by the Forestry Commissioners to inspect the effect of forestry operations on the landscape around Strathyre. The visit resulted in another agreement between the Forestry Commission and the APRS that secured the preservation of certain stands of pine and deciduous trees around Strathyre for aesthetic purposes.[55]

The APRS also received the occasional complaint about the negative impact of forestry operations in the Highlands. In the summer of 1933 an APRS member, Hugh Gardener complained about the extensive operations of the Forestry Commission and the effect on Highland scenery. During a meeting of the APRS council, the view was expressed that blanket afforestation of large areas with conifers was undesirable in Scotland. Surprisingly, after some consideration it was decided that no further action was to be taken on Gardener's letter, because it was believed that the Forestry Commission took care of amenity where possible and in line with the economics of afforestation.[56]

Sometimes complaints were sustained, for example in the case of APRS member Mr. Seton Gordon from Inverness, who reported that the Forestry Commission was ring-barking birch and allowing them slowly to die amongst the young conifer plantations.[57] Forestry Commissioner Major Strang Steel responded to

---

54 'Forestry and Amenity', *The Scotsman*, Mar 15, 1934, p.10.
55 APRS, *Annual Report 1934*, p. 14; Forestry Commission, *Annual Report* (London: HMSO, 1935), p. 9.
56 Archives APRS: Minutes Council meeting APRS, 27 September 1933.
57 Ring-barking is the practice of remove a ring of bark around a tree trunk in order to kill the tree.

the APRS in a letter encouraging the Association to draw the Commission's attention to complaints concerning ring-barking so that they could prevent foresters from killing trees.[58]

The two complaints mentioned above are the only objections to forestry recorded in the *Annual Reports* or minutes of the APRS during the 1930s. Similarly, the National Trust for Scotland archives in Edinburgh does not contain a single letter of complaint about forestry during the first decade of the Trust's existence. The issues of concern mentioned above were pretty insignificant and on the whole the impact of forestry on the landscape was simply not an issue for the conservation organisations and the wider public in Scotland during the 1930s. We can only speculate why this was the case but it is likely a combination of the effects of the depression and the view that forestry would bring jobs to the Highlands. And indeed, the APRS Council was convinced that forestry would bring economic advantages:

> Appearance, to a certain extent, may be scarified, but a countryside re-populated and turned to greater economic account seems preferable to vast areas of relative sterile moorland.[59]

An additional factor in the absence of opposition to afforestation is caused by the fact that rural landowners, who made at least part of their living from the land, dominated conservation organisations in Scotland. It was not in their interest to wage campaigns against forestry operations despoiling landscapes of outstanding beauty, as was the case in the Lake District. In contrast, the leaders of conservation organisations in the Lake District, such as the Association for the Protection of Rural England and the Friends of the Lake District, were outsiders, people who had settled in the region or who were visitors from urban areas. For these reasons, public objections to forestry only gradually emerged in Scotland after the Second World War.

---

58   Archives APRS: Minutes Council meeting ASPRS, 5 January 1938.
59   APRS, *Annual Report 1934*, p. 14.

7. Landscape aesthetics, conservation and public access after 1940

After the Second World War the Nature Conservancy's Scottish Committee emerged as a new major player on the conservation and land management stage in Scotland. The Nature Conservancy was established in 1949 and its mission was to create and manage nature reserves, which preserved flora and fauna, geological and physiological features. The Conservancy was also charged with conducting research and advising planning and land management authorities on Sites of Special Scientific Interest (SSSI).[1] It was set up as a nation-wide organisation but the Scottish Wildlife Conservation Committee (the Ritchie Committee), which advocated the creation of a single conservation service for Britain, concluded that a Scottish Division was needed to carry out an effective conservation policy in Scotland. According to Donald Mackay, the Scottish Committee was unique within the Nature Conservancy because it was virtually autonomous.[2]

As in the case of the Association for the Preservation of Rural Scotland (APRS) and the National Trust for Scotland before the war, the personalities involved with the Scottish Committee of the Nature Conservancy were of some importance to its influence and objectives. The list of members reads like a shortlist of the post-war scientific and land-owning establishment in Scotland. John Berry, a biologist and former environmental advisor to the Hydro-Electric Board, was chairman of the Scottish Committee. Other members included the Earl of Wemyss and March, Sir Henry Beresford-Peirse, Director General of the Forestry Commission, Sir Basil Neville-Spence, along with ecologist Frank Fraser Darling, biologist Donald McVean and Professors Ritchie (Zoology, Edinburgh) and Matthews (Botany, Aberdeen), one of the leading ecologists of his time. A Committee of this calibre was necessary for gaining the confidence of major landowners in Scotland.[3]

Berry was a good choice for leading the Scottish branch of the Nature Conservancy because he was well connected with land-owners and other land-use agencies in Scotland. He was on the Council of the APRS, an advisor of the

---

1 SSSIs protect specific features such as flora and fauna, geology or shape and form of the landscape. See glossary for detailed description.
2 Mackay, *Scotland's Landscape Agencies*, p. 109.
3 Ibid.

Forestry Commission and also a member of the Scottish Landowners Federation.[4] Under Berry a policy emerged of creating much larger National Nature Reserves (NNR)[5] than in England and Wales, beginning with the purchase of a complete mountain, Beinn Eighe, in 1951. Three years later an even larger National Nature Reserves was created in the Cairngorm Mountains, next to the Forestry Commission's Glen More National Forest Park.[6]

Beinn Eighe was destined to strain the relationship between the Forestry Commission and the Nature Conservancy. Long before the purchase it had been recognised that the remnants of an ancient Scots pine woodland had to be protected and preserved. During the war the southeast end of the Beinn Eighe wood was partially felled and the Nature Conservancy believed that this wood had to be restored. The condition of the pinewood remnants can be deduced from comments by Henry Beresford Peirce, director of the Scottish branch of the Forestry Commission, recorded in the minutes of a meeting with the Scottish Branch of the Nature Conservancy in the autumn of 1952:

> In the seven years since the last heavy felling, the wood had deteriorated so much that [Beresford Peirse] feared it might revert to moorland or to birch scrub if no active steps were taken to protect the natural regeneration of Scots pine.[7]

The Forestry Commission agreed with the Nature Conservancy that action was needed to prevent further loss of old growth pines. The discussion about how to prevent further loss focussed on the question of whether to actively interfere by means of planting to allow natural regeneration. It was here that the Forestry Commission showed its true face as an organisation focussed on timber production and not conservation. This is not surprising because building up a timber reserve was the *raison d'être* of the Commission.

During a visit to Beinn Eighe in July 1952 Beresford Peirce, stated that 'the actual regeneration of this area could [...] be done by the Forestry Commission'.[8] The Forestry Commission felt that a forestry project should not be undertaken by two different organisations, but by the appropriate agency that was specially set up to carry out state forestry in the United Kingdom: itself. Beresford Peirse saw two advantages in doing this, the first being 'that the Nature Conservancy

4   T.C. Smout, *The Highlands and the Roots of Green Consciousness, 1750-1990* (Edinburgh: SNH, 1993), p. 23; John Berry, Personal Comment, Letter dated 26-05-1999.
5   National Nature Reserves are created with the sole purpose to protect special biological features and ecosystems and excludes other uses. National parks are open to the public and mix conservation with other activities such as agriculture and forestry. National parks in Britain are 'working landscapes'.
6   Mackay, *Land use Agencies*, p. 109.
7   NAS: SNH1/1, Signed minutes of first and subsequent meetings, meeting 25 Sept 1952.
8   Quoted in: Tim Clifford and Andrews Foster, 'Beinn Eighe National Nature Reserve: Woodland Management Policy and Practice 1944-1994', in: Smout, T.C., *Scottish Woodland History*, p. 194.

would be relieved of a heavy expenditure'.[9] Secondly, the Commissioners believed that the Nature Conservancy was not created to manage forests and would better leave the difficulty of arranging management and supervision of the woodlands in the capable hands of the Forestry Commission.

Figure 7.1: Pinewood with Beinn Eighe in the background.

Photo: Bob Jones, from www.geograph.org.uk with permission.

With this proposal Beinn Eighe was in fact close to being taken over by the Forestry Commission. However, the Nature Conservancy was concerned that the activities of the Forestry Commission would result in the loss of the ancient pine woodlands in the nature reserve. It was due to the intervention of Captain C. Diver, Director General of the Nature Conservancy, that the Conservancy in Scotland was forced to re-think its position with regard to Beinn Eighe in late 1952. He believed that a survey of the pinewoods in the nature reserve had to be carried out before further action was taken. In early 1953 Donald McVean started his now famous study on the ecology of Scots pine at Beinn Eighe. The resulting report concluded that large-scale forestry operations were not necessary to ensure the continued existence of the ancient pine woodlands.

---

9   Ibid.

He recommended a non-interventionist management strategy for these woodlands and this became the basis for the Beinn Eighe reserve's woodland management plan as it finally appeared in 1954.[10]

After the Beinn Eighe episode, the Nature Conservancy developed a cautious attitude towards the Forestry Commission. A 1953 plan by the Forestry Commission and the Department of Agriculture to place the whole of the Spey catchment area under forest was not received with enthusiasm by the Nature Conservancy.[11] It was for this reason that McVean drew attention to the need for closer liaison with the Forestry Commission to gain a fuller understanding of the forestry agency's activities. The Chairman, John Berry, stressed the need to secure woodlands as nature reserves before they disappeared.[12] The result of these two experiences of the Nature Conservancy was that the Forestry Commission lost its primacy over forest management. It confirmed that ecologists as well as foresters had the right to manage state owned woodlands.[13]

The 1958 Working Party

The Forestry Working Party that was set up after the Zuckerman Report had the task of advising the government on future forest policy. In order to gain a proper picture of forestry in the United Kingdom the Working Party invited organisations involved in forestry, landscape management or conservation to submit a memorandum with their views on the work of the Forestry Commission. The Nature Conservancy acted swiftly and submitted their memorandum of evidence in February 1958. In this piece the Nature Conservancy presented its views regarding the scope and activities of the Commission and its relationship with them.

The memorandum opened by stating that the Forestry Acts of 1919 and 1945 took some account of amenity, but that they failed to anticipate the problems related to the integration of forestry and nature conservation. It was also observed that the Forestry Commission underestimated the pressures on the forest estate caused by a rising demand for use of the forests for recreation. This failure was most noticeable on the ground. In their many dealings with the Forestry Commission, the Nature Conservancy had found that the readiness of the Commission's staff to co-operate in matters important to nature conservation were often hindered by the Commission's statutory powers or financial restrictions. The major obstacle seemed to be that the Commission was too

---

10   Ibid., p. 196.
11   NAS: SNH1/1, Signed minutes of first and subsequent meetings, meeting 29 January 1953.
12   Ibid., meeting 5 November 1953.
13   Smout et al., *A history of the native woodlands*, pp. 287-288.

narrowly restricted to activities directly concerned with producing timber at the quickest possible rate. The Nature Conservancy concluded that this was misguided forestry practice and urged for a forest policy with a much wider scope that included the conservation of ancient woodlands and veteran trees, and provision for recreation. The memorandum also suggested that forestry could help to develop a more balanced rural economy and landscape, possibly added to satisfy the Treasury.[14] But how could this be achieved? To address this practical question the Nature Conservancy referred to a development on the other side of the ocean. In the United States the Forest Service was developing a management system that was known as 'multiple use'. The main principle of this system was that all resources and values in the landscape are managed under an integrated management plan. The intent was that this would produce sustainable forests that provided the greatest overall benefits, economically, socially and environmentally. It was suggested that the Forestry Commission introduced this type of management system in Britain.

Another aspect criticised by the Nature Conservancy was the attitude of the Forestry Commission to 'vermin': 'the vague language in the Forestry Act of 1919 regarding damage by rabbits and hares or other vermin has an almost medieval flavour'.[15] It was recommended that the Forestry Commission should draw up a list with species that could be hunted and those that had to be protected and the Nature Conservancy was happy to assist the Forestry Commission in this. However, it took, six years before the Commission looked seriously into the matter of wildlife hunting and protection. In February 1964 the Forestry Commission announced that it had appointed Peter Garthwaite, division officer at Basingstoke, to the new post of Wildlife Officer. His responsibility was to coordinate and develop the Commission's policies and practices of wildlife conservation and management in England, Scotland and Wales, in liaison with the Nature Conservancy and other bodies. The aim of the Commission was to develop methods of control to harmonise the conservation of wildlife with the need for timber production.[16]

The Nature Conservancy concluded the memorandum stating that the relations with the Forestry Commission were excellent and that it was '…unnecessary here to refer to the numerous problems of mutual interests which constantly arise and are settled by mutual arrangement'.[17] Like the relationship between the Forestry Commission and the conservation bodies in the inter-war years,

---

14   TNA: PRO F18/817, Forestry Working Party on Forest Policy, *The Nature Conservancy's Memorandum of Evidence*, pp. 1-2.

15   Ibid., p. 11.

16   Forestry Commission, *Annual Report 1964*, p. 11; TNA: PRO FT3/124, Joint Management Committee Scotland 1962-1968, Forestry Commission and Wildlife, Memorandum by the FC, 12-2-1964.

17   TNA: PRO F18/817, Forestry Working Party on Forest Policy, *The Nature Conservancy's memorandum* p. 11.

most disagreements were solved discretely, in a conciliatory manner. But this was all going to change with the democratisation and increased mobility of society that would follow in the 1960s and 1970s.

The inter-war conservation organisations

The conservation organisations that emerged during the 1920s and 1930s largely continued after the war as they had done before. But there was a major change: the momentum of action had shifted away from the 'old' conservation organisations to the newly formed Nature Conservancy. However, the Association for the Preservation of Rural Scotland and National Trust for Scotland as well as the closely related Glasgow Tree Lovers Society continued to exert some influence in matters of landscape conservation and amenity. The protection of broadleaf trees continued to be an important issue for these organisations and there was some disquiet about the under planting and felling of oak trees in Scotland by the Forestry Commission. But in 1950 the responsibility for timber felling licenses was transferred from the Board of Trade to the Forestry Commission. In a letter to *The Times*, the Honorary Secretary of the Glasgow Tree Lovers Society, Evelyn MacKenzie Anderson, expressed the hope that these new powers would make the Forestry Commission 'come alive to the dangers of wholesale felling' and to 'the value of hardwoods among the conifers'.[18] This suggests that the Commission had not much interest in the preservation of native broadleaf trees and amenity aspects.

Forestry and landscape aesthetics was still very much the preserve of the privileged and wealthy; public complaints about forestry were few, increasing little during the immediate post-war years. In the decade before the war the APRS and National Trust for Scotland combined received only a handful of complaints about Forestry Commission plantations disfiguring the landscape. In the period 1945-1970, the number of complaints recorded increased only slightly, with only five complaints recorded.[19] A survey of two national and two regional Scottish papers (*The Glasgow Herald*, *The Scotsman*, the *Stirling Observer* and the *Oban Times)* confirmed this lack of concern about forestry plantations. The survey yielded only one letter and one article critical of the impact of forestry in the period 1945-65, which both appeared in the *Oban Times*. The article, published in 1955, relates to the impact of the massive afforestation programme on sheep farming and largely concerned a dispute between farmers on the West Coast and Western Islands and the Forestry Commission. The farmers were concerned that

---

18   Evelyn MacKenzie Anderson, 'Preservation of Trees', *The Times*, 14 January 1950, p. 7.
19   Archives APRS and NTS.

they would be pushed out of business if the Forestry Commission bought more land for planting. The sheep farmers doubted if forestry could compensate for the economic loss that would follow the disappearance of sheep farming.[20]

More relevant to this discussion is a letter on forestry planning that was published in the *Oban Times* in August 1965 in which a holiday maker from Cheshire, a certain Mr. Hall, complained about the conifer plantations on the west coast of Scotland. He wrote that he was 'very dismayed to see new planting on the seaward side of ...the coast'. He continued:

> Trees are an economic necessity but for goodness sake let us keep a sense of proportion. Often the strip of land to seaward is narrow and, if left unplanted, would surely be but a modest price to pay toward the saving of a superb view.[21]

The man was clearly not opposed to forestry, but disliked the coniferous plantations obscuring a nice view, as well as the changing the landscape he had become familiar with through many holidays in Scotland. It is interesting to note that the author of the letter was from England and not a Scotsman. He complained as an outsider and aware of this he finished his letter with the observation that:

> It seems to me that there is a great deal too much apathy on behalf of the people [...] who stand to lose their present enjoyment [of the Scottish countryside]. Raise your voice, Scotland![22]

This one lone voice contradicts a survey that was conducted by Chris Yarrow, a forestry student at University College of North Wales, Bangor, in 1964. This survey asked a sample of 214 people across Britain, including 32 who know Scotland well, what they thought of afforestation and the visual impact of forest plantations on the landscape. Afforestation was generally accepted as 'desirable' but not everywhere. Forestry in mountainous areas was for most respondents more acceptable than that on downs, moorland or in agricultural areas. A majority of 60 per cent of respondents thought that the Highlands were the most favourable region for large-scale afforestation while 40 percent thought it was not a good idea.

In terms of the choice of tree species an overwhelming majority of 97 per cent of respondents preferred pure stand conifer plantations in mountainous areas and only three per cent were against this. However, when given a choice of pure or mixed plantations, a large majority favoured mixtures, seemingly contradicting

---

20 'Sheep Breeders and Forestry. Request for Impartial Inquiry', *Oban Times*, 23 July 1955.
21 'Forestry Planning' *Oban Times*, 5 August 1965.
22 Ibid.

the previous statement. In terms of visual impact of forestry on the landscape 60 percent of respondents disliked trees geometric patterns, although some 40 per cent were indifferent or found straight rows of trees pleasing.[23]

Jim Atterson, former Conservator for Scotland, confirmed the virtual absence of resistance against the planting of conifers in Scotland. Through the 1960s and 1970s he could not remember 'much being said against planting in Scotland by the general public, even conservationists'.[24] Atterson believed that even ecologist Frank Fraser Darling did not object to the activities of the Forestry Commission. Indeed, Fraser Darling was not against forestry *per se* but he was probably one of the Commission's most severe critics. In his book *Highlands and Islands* he criticised the Commission's planting policy for being ecological primitive, as the principle of planting monoculture high forest, 'has been obsolete for half a century on the Continent'.[25] Although Fraser Darling was sceptical about certain aspects of the work of the Forestry Commission, he still believed that afforestation was in essence a good thing. He believed that the mistakes of the past could be corrected and by the 1960s he was already seeing signs that the Forestry Commission was trying to introduce a more holistic approach encompassing considerations of amenity, recreation and conservation:

> As the Commission develops and widens its outlook it will be solving [...] part of the problem for the caring for the wild life [of the Highlands]. Already the Forestry Commission has done more towards the establishment of national parks and [...] reserves than any other body.[26]

However, others did not share Darling's opinion and by the early 1960s the National Trust for Scotland indicated that it was not entirely happy with the achievements of the Forestry Commission. In June 1961 the National Trust for Scotland commissioned a landscape survey to William H. Murray, one of Scotland's most distinguished mountaineers, with the aim '... to delineate areas of outstanding natural beauty, to report on the distinguished character of these areas, and to assess change'.[27] The survey was completed by the autumn and the results were published in a booklet in early 1962, and contained some very critical observations of the plantations created by the Forestry Commission.

The areas of the survey were confined to the Highland region because it was thought that this area of unspoiled country was most vulnerable to the

---

23   Chris Yarrow, 'A Preliminary Survey of the Public's Concepts of Amenity in British Forestry', *Forestry*, 39 (1966) 1, 59-67, pp. 61-62.
24   Personal comment Jim Atterson.
25   Frank Fraser Darling, and Morton Boyd, *The Highlands and Islands* (Revised edition; London: Oliver and Boyd, 1969), p. 260.
26   Ibid., p. 260.
27   William H. Murray, *Highland Landscape. A Survey* (Aberdeen: NTS, 1962), p. 9.

modern world and 'most likely to be overtaken by change'.[28] Murray was an active campaigner to protect wilderness areas of Scotland from ill-considered development, including forestry. He observed to his regret that the face of the Scottish Highlands was changing markedly due to the activities of the Forestry Commission and the North of Scotland Hydro-Electric Board, who were building large dams for the generation of electricity. He found that the layouts of the forests were often highly regular, with rectangular blocks of conifers, vertical fence lines and horizontal upper margins where the trees were planted up to a contour line. That was a complaint often heard since the publication of Murray's report and it was not going to disappear for the rest of the 20th century.

Murray's assessment of the Forestry Commission was not all negative, and like Darling, he saw some of the afforestation activities of the Commission as an effort to improve the beauty of the landscape. Murray thought that some of the planting would bring back the forests to Scotland and 'in them [...] is the main hope for the restoration of woods and other flora and fauna that would otherwise be lost'.[29] In Murray's opinion this woodland restoration had to be carried out carefully, but he doubted if the Forestry Commission was the right organisation for the job as he observed that in some cases valuable old stands of Scottish pines had been lost when under planted with exotic conifers. To prevent the loss of valuable woodlands and to protect the landscape Murray advised that the activities of the Commission were inconsistent and should be monitored and warned that 'mere declarations of policy on amenity by the [...] Commission can never be taken on trust, [...] for their work has been too unequal to justify trust'.[30]

Murray concluded his assessment by calling for a central planning body to protect Scotland's natural heritage, otherwise he feared that the combined activities of the Forestry Commission and the Hydro-Electric Board, would irreparably damage and destroy Scotland's natural heritage.[31] The survey itself did not make a huge difference with regard to the attitude of indifference of the general public towards forestry in Scotland, but it was clearly a sign of a growing awareness of the impact of forestry on the Highland landscape.

At the same time the complaints concerning the activities of the Forestry Commission received by the conservation organisations in Scotland remained, not surprisingly, low in the period between 1945 and 1970. The handful of complaints that were received and the way they were dealt with followed a similar pattern as before the war. In the autumn of 1952 Isabelle Lindsay from

---

28   Ibid.
29   Ibid., p. 17.
30   Ibid., p. 17.
31   Ibid., p. 19; The Hydro-Electric Board was responsible for the construction of many large dams all over the Highlands for the generation of electricity.

Bearsden had sent a letter to the National Trust for Scotland to complain about the fact that the Forestry Commission did not allow natural regeneration in Glen Falloch, west of Loch Lomond. Both the Association for the Preservation of Rural Scotland and the National Trust for Scotland had high level contacts in the Forestry Commission and therefore the Trust referred the letter to Beresford Peirse, Director of Forestry for Scotland. He took the matter very seriously and even found time to visit the forest by, and replied to the complainant, inviting her to meet with Mr. James, conservator for the south of Scotland and the Glasgow area, to discuss her objections.[32] There is no record of this meeting, so it unclear whether this meeting ever took place.

In another case the APRS responded in similar fashion. In April 1960 the Association received a letter from a member of the Glasgow Tree Lovers Society drawing attention to the felling of broadleaves by the Forestry Commission in the Queen Elizabeth Forest Park (Ard Forest).[33] Sir Samuel Strang Steel, Former Chairman of the Scottish National Committee of the Forestry Commission, pointed out that this was probably only a selective felling and suggested asking the Commission for further information. In a reply the Conservator of Scotland West explained that it was the policy of the Commission to grow hardwoods where the soils allowed and that some selective felling was indeed carried out. The Conservator offered to talk with the correspondent.[34]

This was the typical pattern of interaction between the Forestry Commission and the conservation organisations: if an individual had some complaint about forestry practices, he or she was invited to discuss their concerns with forestry officers. The Forestry Commission appeared to take complaints seriously and to encourage its officers to look into these matters. This also applied to concerns raised by local councils, as indicated by an internal memo of the Assistant Forestry Commissioner for Scotland, Mr. Forres, in December of 1961:

> … local authorities have certain responsibilities in the matter, and it is important that their views should be sought in all appropriate cases as well as considerations being given to any representations they may make to us.[35]

They could probably deal with individual complaints because the numbers were so low that it was easy to handle.

At the highest political levels the views of the well established organisations, such as the National Trust for Scotland and the APRS, were actively sought.

---

32   Letter from Sir Henry Bereford Peirse, Director of Forestry for Scotland, to the National Trust, 17 October 1952, Archive National Trust for Scotland.
33   Minutes Council Meeting APRS, 3 May 1960, Archives APRS.
34   Ibid.
35   NAS: FC11/24, Amenity, Memo by Assistant Commissioner (Scotland) 20th December 1961.

When the Government Working Party on forest policy was set up in 1962, the Association for the Preservation of Rural Scotland were invited to submit their views on amenity and forestry. The Working Party was informed that the council of the APRS '[…] were strongly of the opinion that more planting of broad-leaved trees of hardwoods should be undertaken'.[36] The APRS also stressed that popular viewing points should be left unplanted in new forestry schemes. In addition, the opportunity was taken to express concern about the gradual disappearance of hedgerows from the landscape because pastoral landscapes were being replaces by forestry.[37] The hedgerows remained an important topic for the APRS throughout the 1960s, but other issues were starting to eclipse the concern over the impact of forestry on the landscape. In the wake of the public concerns over pesticides in the wake of Rachel Carson's publication of *Silent Spring*,[38] the APRS became involved in a campaign against water pollution by chemicals, while the National Trust for Scotland focussed increasingly on the management of its own properties. In the case of forest restoration and landscaping the Trust asked for advice from well-known landscape architect Sylvia Crowe about how to make its forests blend into the landscape. Crowe was a distinguished landscape architect and the author of a standard work on landscape design entitled *Tomorrow's Landscape*. It was in this book that she first defined the principles of how to fit forest plantations more naturally and less intrusively into the landscape.[39]

Although the Forestry Commission would later hire Silvia Crowe as well, it did not necessarily mean that the National Trust for Scotland entirely agreed with the Forestry Commission's policies and practice. It criticised the commercial plantations of the Commission and thought that this was not an example the Trust had to follow on its own properties. By the start of the 1970s, most of Scotland's traditional conservation bodies, such as National Trust for Scotland and the APRS were preoccupied with issues other than forestry, such as environmental pollution or management of their own estates. It was public opinion by the end of the decade that became the most critical voice in issues of forestry and landscape impact. This was the result of the democratisation and increased participation of all sectors of society during the 1960s and 1970s, including nature conservation and environmental activism, ending the era in which 'gentlemen conservationists' were the guardians of nature.

It was a Britain-wide organisation, the Ramblers Association, which staged a first campaign against blanket forestry in the early 1970s. In the autumn of 1971 the Association published a pamphlet entitled *Forestry: time to rethink*,

---

36   APRS, *Annual Report 1963*, p. 21.
37   APRS, Leaflet, *1926-1996, 70th Anniversary*.
38   Rachel Carson, *Silent Spring* (Boston: Houghton Mifflin Co., 1962).
39   Sylvia Crowe, *Tomorrow's Landscape* (London: The Architectural Press, 1963).

in which they argued that indiscriminate planting of the Scottish Highlands with fast-growing conifers was doing great damage to the countryside. The pamphlet attacked all arguments that the Commission had used to justify their afforestation programme, including the need for strategic reserves, less reliance on imported timber, employment, and provision for recreation. The Association called for an immediate stop to the further expansion of the afforestation programme and called for a full-scale Government enquiry into the affairs of the Forestry Commission.[40]

In response to the Ramblers Association's pamphlet Lord Taylor of Gryfe, the then Chairman of the Forestry Commission, issued a statement to the press. He argued that the claims made by the Ramblers were unjustified and that the Commission's activities provided employment, recreational opportunities and would decrease the reliance on timber imports in the long term. Most importantly, he stated that forestry did not harm the landscape and that forest plantations increased biodiversity harbour 'a wide range of flora and fauna', to a greater extent than the bare moorland they had replaced. Lord Taylor added that the Commission did not fell any deciduous trees in 'areas of amenity importance' and left many wilderness areas unplanted and delegated the management of these areas as nature reserves to the Nature Conservancy or local conservation groups.[41] By the early 1970s the top-down approach to landscape management was still very much alive within the Forestry Commission and any criticism was met with a reiteration of the often-cited justifications for the forestry policy that had been used since the inter-war years.

A second response to address criticism of forest policy or forestry operations was technocratic in nature. For example, in the early 1960s the Forestry Commission had appointed a landscape architect to make their forests aesthetically more pleasing in response to long-standing criticisms of the appearance of forest plantations and, more importantly, to increasing numbers of tourists visiting the forests.

Landscaping the forests

In February 1944, Desmond Heap, a well-known planning lawyer, made some critical observations on the appearance of the conifer plantations created by the Forestry commission.[42] In a speech delivered in Leeds to the North of England Division of the Town Planning Institute he stated:

---

40 Ramblers Association, *Forestry: time to rethink* (London: The Ramblers Association, 1971).
41 Bruce Campbell, 'Forests under Fire', New *Scientist*, 53 (6 January 1972) 777, 22-23, p. 23.
42 Heap was a lawyer, the Comptroller, and City Solicitor to the Corporation of the City of London and the former Deputy Town Clerk of Leeds.

... I do know that the ranks of coniferous trees planted by the Forestry Commission in pursuance of what are supposed to be the best interests of afforestation are a perfect eyesore wherever I have seen them and are definitely prejudicial to the amenities of the countryside [...] and so, as I reflect on planning matters, I often think what a pity it is that some better method of afforestation could not be thought of [...] than the setting up of row upon row of coniferous trees.[43]

These criticisms of the appearance of the forestry plantations did not dissipate during the decades following the Second World War, and in 1964 the Forestry Commission appointed Sylvia Crowe as landscape consultant. Her appointment was a direct result of the ministerial statement on forestry of July 1963 following the first five-year Forestry Review. This statement included for the first time the provision of recreational facilities and aesthetic considerations in forest policy and was also a response to the objections of the highly regular and rectangular forest plantations that were found in the Highlands.

Crowe's task was 'to assist [the Commission] in making their forests as attractive in appearance as they must be efficient in production'.[44] According to Crowe, landscape patterns evolved naturally by geological and climatic processes and in order to make sound decisions on amenity issues it was necessary to analyse and understand the character of the underlying landscape. She argued that the constituent landscape elements, such as existing types and patterns of vegetation and land use and the colours of the rocks and the soil, and the shape of the relief, define the visual character of a particular landscape. In Crowe's opinion the distribution and combination of these elements determined the pattern and the nature of the forest, for example a particular mix of tree species or homogenous stands, to make it look right in any given landscape.[45]

The method that Crowe used to fit forests into the landscape was based on three interrelated principles. The first of these principles was the introduction of contrast between different landscape elements. In her opinion this was essential to maintain a balanced and attractive landscape pattern and to achieve this there had to be a contrast between areas of open ground and of planting and variation in the type of tree species, farm crops and other vegetation.[46]

---

43 Desmond Heap, 'Planning – A Lawyers Reflections, 1944', *Journal of Planning and Environmental Law*, Special Issue, November 1983, 8-14, p. 9.

44 Forestry Commission, *Forty second Annual Report of the Forestry Commissioners* (London: H.M. Stationery Office, 1963), p. 9.

45 Silvia Crowe, *Tomorrow's Landscape* (London: Architectural Press, 1956), p. 16.

46 Silvia Crowe, *Forestry in the Landscape* (London: HMSO, 1966), p. 6.

The second principle, the choice of species with relation to the landscape, determined the appearance and character of that landscape. Crowe believed that the character of th forests in Scotland was mainly determined by conifers but that hardwoods had to be used where possible to break the monotony:

> Over the great majority of Forestry Commission land in Scotland, [...] where conifers can be accepted as the only possible timber trees, the landscape requirements can be met by the occasional introduction of hardwoods related to access routes, [...] and the retention of existing hardwoods where they make an important contribution to the pattern of the landscape.[47]

In Crowe's view, the trees had to be matched to the site, not with regard to the soil, aspect or biological considerations, but to make it blend with the existing landscape elements and forms. She also advised the Commission to keep the existing hardwood trees in place when a new plantation was started and not to under-plant these with conifers, which made them invisible in the landscape. Crowe concluded that under-planting and ring-barking were undesirable practices and that broadleaves had to be saved and integrated into plantations. Apart from aesthetic considerations, Crowe recognised the importance of hardwood belts in coniferous forests for linking habitats and concluded that 'this pattern also provides the ideal habitat for bird and animal populations'.[48]

The third principle considered by Crowe was the shape of forestry plantations in the landscape. 'Planting shapes' refer both to the pattern of different species within the forest and to the outline of the forest as a whole. Crowe advised the Commission to follow the natural variation of soil and topography and that size and shape of plantations should be related to the shape and scale of the terrain. She used the pattern of planting to avoid straight lines and the creation of forest blocks and to accentuate the shape of the hills instead of blanketing them.[49]

Finally, felling operations have an extreme impact on the landscape and to avoid damage to the scenery, Crowe applied the same principles used to create new plantations. In Crowe's opinion, harvesting operations could be used as an opportunity to erase straight lines in the landscape and rectify the shape of plantations.[50]

Crowe's ideas evolved over time from landscape design, which is fitting forests into the landscape and beautifying them, towards an objective of multi-purpose forestry with more emphasis on nature conservation. Crowe recognised the

---

47   Ibid., p. 13.
48   Ibid.
49   Ibid., p 18.
50   Silvia Crowe, *The Landscape of Forests and Woods* (London: HMSO, 1978), pp. 32-35.

importance of forests for timber production but also for nature conservation and recreational purposes.[51] In order to do so Crowe advised the Forestry Commission to draw up a long term management plan to make the best use of all forest resources and 'to ensure that no one use will conflict with another, and to bring all uses together into a landscape which will both function well and look well'.[52] But Crowe never lost sight of the prime objective of her employer and she realised that nature conservation and recreation were always subsidiary to the prime aim of producing timber. In this context she observed that 'conservation of resources should always take precedence over demands for [recreational] use'.[53]

During a meeting on multi-purpose forestry organised by the Royal Scottish Forestry Society in 1972, an officer from the Forestry Commission, Brian Holtam, acknowledged the importance of Crowe's work in educating the Forestry Commission and giving its officers 'a better understanding of the landscape and some of the simple measures which could be [...] effective in making improvements'. But he continued by saying that there was a 'danger of losing sight of the prime object for most of British forests'[54] — the production of timber. Nevertheless, the influence of Crowe's ideas spread gradually through the Forestry Commission, which undertook landscaping projects and design courses for foresters. In 1972 a forest officer was sent on a landscape design course at Newcastle University. By 1978 he was involved in a wide variety of tasks, including the design of an important planting scheme at Beinn Ghuilean on the Kintyre peninsula in western Scotland.[55] The Forestry Commission introduced a landscape design policy in 1978 but the initial focus was lost as emphasis on financial objectives increased during the early 1980s. Subsequently the importance of landscape aesthetics was re-established but now in connection with a whole body of environmental policies that would be implemented by the late 1980s.[56] These developments will be explored in more detail in chapters nine and ten.

---

51 Sylvia Crowe, 'The Multi-purpose Forest', *Scottish Forestry*, 26 (1972) 3, 213-216.
52 Crowe, *The Landscape of Forests*, p. 41.
53 Ibid., 41.
54 Crowe, 'The Multi-purpose Forest', p. 215.
55 Forestry Commission, *Fifty seventh Annual Report of the Forestry Commissioners* (London: H.M. Stationery Office, 1978), p. 18; Oliver Lucas, 'The Forestry Commission', *Landscape Design*, 150 (August 1984), 10-11, p. 10.
56 Oliver W.R. Lucas, 'Aesthetic considerations in British Forestry', *Forestry*, 70 (1997) 4, 343-349, p. 347.

8. Foresters as naturalists

The massive afforestation programme that started in 1919, and speeded up after the Second World War, had a direct impact on the landscape. The most visible of this impact is, of course, the change in the landscape that comes with the planting and harvesting of forests. There is a sense of loss when a familiar landscape is transformed by forestry operations such as planting and tree harvesting. It is for this reason that the visible impact of forestry operations sparked off the earliest debates about landscape aesthetics and amenity in relation to forestry. In the previous two chapters we explored the response to the forestry plantations among external organisations and the general public up to the 1970s, but the discussion about the visible impact started immediately after the Forestry Commission was established, almost before the first trees had gone into the ground. The impact of the monotony of rectangular blocks of dark conifers across the land was first stressed by John Perkins, a member of the Linnean Society and an accomplished botanist, published in the *Quarterly Journal of Forestry* in 1920. He warned about the effect of large single species plantations on the landscape:

> To plant pure is a sound silvicultural maxim. To follow this out to the letter will result in plantations of a severe type - largely consisting of rectangular areas of a single species of conifer.[1]

He predicted that the result would be:

> A closely grouped mass of trees of the same kind and pattern with no relief to cheer the eye.[2]

This article set the tone for the discussion about the visual impact of forestry on the landscape in the decades that followed.

In 1927 another outsider, William Dallimore, a well known botanist from the Royal Botanic Gardens, Kew, published an article entitled *Aesthetic Considerations in British Forestry*. Dallimore criticised the dark, uniform and geometric plantations of non-native conifers that were planted with the sole purpose of making money:

---

1   John Perkins, 'A Plea for the Consideration of the Aesthetic Side in Restocking Our War-felled Woods', *Quarterly Journal of Forestry*, 13 (1920), p. 255.
2   Ibid.

Fancy block after block of the same kind of tree, the trees spaced with mathematical accuracy, and only relieved by other blocks of another kind of dismal uninteresting tree that can be only looked upon as representing so many pounds shillings and pence.[3]

Figure 8.1: Geometric blocks of conifers in the landscape, Sutherland, northern Scotland.

Photo: Jan Oosthoek.

Dallimore goes on to suggest alternative approaches to the geometric layout of plantations and the use of shrubs and native trees to make the forests fit better into the landscape. Thirty years before Sylvia Crow, Dallimore wrote:

> [Foresters] can aim at informal outlines with the dense forest merging naturally by groups and isolated trees into farm-land; they can plant about the borders of their woods and forests groups of attractive and interesting trees or large shrubs, and where vantage points occur they can introduce groups of brighter coloured trees amongst those of sombre hue.[4]

Dallimore made no apologies for the use of non-native conifers and the creation of production forests but he advocated development of a more diverse-looking forest landscape. In another article published a year earlier, Dallimore recognised that this would be more expensive but that it was essential in areas of natural beauty that are popular as a tourist destination. He also regarded old

---

3   William Dallimore, 'The Aesthetics of British Forestry', *Forestry*, 1 (1927) 1, 53-54, p. 53.
4   Ibid., p. 54.

trees as essential in preserving the character of the landscape and advocated the preservation of old trees in the landscape five decades before the preservation of so-called veteran trees became an important conservation issue in Britain.[5]

Dallimore and Perkins were not connected to the Forestry Commission and their ideas about aesthetics of forestry in the landscape appear to have been largely ignored. As the post-war planting programme progressed with a great sense of urgency to establish the strategic reserve of timber, the simple direct and cost conscious approach of planting monoculture forest plantations created large blocks of conifers in the landscape. Nowhere was this more publicly visible than in the Lake District; as discussed before, by 1935 the Forestry Commission was involved in a conflict with conservationists. These negative effects of forestry on the landscape were increasingly recognised by foresters and gradually the ideas of the organic integration of forests in the landscape emerged. By the mid-1930s Lord Clinton, one of the original Forestry Commissioners and former Chairman of the Forestry Commission, wrote in response to the Lake District conflict that:

> One really valid objection to modern planting from the artistic point of view is the hard margins and rectangular figure which are generally adopted in the layout.[6]

To prevent hard margins and straight lines Clinton proposed to plant or regenerate several species that differ in colour, shape and size in irregular patterns at the boundaries of plantations to 'disguise any straightness in outline or sharpness in angle'.[7] By writing this Lord Clinton followed in the footsteps of Dallimore, Perkins and Sir Walter Scott.

Forestry on ecological basis

Instead of deliberately planting trees in irregular patterns and using a variety of species to make forests fit into the landscape, some proposed a more natural method to achieve this. This method was Mark Anderson's forestry on an ecological basis, which approaches forests as ecosystems and advocated to plant tree species that match the site conditions. Forestry on an ecological basis does not seem extraordinary nowadays, but was quite extraordinary for its time and according to William Mutch, a former colleague at the University of Edinburgh, Anderson was a 'prophet crying in the wilderness' in the 1950s.[8]

5   William Dallimore, 'The Aesthetic Value of Trees', *Transactions of the Royal Scottish Arboricultural Society*, 40 (1926) 2, 90-105.
6   Lord Clinton, 'Trees and Landscape', *Quarterly Journal of Forestry*, 30 (1936), p. 200.
7   Ibid.
8   Personal comment William E.S. Mutch, 12 August 1998.

Mark Anderson is probably the most famous forester Scotland has ever produced and started his career as a research officer with the Forestry Commission in Scotland. In 1932 he resigned from the Commission frustrated that he was not allowed to do more scientific research into forest genetics and forest ecology.[9] Another factor seems to have been his dislike for the then Chairman of the Forestry Commission, Roy Robinson. Anderson disagreed with the vision of Robinson, who was concerned with large-scale plantations and the use of exotic trees, in particular Sitka Spruce.[10] After Anderson had left the Forestry Commission he took up a position in the Irish Forestry Service which culminated in his promotion to a directorship. After the war he returned to Britain to become a lecturer in forestry at the University of Oxford. He did not feel at home in the college world of Oxford and was about to leave Britain for Australia when he was appointed to the Chair of Forestry at Edinburgh University in 1951.[11]

One of the key texts for understanding Anderson's ideas is his *Guide to the Selection of Tree Species*, from which we gain a good understanding of what is meant by forestry along ecological lines, or naturalistic forestry as it was called in Germany. Naturalistic forestry is not aimed at fitting forests aesthetically into the landscape or the protection of habitats of wildlife; instead it propagated the selection of tree species based on a detailed assessment of the local environmental conditions, including the biological, ecological, meteorological and soil conditions in order to create healthy and productive forest ecosystems.[12] Anderson's whole outlook on forests was what we call holistic nowadays. In a radio talk he described forests as 'extremely complex associations of organisms, living in a delicately balanced harmony, amongst which the trees are merely the most conspicuous components'.[13]

Anderson regarded forests as living communities, a term used by German forester Josef Köstler in his book *Silviculture*, which Anderson had translated into English. The concept of the living forest community recognised the reciprocal dependence of all biotic and abiotic parts upon the whole of the forest ecosystem. Köstler writes in his book that 'silvicultural thought and action must deal with living communities; it must take the laws of nature into account and adapt itself to them'.[14] He makes a distinction between the mechanical outlook of forestry and the biological outlook. The mechanical outlook regards the forest as a productive system controlled by humans and yielding timber as an

---

9   Charles J. Taylor, 'M. L. Anderson', *Scottish Forestry*, 15 (1961) 4, 260-262, p. 261; Taylor, *Forestry and Natural Resources*, p. 26; Personal comment William E. S. Mutch; Charles Taylor, 'Mark Anderson - Scottish Forester', *Scottish Forestry* 36 (1982) 4, 297-303, p. 298.
10   Taylor, 'Mark Anderson', p. 299; Personal comment William E. S. Mutch.
11   Taylor, 'M. L. Anderson', p. 261; personal comment William E. S. Mutch.
12   Mark L. Anderson, *The Selection of Tree Species* (Edinburgh: Oliver and Boyd, 1950), pp. 4-17.
13   University of Edinburgh Special Collections: GEN 1971/6, 'Time for Forestry'. Broadcast talk by Professor M. L. Anderson, Monday, 2 January 1956.
14   Köstler, Josef, *Silviculture*, Translated by M. L. Anderson (Edinburgh: Oliver and Boyd, 1956), p. 3.

end product, one treating trees in the same way as grain and other agricultural crops. The biological line of thought regards forests as part of the natural world. It was thought that in a natural state, undisturbed by humans, forests renew themselves in perpetual harmony. Köstler regarded the careful study of natural forests as essential for learning how to imitate the natural processes in artificial forest plantations as a way to secure the health of these forests and the balance of nature in these living communities.[15] The main aim of these so called naturalistic practices was to produce timber without compromising the capability of a locality to grow a new crop, a concept that we now call sustainability. Köstler's ideas were rooted in the concept of the *Dauerwald*, or 'perpetual forest' that was first proposed in Germany by Alfred Möller in 1913.[16]

Anderson used Köstler's distinction between the mechanical and biological approach of forestry, although he called it the economic and protection functions of the forests. In Anderson's view, the economic function is obviously concerned with the production of timber. Anderson defined the protection function as all the benefits of forestry other than wood production: the influence of the forest on climate, on soil, water supply, and the provision of recreational areas for the community, the improvement of amenity, rural scenery and country life, the provision of habitats for plants and animals. Anderson was concerned with forestry on an ecological basis and he defined forest ecology as the relationship of the forest to its wider environment.[17]

Anderson's ideas had developed during the inter-war years long before he translated Köstler. He drew heavily upon the forestry tradition that was developed in the colonial context, on the continent and from long standing Scottish estate forestry practices. This can be observed in his Oxford lecture notes of 1928, in which he stated:

> ...the ideal forest is one which is capable of regenerating itself without man's assistance. With such forests [...] the condition of the stand and the soil and the nature of local climate are such that seed is produced plentifully and germinates abundantly. The balance of nature is such that sufficient seedlings survive to form a new stand.[18]

At the same time, Anderson realised that this was quite impossible in Scotland where most forests had to be grown from scratch because there were no forests in existence on the elevated areas where afforestation was to take place.

---

15   Ibid., p. 11.

16   A. Pommering and S.T. Murphy, 'A Review of the History, Definitions and Methods of Continuous Cover Forestry with Special Attention to Afforestation and Restocking', *Forestry*, 77 (2004) 1, 27-44, p. 28.

17   'Time for Forestry'. Broadcast talk by Anderson; Interview Mutch.

18   M. L. Anderson, Lecture notes on nursery management, 1928. University of Edinburgh Special Collections, miscellaneous papers Department of Forestry, not catalogued.

There could be no natural regeneration without an existing forest. 'In such cases', he wrote, '[the forester] resorts to artificial regeneration [...] by planting out in an area of ground specially set aside for the purpose'.[19]

The young trees grown in these nurseries had then to be planted out to form new forest plantations. This was acceptable for Anderson in the Scottish context, but he was not very keen on the uniform blanket forests that the Forestry Commission created, especially after the Second World War. Anderson opposed the management of blanket forests under a system of clear felling because he disliked uniform single species forest plantations and regarded these as unsustainable. Anderson thought that uniform plantations were undesirable and even impossible in the Scottish context because site conditions are so extremely varied and complicated throughout the country that Anderson proposed to adapt forestry practice and the species used to the local environmental conditions.[20] That meant in practice that a forest could become a patchwork of different species because soil and aspect, the orientation of a slope to the sun, can change considerably over short distances.

Anderson advocated a forestry practice that was able to grow trees, fulfil a number of non-economic functions, such as recreational use and wildlife habitats, produce timber and was capable of regenerating itself by natural means after it was properly established. Anderson summarised his ideas as follows:

> Some foresters, notably the French, are in general opposed to such a system [of monocultures and clearfelling] and in favour of a system of management which involves no clear felling but clearings over small areas only and use the greatest extent possible of the natural process of regeneration of the forest.[21]

Anderson's maxim, 'study nature, follow her if you can, but guide her where need be and record what is done and achieved', was very much in line with Köstler's advice to study natural forests.[22]

Anderson felt that the tide of history was against forestry on an ecological basis after the Second World War. He believed that post-war forestry policy led foresters to create forests with the sole purpose of 'producing a certain minimum amount of produce annually [...] enough to pay the annual expenditure [...] plus compound interest'.[23] New economic ideas about return on invested capital had emerged during the years before the war and new technology had made

19   Ibid.
20   Anderson, M.L., *The Selection of Tree Species.*, p. xi.
21   University of Edinburgh Special Collections: GEN 2158/1, M. L. Anderson, Miscellaneous notes, lectures, etc. on forestry.
22   Taylor, 'Mark Anderson - Scottish Forester', p. 302.
23   'Time for Forestry'. Broadcast talk by Anderson.

it possible to prepare large tracts of land and to wipe out local environmental variations. The practice of short rotations of single species was a reaction to the demands of post-war forest policy of rapid expansion of the forests and pressure from the Treasury to make forestry pay.

To reach the post-war planting targets and to pay the annual expenditure foresters faced the task of speeding up the growth of trees. Therefore experiments were staged with fast growing exotics and new thinning techniques and the application of fertilisers. This fitted in very well with the emergence of Sitka spruce as a more robust productive species and the emergence of large scale plantations, 'Canadian style'.[24] These forests were treated as a crop, a collection of trees grown in a timber farm, which can be removed and converted for use and re-sawn like a crop of wheat. Anderson warned against these practices and doubted if stimulating fast growth and large scale exploitation saved time and money. He stated in a radio talk that any advantage in the rapid growth of forests and production of timber 'may be more than offset by serious troubles later'.[25] With these 'troubles' he meant unsustainable practices leading to exhaustion of the soil and erosion, attraction of diseases and pests and increasing risks of the trees blown over. Anderson did not wish to treat a forest as a crop but instead as a

> ... stand to be conserved in such a way that the material that is removed can be replaced with no irreparable damage to the forest as a whole, that is to say, either to the soil or to the stock growing on it. [The forester's task] is not to exploit the forest but to ensure its perpetuation as a production unit.[26]

In this quote Anderson describes sustainable forestry long before the modern meaning of the concept was introduced in the 1980s! That does not mean that he was not interested in the commercial exploitation of the forests. Anderson's aim was not different from the people who advocated large-scale monocultures of fast growing species: the production of timber to make a profit, although in order to achieve this goal he advocated a different management strategy based on ecological considerations. Anderson was convinced that an income could be drawn from a balanced and healthy forest in perpetuity and he was not concerned with the short-term return on invested capital. Like ecologist Frank Fraser Darling, Anderson believed that it would take a long time and several forest rotations of 100 to 150 years to create a viable forest ecosystem. For Anderson it was the long term that counted and that the creation of healthy forests was for the benefit of humankind.[27]

---

24 Personal comment William E.S. Much, 12 August 1998.
25 Radio talk Anderson, 2 January 1956.
26 Ibid.
27 Personal comment William E. S. Mutch; Personal comment Jim Atterson, 13 August 1999.

In a review of Anderson's translation of Köstler's book, J. Alan B. MacDonald, Conservator of South Scotland, observed that the forestry plantations of the Forestry Commission were a far cry from Anderson's ideas:

> We have, however, less reason to be proud of our record for disregarding natural laws of the forest in our plantings and clear fellings. For even if we admit the necessary and catastrophic war fellings - how many of us knew better or felt keenly enough that other and less vandalistic methods of reaping and replenishing were possible? Loyalty towards sustention scarcely existed then; do we yet possess the 'strong personalities' so truly required?[28]

The rapid expansion of monoculture forest plantations in the Scottish uplands in the decades that followed since these words were written suggests that there were not many 'strong personalities' within the Forestry Commission to move away 'from the crude mechanistic ideas of clear felling and low thinning which have long cursed our forestry'.[29] However there were in fact a good number of 'disobedient foresters' within the ranks of the Forestry Commission who experimented with the less formal methods based on naturalistic forestry proposed by Anderson and Köstler and who believed that forests were not just production units but ecosystems with additional functions.

Forest ecology

In 1954, in the midst of the post-war planting bonanza James Macdonald, Director of research and education of the Forestry Commission, argued that research should not just be aimed at nursery problems, pests and diseases, genetics and mechanical development and other plantation techniques, but that more research should be devoted to increase the ecological knowledge of the forests. Macdonald added that successful afforestation of bare hill land and moorland depended on the understanding of ecological processes, and he regretted that so little work had been done in this field.[30] This statement is significant because it came from one of the most senior officers of the Forestry Commission.

As our discussion of Anderson's ideas has already highlighted, the importance of ecology in forestry was recognised in the inter-war years. Anderson was not the only forester to do so. In 1933 A. C. Forbes, Assistant Commissioner for Ireland until 1922, published an article entitled 'Silviculture on Natural Lines'

---

28   J. Alan B. MacDonald, 'Silviculture (Josef Köstler)', *Forestry*, 30 (1957) 2, 195-198, p. 197.
29   Ibid., p. 198.
30   James Macdonald, 'Forestry Research and Experiment in Scotland 1845-1953', *Scottish Forestry*, 8 (1954) 3, 127-141, p. 130.

in an issue of *The Scottish Forestry Journal*. In this article Forbes discussed a visit to a Scottish forest, managed by a system of forestry on natural lines including the planting of species related to site conditions and natural regeneration. Forbes observed that the result of this type of management was 'extremely attractive' and concluded that 'the wood is now practically uneven-aged, and resembles a natural woodland in every respect'.[31] About a decade later Arthur Geddes outlined the theory behind this type of forest management in an article published in the *Scottish Forestry Journal* with the title 'Landscape and Ecology in relation to Afforestation'. Geddes explained in this article that the utilitarian ideas of forestry with their straight-line boundaries and uniform plantations were a mistaken philosophy. He linked forestry on ecological lines with aesthetic considerations and argued that the adaptation of a forestry practice that matched tree species to the site would create a forest that looks more natural and blends better into the landscape. He based this on the experience gained at Inverliever, on the west coast of Scotland, which showed that uniform plantations were no longer uniform after ten years due to local differences in site conditions. Almost every block at Inverliever showed variable growth and some blocks had simply died. A few years later, a new planting method had been worked out linking the assemblage of the natural main plant communities on the site with the tree that grew best as a part of these ecosystems. The application of this method led to the creation of mixed woods and curved lines, not by means of planting but by using ecological principles, following the natural boundaries of plant communities and soils, which allowed nature to do the landscaping.[32]

Immediately after the Second World War W. H. Rowe, a forester from Oxford, wrote about forestry on an ecological basis in his book, *Our Forests*. He stated that forests are 'a living community throbbing with life', and continued: 'for here, indeed, is a colony of individuals - plants, trees and animals, co-existing in a communal life'.[33] To preserve this, Rowe advocated the use of mixed woods and, where possible, natural regeneration to avoid monotonous forests planted in straight lines and geometric patterns: 'The new forests need not become monotonous blobs obscuring a favourite view or marring a familiar landscape'.[34] But at the same time the prime objective was in Rowe's eyes the production of timber and selecting tree species based on site conditions was the most suitable method for achieving this. This was all very much in line with Anderson's ideas and made the latter less of a prophet crying in the wilderness.

But how common was the *practice* of planting of trees according to site conditions? The conclusion depends on where you look and at what time.

---

31   A. C. Forbes, 'Silviculture on Natural Lines', *The Scottish Forestry Journal*, 47 (1933) 1, p. 1.
32   Arthur Geddes, 'Landscape and Ecology in Relation to Afforestation', *The Scottish Forestry Journal*, 58 (1944) 1, 53-57.
33   W.H. Rowe, *Our Forests* (London: Faber & Faber, 1947), p. 11.
34   Ibid., p. 23.

During the inter-war period there was a general tendency to match trees to the conditions at the site, like in Strathyre in Perthshire. The Strathyre working plan of 1951 notes that 'great care was taken to plan species according to the indications of even small vegetational changes'.[35] It was here that the local forester, Alistair Cameron, the son of Simon Cameron who helped create the experimental forests at Corrour, planted trees according to the site. He used the local plant communities and soil differences to define where to plant a certain tree species and he took also the topography and the resulting microclimates into consideration. Cameron believed that planting trees in compact and regular blocks of single species would not work very well in the context of the environment and landscape of Strathyre because of its varied topography and soils, and vegetation assemblies that as well as severe exposure on the upper slopes of the mountains. The foresters in Strathyre followed this natural pattern of soil, vegetation and climatic variation in order to plant trees to the best advantage and an effort was made to match the trees to the site and thus created the diverse forests we see at the present day. Although the main species used were conifers, on the lower slopes and on the roadsides native broadleaves were planted to increase the variety and beauty of the forests.[36] The planting method used in Strathyre did not go unnoticed and Fraser Darling commented in his book *Natural History of Highlands and Islands* that:

> Such is the country either side of Loch Lubnaig where the Forestry Commission is changing the face of the hillsides. The varied scheme of plantings here can serve as a model to confound those who hold that forestry spoils the scenery.[37]

A 1951 a Forestry Commission guide to Strathyre forest stated with pride, that this forest 'shows how forestry can be enhancing a Highland landscape when forethought is given to its future effects'.[38]

North of Loch Ness, in Glen Urquhart, the Commission's foresters took a similar approach. The Forestry Commission acquired the first part of this estate in 1923 and the remainder in 1944. Most of the planting here was a mix of conifers, of which Scots pine was the dominant species. Where and what kind of species were planted depended in the local variations of vegetation and soil conditions.[39]

The forests around Fochabers in the Speymouth area of northeast Scotland are another example of trees matched to the site. The forester in charge of this wood, Bob Allison, planted 400 hectares per annum around Fochabers

35 NAS: FC7/9, *History of Strathyre Forest, 1934-1951*.
36 NAS: FC7/9 *History of Strathyre Forest*; Macdonald, *The Forestry*, p. 49.
37 Darling, *Highlands and Islands*, p. 23.
38 Forestry Commission, *Britain's Forests: Strathyre* (London: HMSO, 1951), pp 5-6.
39 NAS: FC7/35, Working Plan Glen Urquhart 1950-1965.

during the 1950s. The planting of these extensive areas was possible due to the introduction of large-scale cultivation by means of ploughing, but that did not make much difference to the choice of species with regard to the site conditions. Allison wanted to plant the most suitable species with respect to soil and climatic conditions but the problem was that the nurseries did not always supply what he needed. The nurseries mass-produced seedlings and consequently foresters had to take the trees that were available, but despite this problem and the commercial objectives of the Forestry Commission, the forests around Fochabers are remarkably diverse. The forests started as plantations of spruces, chiefly Sitka, mixed with Scots pine and on the higher slopes lodgepole pine. Although the area was ploughed, in order to improve drainage, trees were still planted taking soil and climatic conditions in to consideration. A careful thinning regime and natural regeneration allowed the invasion of shrubs and the creation of uneven aged tree stands, which attracted in turn birds and wildlife. The development of a diverse forest happened despite the commercial objectives applied to the forests around Fochaber, creating the diverse and mixed forests we see today. This was in large part the result of the way that local foresters had managed the forests and actively encouraged it to develop into a more diverse forest ecosystem.[40]

However, the conditions in Strathyre, Glen Urquhart and around Speymouth are not as wet and windy as along the west coast or in the far north of Scotland. In these areas matching trees to the site was practised, but did not result in a mix of different species. In Benmore Forest in Argyll very little mixing of species was carried out, and planting was almost entirely confined to pure blocks of different common conifers, generally large blocks of spruce and smaller compact blocks of pines, larches and Douglas fir. During the inter-war period most trees here were planted in turfs to deal with the wet and peaty conditions. After the war the introduction of new cultivation techniques allowed larger planting programmes to be initiated, mainly of spruce. The reason for the predominant use of spruces is simply dictated by the fact that these trees as better suited to survive the wet and windy conditions of the west coast. The same story applies to Ardgartan Forest, part of Argyll Forest Park, where initial planting by the Forestry Commission was spruce planted in turfs.[41]

Loch Ard Forest is situated in the heart of the Queen Elizabeth Forest Park, now part of the Loch Lomond and Trossachs National Park, in the upper Forth basin. The forest is predominantly one of spruces, which accounted for more than two-thirds of the planted area in 1960. The area planted during the inter-war period

---

40   J.L. Fergusson, 'The 69th Annual Excursion in the North-east', *Scottish Forestry*, 20 (1966) 1, 248-254, p. 253; Personal comments Bob Allison, 21 July 1999.
41   NAS: FC7/3, Forest History Glen More Forest, 1925-51; NAS: FC7/1, Forest History Ardgartan Forest, 1924-51.

was described in the forest working plan as 'diverse in character' and that 'a very intimate choice of species related to site variation was practised resulting in a form of group mixtures'.[42] After the war the 'choice of species related to the site' philosophy was abandoned in favour of the large-scale cultivation that was made possible by the introduction of ploughing. The working plan described this shift in cultivation techniques as follows:

> Due to the nature of the sites being planted, their remoteness, plough draining and cultivation techniques, combined with manuring, the choice had normally been spruce or pine.[43]

It was the new cultivation techniques that made foresters shift from a forestry based on ecological lines to a forestry that was mechanised and able to create site conditions that were as uniform as possible over large areas. During the inter-war years the choice of species related to the site was the most economical way to grow timber, but after the war the new cultivation methods looked more promising to create profitable forests because it was more efficient and reduced growth times and cost. This can also be observed in the Carron Forest, in Wester Ross in northwest Scotland, were most forests were established by means of ploughing after the Second World War. The majority, a staggering 93 per cent, of all trees planted in Carron Forest were spruce species, of which 79 per cent was Sitka spruce.[44]

The same happened in the forests of Mid-Argyll around Kilmartin, north of Lochgilphead, where the plantations are for more than 80 per cent composed of spruces planted on ploughed ground. The management objective of these forests was to 'supply the maximum pulpwood to the Fort William pulp mill', highlighting the shift towards an industrial-scale timber production by the beginning of the 1960s.[45] However, foresters realised that the new mechanical forestry practice did often produce forests that were not very suitable for multi-purpose use, including the protection of wildlife and the conservation of landscapes of outstanding natural beauty.

In 1964 Andrew Watt, Forestry Commission Director for Scotland, suggested that forest research could not afford to neglect the need of more basic knowledge on climate, soils, ecology and tree physiology, repeating what James Macdonald, Director of Research and Education of the Forestry Commission, had argued ten years earlier.[46] Macdonald had argued that research should not only be aimed at creating efficient forests by developing mechanical and other

---

42 NAS: FC7/48, Working plan Loch Ard Forest.
43 Ibid.
44 NAS: FC7/52, Working Plan Carron Valley, 1966.
45 Working plan for mid-Agyll, 1966, NAS FC7/59.
46 Andrew Watt, 'Some Aspects of Forest Research in Great Britain', *Scottish Forestry*, 18 (1964) 2, 105-110.

plantation techniques, but that a better ecological understanding of the forests was also necessary for successful forestation of bare hill land and moorland.[47] At about the same time there was considerable discussion between proponents of ecological forestry and the more economically oriented foresters and part of this debate took place in the public sphere through correspondence in newspapers. In July 1956 John McEwan, a forester in the west of Scotland, attacked the movement opposed to rapid development of highly productive forests in a letter to the *Glasgow Herald*:

> This ecological school of thought plans for protective forestry and places [it] on a much higher plane than money-making policy.[48]

In a reply to McEwan, C. Brenshaw, a forester from Perthshire, defended the ecological school by stating that, in line with Anderson, long rotations and use of native deciduous trees would improve the soil. Brenshaw thought that ecology was a necessary component in forestry and that 'it would be pathetically foolish to neglect its revelations'.[49] But the tide was against ecological forestry and short rotation forestry based on large-scale mechanical cultivation, and the use of Sitka spruce became firmly established by the early 1960s.

The break in forestry practice is less dramatic if we bear in mind that both the practices of ecological forestry and the new mechanical forestry had the same objective: the production of timber to create a strategic timber reserve and to make a profit. Despite that their aims were similar, the new forestry practice had a profound impact on the appearance and function of the forest. The forests became less diverse, larger and their shape had to be rectangular because this was easier for ploughing operations. However, the changes do not tell us much about the attitudes of foresters towards nature conservation, wildlife management and nature in general.

Disobedient foresters

The famous Scottish ecologist Frank Fraser Darling described the upland moors and peatlands in a vivid phrase as a 'wet desert' and was convinced that these areas had to be reclaimed for the restoration of the forests that had once thrived there, and he believed if that could not be done through natural regeneration then it had to be done artificially. The main purpose of forest re-creation was the production of timber, but Fraser Darling was convinced that this would

47 Macdonald, 'Forestry Research and Experiment in Scotland', p. 130; James Macdonald, 'Progress in Forestry Research', *Scottish Forestry*, 4 (1950) 2, 40-48.
48 John McEwan, 'Forestry and land use in Scotland. Attack on the "Ecological School"', Letter to the *Glasgow Herald*, 18 July 1956.
49 C.M.B. Brenshaw, 'Case for Native Deciduous Trees', Letter to *Glasgow Herald*, 21 July 1956.

also increase biodiversity in the Highlands, and it was for this reason that he regarded the work of the Forestry Commission as important and valuable.[50] In the 1969 BBC Reith Lectures he praised the Commission by saying:

> [The Forestry Commission] preceded State action in establishing its own National Forest Parks, which in Scotland have to make do for the National parks that the country has been denied. Furthermore, in the last twenty years the Commission has planted its new forests with much more ecological awareness, using different species.[51]

From the early years of the Forestry Commission, its foresters had showed an interest in other aspects of forestry than simply growing telegraph poles. The Forestry Commission used the high forestry system managed with regular thinning and clear cutting of the final crop in the hills of Scotland, although this system had a few disadvantages. The high forestry system can easily turn into a kind of forestry dictated by textbook calculations and data in yield tables, turning forestry into a hard-fact science with the aim of producing the most desirable product in the most economic time. This was observed by F. Oliver, a district officer of the Forestry Commission,[52] and he wrote a provocative article in the *Forestry Commission Journal* in 1939. In this article he questioned the outcome of the existing forestry management system in use. Oliver was surprised that so much forestry literature suggested that foresters have to imitate nature, but in his experience the reality was quite the opposite:

> ... to a forester nature is everything that is bad: she is slothful, wasteful, careless, extravagant, and the results she obtains are often deplorably poor.[53]

He continued by stating that this is quite obvious because in natural forests developments occur randomly and result in unpredictable outcomes. In nature, trees are never arranged in geometric patterns; it would be 'uneven, patchy and blanky, with much variation of species'.[54] The result of the high forestry system is the very opposite of irregular natural forests; their whole management is tailored to make the plantations as productive as possible. Oliver believed that high forests were degraded into 'pole factories' and that forestry 'has inevitably become something resembling a mass production business'.[55] He even went as

---

50   Darling and Boyd, *The Highlands and Islands*, pp. 66, 69-70, 73-74; Smout, T.C., *The Highlands and the Roots of Green Consciousness*, p. 9.

51   Frank Fraser Darling, *Wilderness and Plenty, The Reith Lectures 1969* (London: BBC, 1970), p. 67.

52   F. Oliver started his forestry career as a District Offices of the Forestry Commission in Inverness. In 1937 he moved to Dumfries to head the forestry district in the South of Scotland. After the war the was the chief controller of wood exports in Hamburg, Gemany, before becoming conservator of the East of Scotland in1947. He retired in 1964.

53   F. Oliver, 'Thoughts on Afforestation', *Forestry Commission Journal*, 18 (1939), p. 123.

54   Ibid.

55   Ibid. p. 224.

far as saying that 'proper' forest management could become mismanagement, ultimately doing harm to the landscape and ecosystems. Oliver observed further that, under the label of proper silviculture, healthy birch forests were removed or ring barked followed by planting with conifers. He concluded his article by suggesting that forestry should be less mechanical and allow more natural development of the forests. He argued that 'a measure of untidiness may be good forestry, and may be sound both silviculturally and economically. It would certainly improve in amenity'.[56]

Oliver was not the only forester appalled by the ruthless suppression of vegetation other than commercial trees. By the beginning of the 1950s, Arthur Cuthbert, a former district officer in Perthshire, was employed as a young forester in a large woodland survey. In many areas he observed that before planting the existing trees were ring-barked. He was appalled by this practice and included a long personal letter in the final draft of a survey presented to the Forestry Commission to support and official protest against this practice. Cuthbert felt that he had not gone into forestry to kill trees but to plant new ones and to care for the existing forests.[57]

Many foresters felt the same way as Cuthbert and wanted to create forests, not destroy them, and they had also a general interest in natural history.[58] John Davies, former Conservator for the west of Scotland, explained in this context:

> I think that you must keep in mind that most foresters are keen naturalists. I never met a forester that was not interested in birds or something like that and therefore were pretty good custodians of what they had.[59]

These words contain the echo of George Ryle, the later Deputy General Director of the Forestry Commission, who wrote in 1927: 'a naturalist is born and not made'. He continued:

> … and in most cases the factors which go to make the born forester also bring out in him the instinct and feelings of the born naturalist. In fact, the very life which he leads, with his unique opportunities for first-hand observation during all seasons of the year, cannot help but to inculcate in him a degree of insight into the ways of the wild which few others could obtain in a lifetime of book learning.[60]

---

56 Ibid. p. 225.
57 Personal comment Arthur Cuthbert.
58 Personal comment Jim Atterson.
59 Personal comment John Davies.
60 George B. Ryle, 'The Forester as a Naturalist', *Forestry Commission Journal*, 6 (1927), 21-22.

Ryle, like Davies, suggests that good foresters must be keen naturalists with the desire not only to create forests but also to enhance and protect the life contained in them. Ryle also expressed his concern that the conversion of bare ground into forests would change the local flora and fauna. Therefore, he thought that 'foresters and naturalists will be losing opportunities if they do not make a study of the changes they are causing to take place in both fauna and flora of their charges'.[61] He believed that foresters were the custodians of their estates and decided what nature should look like. If species declined because of the creation of new forests the forester was only following nature by doing nothing to prevent this, but if 'by accident the Forestry Commission is instrumental in saving from extinction such creatures as the wild cat, the pine marten, the badger and others, every lover of Britain's small fauna will thank them'.[62] The forester is here the custodian and creator of nature; a nature that was concerned with silviculture guided by the principles of nature itself.

At the forest level there were foresters studying and protecting the wildlife of their forests, for instance Donald MacCaskill who studied and recorded small mammals and birds living in the forests under his care. MacCaskill was a keen naturalist and wildlife photographer who published books on wildlife and birds and helped the BBC with the production on a number of wildlife films. MacCaskill continued the work that Cameron had started around Strathyre, where he was head forester in the 1960s and 1970s until his retirement. However, he went a step further than Cameron in that he not only tried to fit the forest organically into the landscape but also to have consideration for wildlife. In the case of a glen where eagles were known to be nesting he had designed the forest so that the eagles were not disturbed. It may not have been the most efficient way to plant a production forest but MacCaskill believed that a forest is more than a collection of potential telegraph poles.[63] The forestry practice he advocated did not always find favour with his superiors but that did not stop him from practising it. Earlier in his career when he was ordered by his superiors to cut down some semi-natural oak woods the banks of Loch Awe he prevaricated and delayed because he believed that these trees should be protected. This attitude amounted to a refusal to carry out formal forestry policy and by doing so he won in the end and the oak trees were saved.[64]

MacCaskill was not a lone forester interested in forest wildlife and the protection of semi-natural woodlands. John Davies recalled the observation of wild cats in the Central Belt of Scotland and pine martens in the Great Glen where they had been absent for a long time. He wrote about the wild cat:

---

61 Ibid., p. 20.
62 Ibid., p. 21.
63 Jim Crumley, 'Don MacCaskill', *The Scots Magazine*, 134 (2000), 96.
64 Rennie McOwan, 'Don MacCaskill', *Herald Scotland*, 16 May 2000.

I well remember the excitement we felt in the 1960s when we found them breeding in Carron Valley Forest, outside Falkirk. I have no doubt they will continue to move south.[65]

He attributed the spread of these and other animals to the expansion of the forests since 1919 and was convinced that the process would continue with the creation of new forests. Forester Fred Donald, Assistant District Officer in Kincardine and Angus, recalls that one of his foresters, Struan Stewart, was an expert on deer and he would stay up all night to see the deer, record their numbers and study their foraging pattern.[66]

In a 1960 article in *Scottish Forestry* MacDonald Lockhart, President of the Royal Scottish Forestry Society, stressed the benefits of afforestation for Scotland's wildlife. He argued that the newly planted forests would provide shelter for wildlife such as birds, small predators and deer. He was convinced that rare animals, like the badger, 'will increase as our forest area does'.[67] However, these statements must be approached with caution because Forestry Commission sources, such as the annual reports, are silent on wildlife numbers in the forests during the 1960s and 1970s. Beyond the concerns of individual foresters, wildlife protection was still not part of the merit of the Forestry Commission. It is also silent about the attitudes toward ancient woodlands and native broad leave trees, which were in many cases under planted with conifers or removed as late as the 1980s.

The foresters mentioned here is only a small sample of the many foresters who were keen naturalists with an interest in the conservation and protection of forest ecosystems. If this is anything to go on it seems that there was a general belief among foresters working in the forests that there should be more concern for nature conservation within the Forestry Commission. George Peterken also suggested this when he wrote that many foresters were (and are) sympathetic towards nature conservation.[68] According to Jim Atterson, the foresters at headquarters had exactly the same ideas as foresters out in the forests, but it was just that foresters on the ground could actually do something, although perhaps in a small way. They could not really protect wildlife because it was not part of their main programme and it was not budgeted for and therefore they had to do it during their own time.[69]

However, during the 1960s this started to change and the protection and conservation of flora and fauna became an issue within the Forestry Commission.

---

65 Davies, *The Scottish Forester*, p. 52.
66 Personal comment F.T. Donald, 13 July 1999.
67 S.F. Macdonald Lockhart, 'Forestry and Wild Life', *Scottish Forestry*, 14 (1960) 1, 199-204, p. 203.
68 George F. Peterken, *Woodland Conservation and Management* (London: Chepman and Hall, 1993, 2nd edition), p. 198.
69 Personal comment Jim Atterson.

In 1964 the Forestry Commission appointed a Wild Life Officer with the task 'to harmonise the conservation of wild life with the need of timber production'.[70] For more than forty years there was no official conservation policy but many foresters were keen naturalists. That they did not act like national park rangers is understandable because their job was to create new forests and produce timber, not to create national parks and conserve wildlife. If that happened incidentally foresters regarded this as a bonus. Different attitudes later prevailed in the Forestry Commission, and many foresters played an influential part in scenic and ecological planting where commercial plantations were fringed by deciduous trees or had clumps of mixed species inserted in suitable spots and where the needs of wildlife were taken into account. These attitudes formed the basis of the remarkable transformation of the Forestry Commission during the 1980s and 1990s, the subject of the next chapter.

70   Forestry Commission, *Annual Report, 1964*, p. 11.

9. The end of monoculture forestry

By 1978 a landscape design policy had been introduced by the Forestry Commission and by 1984 the Commission had a landscape design team of three foresters with landscape design qualifications. Between 1975 and 1982 this team was able to design about 7,300 hectares of new planting and 7,100 hectares of felling and replanting, concentrated in the most beautiful and prominent landscapes in Scotland and England.[1]

However, the ideas of landscape design were still not fully accepted by the Forestry Commission as being part of its role, and were regarded as rather separate from production forestry. Forestry had become so highly scientific, quantified and logical that the qualitative, multi-purpose forestry approach was difficult to accept, especially in a professional activity as fundamental as forest planning. Through the early 1980s there still existed a strong dichotomy between commercial forestry and environmental and landscape concerns and it was difficult to give up such a firmly held position after sixty years of planting monocultures in the most efficient way, i.e. geometric blocks.[2] This attitude was going to change rapidly in response to a coincidence of pressures which led to significant changes in forestry policy during the 1980s with the development of the Forestry Commission's broadleaf policy, and in particular the conflict over the planting of the wetlands in the far north of Scotland.

Forestry tax breaks

Between 1977 and 1980 two influential reports on forestry policy were published: *The wood production outlook in Britain* by the Forestry Commission and the *Strategy for the UK Forest Industry* by the University of Reading's Centre for Agricultural Strategy. Both reports advocated the continued expansion of forestry in Britain based on increasing consumption of wood products and of possible pressures on world supplies. The reports saw an equal role for the state and private sector in the expansion of Britain's forestry. By the late 1970s sixty per cent of Scottish forests were owned by the Forestry Commission but the ability to expand state forestry was regarded as limited. In order to expand forestry, forms or partnership and cooperation between landowners, the Forestry Commission and the private sector were seen as essential. To encourage more involvement of the private sector the University of Reading's

---

1 Oliver Lucas, 'The Forestry Commission', *Landscape Design*, 150 (August 1984), 10-11.
2 Oliver W.R. Lucas, 'Aesthetic considerations in British Forestry', *Forestry*, 70 (1997) 4, 343-349, p. 346.

Centre for Agricultural Strategy recommended in a report on forestry strategy a simplification of planning procedures for forestry and the introduction of higher grants and a favourable taxation regime.[3]

The Forestry Commission and Centre for Agricultural Strategy reports were hardly radical documents and elaborated themes such as looming timber shortages and import substitution, which had been used as a justification of state involvement in forestry since the early 20th century. This did not sit well with the proponents of free trade and neo-liberal economics. In 1981 the Institute of Economic Affairs, a free market think-tank, published a report by economist Robert Miller tentatively entitled *State Forestry for the Axe*, which is a radical neo-liberal critique of 20th century forestry policy. Miller proposed the de-nationalisation of the Forestry Commission, the removal of existing planning controls on planting and felling and to 'abolish both grants and tax exemptions', ending all state support for forestry and leaving the industry in the hands of market forces.[4]

However, a year after the coming to office of the Thatcher government in 1979, it was announced that continued forest expansion was 'in the national interest, both to reduce our dependence on imported wood in the long term and to provide continued employment in forestry and associated industries'. In the same policy statement it was also announced that while afforestation would continue at rates similar to those in the past, it would be carried out mainly by the private sector. In order to facilitate this greater 'opportunities for private investment' in forest assets would be created, 'including the sale of a proportion of the commission's woodlands and land awaiting planting'.[5] A year later in 1981 this was formalised when the Conservative Government amended the 1967 Forestry Act, which shifted the emphasis of forest policy to the private sector. At the same time a simplified grant scheme was to replace dedication[6] and part of the Commission's estate was to be sold off to private buyers. This showed that whatever the flavour of government, the forestry lobby would find ways of securing support for upland conifer planting, using job creation and the importance of a state-owned forestry service to appeal to the Labour party and arguing for private investment to secure Conservative support.[7]

---

3   Forestry Commission, *The Wood Production Outlook in Britain* (Edinburgh: Forestry Commission, 1977); Centre for Agricultural Strategy, *Strategy for the UK Forest Industry*, CAS Report no 6 (Reading: University of Reading, 1980).

4   Robert Miller, *State Forestry for the Axe: A Atudy of the Forestry Commission and De-nationalisation by the Market* (London: Institute of Economic Affairs, 1981), p. 63.

5   HC Debate, 10 December 1980, Vol. 995, Column 927-928, *Forestry Policy (Review)*.

6   A woodland owner could dedicate a woodland for the purpose of timber production under a management plan agreed with the Forestry Commission. The Commission would provide the landowner with practical advice and a subsidy for woodland management. See chapter 5.

7   Philip Stewart, 'British Forestry Policy: Time for a Change?', *Land Use Policy*, 2 (1985) 1, 17-29, p. 21.

These changes in forestry policy were only cosmetic and the real driver of forestry expansion during the early 1980s was a system of tax concessions and grants which had been available since the 1950s but only started to be used on a large scale by the 1980s. For larger conifer plantations of ten hectares or more the grant rate was £240 per hectare in the mid-1980s. This would amount to a subsidy of 24 per cent in the case of a typical establishment cost of £1000. This was a substantial subsidy, but it was the tax system that provided the real incentive, particularly for high-income earners, and made investing in forestry very attractive. These tax incentives allowed any losses incurred on forestry operations to be set against other income for tax purposes. In assessing the profits from forestry the value of growing timber was ignored and the inevitable investment, or loss, made during the establishment phase of a new plantation was off set against other income. For example, it was now possible for someone paying 60 per cent income tax to offset the cost of establishing a forest plantation against other taxable income, minus the forestry grant (Based on the example above: £760 x 0.6 = £456). After grant and tax relief, the cost of creating plantations in this example would fall to £304 or just over 30 per cent of the cost without the grant and tax relief. The value of relief depended on the tax rate: obviously it was much greater to someone in the top tax-bracket than to a base-rate taxpayer.[8]

As a result of the tax breaks investors flocked to the new forestry plantations and by the mid 1980s over 90 per cent of all newly planted forests in Scotland were financed with this scheme. However, the scheme would not work on its own because the long rotations of forestry plantations meant that capital would be locked up for periods of more than fifty years, and of course by that time revenue from timber sales would be taxed. However, this tax could be avoided by selling off the land soon after the creation of the plantation. The sale would also unlock the value of the plantation for the initial investor. The new occupier was then entitled to be assessed for income tax based on the value of the land, and not the timber growing on it, and as a result having to pay very little or even no tax on the revenue from timber sales at a later date.[9]

This type of investment was attractive for institutional investors, such as pension funds, who were looking for reliable future revenue streams over the long term. The initial investors moved on to invest in new plantations on even poorer and more remote land and the cycle repeated itself. In other words tax breaks for people in the highest tax bracket encouraged a rapid expansion

8   Alexander S. Mather, 'New Private Forests in Scotland: Characteristics and Contrasts', *Area*, 20 (1988) 2, 135-143, p. 135; G.P. Hill, 'Policies for Small-scale Forestry in the United Kingdom', in: Stephen Robert Harrison, J. L. Herbohn, K. F. Herbohn (eds.), *Sustainable Small-scale Forestry: Socio-economic Analysis and Policy* (Cheltenham: Edward Elgar Publishing, 2000), 138-151, pp. 142-143.
9   Alexander S. Mather, 'The Structure of Forest Ownership in Scotland: A First Approximation', *Journal of Rural Studies*, 3 (1987) 2, 175-182, pp. 181-182.

of new forestry plantations in order to be able to sustain forestry as a tax shelter. This favourable tax regime had unintended consequences because it encouraged the creation of forest plantations on the cheapest land available, which was often land in remote areas that had potentially high wilderness and conservation value. In the late 1970s and early 1980s such cheap land located in the far north came on the market at a time when land available for afforestation in other parts of Scotland declined rapidly. In addition, new forestry ploughing technology allowed the cultivation of deep, wet peats for the first time, and the use of Lodgepole pine (*Pinus contorta*) as a nurse crop for Sitka spruce (*Picea sitchensis*) proved to be a silvicultural breakthrough on deep peat. As a result of the favourable tax regime and technological breakthroughs the wetland areas of the 'Flow Country'[10] in northern Scotland, poorly suited to commercial forestry, were drained and planted with even-aged monocultures of non-native tree species, primarily Sitka spruce.[11]

Figure 9.1: Aerial view of the Flow Country in Sutherland.

Photo: Graeme Smith from www.geograph.org.uk with permission.

---

10 It is thought that the Flow Country takes its name from the Old Norse language and it means 'boggy ground'.

11 Charles Warren, "Birds, Bogs and Forestry' Revisited: The Significance of the Flow Country Controversy', *Scottish Geographical Journal*, 116 (2000) 4, 315-337, p. 316.

The Flow Country is the largest expanse of blanket peat in the Northern hemisphere and is of international significance because it provides a habitat for many unique and rare communities and species of specialised flora and their associated fauna, in particular birds.[12] The cultivation of these areas for forestry was so damaging to the landscape and wetland ecosystems involved that this was going to backfire on forestry when it became clear to conservationists that the tax break system encouraged unsustainable 'rogue forestry' that had no regard for environmental or landscape values.

Controversies

This perception of 'rogue forestry' was fuelled by a condemning forest policy review jointly carried out by the Nature Conservancy and the Natural Environment Research Council in 1978. The review identified over 700 sites of biological importance, covering one million hectares, including 60,000 hectares of Forestry Commission land. The review put emphasis on the importance of broadleaf woodlands and in particular on so called ancient woodlands and concluded that the work of the Forestry Commission was particularly damaging to these woodlands. The Forestry Commission responded by stating that such sites 'are already protected by management plans of one kind or another'. They dismissed the claim that more consideration had to be paid to broadleaves and the value of ancient woodlands was ignored.[13]

In 1979, a House of Lords Select Committee under Lord Sherfield began an investigation into the Scientific Aspects of Forestry. The Committee made the recommendation that:

> The proper objective for those woodlands and old broadleaf plantations which are not specially selected for nature conservation is to manage them productively and profitably in a way that is compatible with maintaining a value for wildlife and amenity.[14]

The House of Lords Committee linked native broadleaves with timber production and amenity, something the Forestry Commission had done seven years earlier after the forestry policy review of 1972 but had not acted upon.

In 1982, a conference on broadleaves in Britain was held at Loughborough. It is interesting to note that the Forestry Commission and the Institute of Chartered Foresters jointly organised this conference. This event can be identified as the turning point against the dominant use of conifers in favour of native broadleaves

---

12   Ibid., p. 319.
13   Forestry Commission, *Annual Report, 1978*, p. 17.
14   House of Lords Select Committee on Scientific Aspects of Forestry, 1979-1980.

and other trees. The Commission recognised the concern of many people over the poor state of much of Britain's broadleaved woodland and, in particular, the loss of ancient semi-natural woodland to agriculture and other uses. Following the Loughborough conference the Commission undertook a comprehensive review, lasting two years, of all aspects that would involve a broadleaf policy. Some fifty organisations, including many major forestry and environmental bodies, were given opportunities to put their views forward.[15] This review culminated in the Government statement on broadleaf policy in July 1985. The Government's Broadleave policy was aimed at:

> Encouraging positively and sympathetic management of the country's broadleaved woodland to arrest depletion, to increase the quality of timber and to expand this valuable national resource to meet the various complementary objectives.

One of these complementary objectives was:

> To encourage the maintenance and greater use of broadleaves in the uplands, particularly where they will *enhance the beauty of the landscape* and the wildlife interest (emphasis added).

The Commission further explained in the policy description that:

> ... woodlands designated as areas of high landscape value require special management attention.[16]

The objectives of the broadleaf policy were impressive. The Commission committed itself to the protection of broadleaved woodlands and trees, especially the so-called ancient woodlands and hardwood trees of high landscape value. But these intentions hardly seemed to apply north of the Scottish border where the Forestry Commission and private forestry alike continued to create large new conifer monocultures. Any criticism was countered with the argument that the work of the Forestry Commission and the industry it supported was simply carrying out forestry policy and fulfilling the government's planting target, then set at 33,000 hectares per annum. In addition it was claimed that cultivation in the far north of Scotland developed unproductive land, which would boost the local economy and provide employment, arguments used to justify state forestry since the early 20th century. In line with forestry policy developed since the 1972 review, further benefits were envisaged from the new forest habitat created, including providing a haven for rare bird species, supporting increased biodiversity and provision of new recreational opportunities.[17]

---

15 Charles Watkins, 'Recent changes in government policy towards broadleaved woodland', *Area*, 18 (1986) 2, 117-122, p. 119.

16 Forestry Commission, *The Policy for Broadleaved Woodlands* (Edinburgh: Forestry Commission, 1985).

17 Warren, 'Significance of the Flow Country Debate', p. 118.

These justifications were just a smokescreen and the Forestry Commission operated as part of a wider 'forest-industrial complex' made up of Scottish landowners, timber processors, private forestry companies, and investors, both private and institutional, all of whom come together to benefit from public subsidies. In the spring of 1985 the Countryside Commission for Scotland expressed its concern about the fact that this forest-industrial complex seemed to becoming increasingly unwieldy and beyond the control of any planning mechanisms. In 1985 at the presentation of its annual report Nature Conservancy Council chairman David Nickson predicted correctly 'that forestry would be the dominating countryside issue in Scotland for the next decade' unless forestry interests became sensitive to public opinion and took planning controls more seriously.[18]

These words were not as prophetic as it seems but simply reflected concerns aired by conservationists and countryside interest groups such as the Ramblers Association and the Royal Society for the Protection of Birds (hereafter RSPB). In 1983, Alan Mattingly, the Secretary of the Ramblers Association called in a letter published in *The Times* newspaper on the gvernment and forestry interests to create mixed species plantations and pay more attention to landscape values.[19] This opposition was still mild compared to what was to follow in the mid-1980s. In July 1985 in an unprecedented move, the RSPB asked the Government to suspend all grants for afforestation in the Flow Country, pending a full review carried out by the Nature Conservancy Council (hereafter NCC), the Government's United Kingdom-wide conservation and wildlife watchdog, of the effects of afforestation of the Flow Country. The RSPB was also talking to the Forestry Commission in a bid to persuade them to stop planting subsidies to forestry companies active in the North of Scotland.[20] This did not achieve the desired effect and the cultivation and planting in the peat lands of northern Scotland continued.

However, the future of forestry in the Flow Country was not as secure as it seemed and a significant change in policy resulted from a coincidence of pressures. In 1986 the existing forest policy started to unravel when the National Audit Office published a review questioning the economic justification of the Forestry Commission investing further public funds in creating new conifer forests on marginal land in the far north of Scotland. The National Audit office concluded that plantings in the future were expected to become increasingly concentrated on sites which were marginal for timber production and would be unlikely to yield an acceptable return on capital.[21] The bottom line was that the

---

18   Ronald Faux, 'Curb Urged on Private Forestry', *The Times*, 16 May 1985, p. 3.
19   Alan Mattingly, 'Fresh Approach on Forestry', letter to the editors, *The Times*, 12 September 1983, p. 11.
20   Anon., 'Saving Scotland for Birds that Hate Trees', *New Scientist*, 1470 (22 August 1985), p. 16.
21   National Audit Office, *Review of Forestry Commission Objectives and Achievement* (London: HMSO, 1986).

planting grants and tax breaks were very costly for the state and in particular the ordinary tax payer, something that was difficult to sell to the general public by a Conservative government that believed in low taxation and laissez-faire. But in the face of opposition of vested interests in the forestry industry, Scottish politicians and local people, it was difficult for the Government to remove the tax scheme.

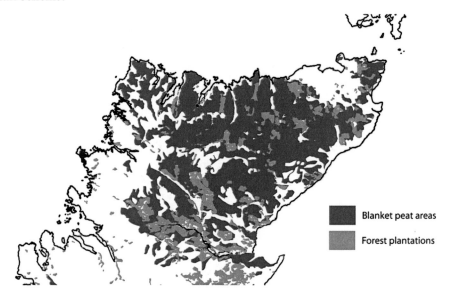

Map 9.1: Blanket peat areas and forestry in the Flow Country of Caithness and Sutherland.

Source: Based on D.A. Ratcliffe and P.H. Oswald (ed.), *The Flow Country of Caithness and Sutherland* (Peterborough: NCC, 1988), fig. 27, 68 & 69.

Around the same time of the Treasury report, the RSPB published a report entitled *Forestry in the Flow Country*. In this report, the RSPB drew attention to the extensive planting undertaken by Fountain Forestry in the Flow Country of Caithness and Sutherland and the damage it did to the local bird populations. The campaign against forestry in the Flow Country was considerably aided by the involvement of certain celebrity investors such as Terry Wogan; by a television documentary presented by the well-known environmentalist David Bellamy in February 1988 entitled *Paradise Ploughed*; and by the publication of an emotively entitled booklet *The Theft of the Hills* written by a concerned former employee of the Forestry Commission.[22] But all this noise was not sufficient to shift the Government's official forestry policy and end the expansion of forest plantations on the blanket peatlands aided by the taxpayer.

---

22   Warren, 'Significance of the Flow Country Debate', p. 118; David Goode, 'Forestry and the Flow Country: Paradise Ploughed – A Television Programme in ITV', *New Scientist*, 1598 (4 February 1988), 85-87.

However, in 1987 the NCCpublicity provided the Government with a perfect opportunity to end the tax breaks for forestry when it published its own report entitled *Birds, Bogs and Forestry*, which criticised forestry in the Flow Country in unusually outspoken terms for a Government organisation. It described the tree planting in North of Scotland as Britain's 'most massive loss of wildlife habitat since the Second World War'.[23] During the presentation of the report in London the Chairman of the NCC, William Wilkinson, called on the government to declare a moratorium on all forest planting and forestry grants in the Flow Country. The publication of the report was accompanied by a well orchestrated publicity campaign, for example a major article in *The New Scientist* by Desmond Thomson, moor ecologist of the NCC, entitled 'The battle of the Bog'.[24]

In the budget of March 1988, the Chancellor of the Exchequer Nigel Lawson, removed without any warning the tax incentives that was driving forestry investments. The move was certainly influenced by the controversy surrounding the planting of the Flow Country, in particular the NCC report, but it was also political damage limitation at a time when a large part of the electorate believed that the Government was subsidising the rich.[25] The Forestry Commission observed properly that this was done to demolish 'arrangements under which tax payers … had been able to shelter other income from tax by setting it against expenditure on forestry, while effectively enjoying freedom from tax on the income from the eventual sale of timber'.[26] The controversy ended with a 'Solomonic judgement' by the Secretary of State Malcolm Rifkind 'dividing the Flows half for the forest industry and half for birds'.[27] This was in an attempt to placate both conservationists and forestry interests, which was made explicitly by the Secretary of State for Scotland even before the budget announcement in February 1988:

> We seek to achieve two legitimate objectives: to meet the ecological criteria, which we have done on a scientific basis, and, at the same time, to take account of the livelihood of those who live in that part of Scotland and who have a legitimate interest with regard to their livelihood and the work opportunities that are available to them.[28]

The Highland and Island Development Board was outraged by these developments and blamed the NCC for undermining forestry development in the Highlands. The chairman of the Highland and Island Development Board concluded that the

---

23   Anon., 'Go-ahead for Forests Threatens Ancient Boglands', *New Scientist*, 1597 (28 January 1988), p. 29.
24   Desmond Thomson, 'The Battle of the Bog', *New Scientist*, 1542 (8 January 1987), 41-45.
25   Warren, 'Significance of the Flow Country Debate', p. 326.
26   Forestry Commission, *Annual Report 1988*.
27   T.C. Smout, *Nature Contested*, p. 62.
28   HC Debate, 24 February 1988, vol. 128, Column 287, *Forestry*.

NCC suffered from 'distant management and policy making'.[29] But his reaction was mild in comparison to that of some sectors of the local population, which was conveyed by headlines in the local press such as 'Farmers fuming over NCC 'green fascists''.[30]

Although the NCC appeared to have won the battle over the Flow Country, the outfall of the conflict would hit the organisation very hard. The tactless press conference of the NCC in London presenting the *Birds, Bogs and Forestry* report and the noisy campaign that followed annoyed many in Scotland. It was experienced as 'Scientific colonisation' from London and in the ensuing months the NCC was warned in the House of Lords about the possible consequences of its actions:

> Recently [the NCC] had a press conference in London to announce the freeze in the development of forestry and consequent loss of jobs in the north of Scotland. It did not consult the Highlands and Islands Development Board. That sort of behaviour provides the necessary propaganda for the Scottish Nationalists.[31]

This warning was not unfounded because the whole Flow Country episode had angered the Scottish political and landowning establishment and they leaned upon the Conservative Government to abolish the NCC, so Scotland could get a wildlife agency of its own that would supposedly be more sensitive to Scottish interests. The Flow Country debate was one of the factors in the decision to break up the NCC and in July 1989, the Minister for the Environment, Nicholas Ridley, quite unexpectedly announced in Parliament that the NCC was to be broken up into three separate councils, one England, one for Wales and one for Scotland. As a result the NCC was dismantled and Scottish Natural Heritage (hereafter SNH) came into being as Scotland's conservation agency in April 1991. Now nature conservation was entirely in Scottish hands and foreshadowed the political devolution by the end of the decade, which also had a bearing on forestry policy in Scotland and the Britain as a whole.[32]

Following the 1988 budget the Forestry Commission, which had supported the tax incentives on forestry, was shaken to the core by the removal of these tax breaks and commented in its annual report that it needed 'a period of adjustment' to the new situation.[33] Luckily the Forestry Commission's period of adjustment was aided by the Government's introduction of the Woodland Grant Scheme to replace the earlier Forestry Grant Scheme and Broadleaved Woodland

29   Quoted in: A.S. Mather, 'Protected Areas in the Periphery: Conservation and Controversy in Northern Scotland', *Journal of Rural Studies*, 9 (1993) 4, 371-384, p. 374.
30   Ibid.
31   HL Debate, 13 January 1988, vol. 491, Column 1268, *Scotland: Devolution*.
32   Mather, 'Protected Areas in the Periphery', p. 374; Warren, 'Significance of the Flow Country Debate', p. 330.
33   Forestry Commission, *Annual Report and Accounts, 1988*.

Grant Scheme. The Woodland Grant Scheme was administered by the Forestry Commission and its objectives were to encourage good management of existing woodland, the creation of new woods for timber production and landscape improvement. Further objectives included the provision of employment through forestry, an alternative use for land in agriculture, habitat for wildlife, and opportunities for recreation and sport. In addition the new grant progamme provided Establishment Grants towards the cost of planting new woods or undertaking work that encouraged natural regeneration.[34]

An additional development that aided the new direction in forestry was the wider problem of the surplus of agricultural land in the European Union. This was regarded as an opportunity to put excess agricultural land to use for forestry and as a result a pilot farming forestry scheme was introduced in 1988 and replaced in 1992 by the *Farm Woodlands Premium Scheme*. The Ministry of Agriculture, Fisheries and Food administered this scheme although applications to participate in the scheme had to be made to the Forestry Commission. The new grant schemes favoured forestry in more fertile parts of Scotland as well as native broadleaf species and ancient woodlands.[35]

In addition to the new grant schemes the Forestry Commission introduced a Community Woodland Supplement for new woods within five miles of the edge of a town or a city and where there were few other woods that could be used by the local community. This was part of meeting the social objectives of forest policy, which were interpreted by the Forestry Commission to mean recreation and amenity, giving precedence to urban interests over rural needs. But this narrow interpretation was challenged by a new group of buyers of Forestry Commission land that was sold under the land disposal programme as part of the Conservative's privatisation efforts in the early 1980s. Although the disposal programme of the FC was mainly aimed at the commercial forestry sector, in 1987 a new group of unexpected buyers of FC estates emerged: local community groups.[36] These community land purchases, although relatively small in number, were part of a broader movement within Scotland for land reform. This development was going to have significant consequences for the development of forest policy during the 1990s.

---

34 S.R. Harrison, P. Hill, P. and K. Herbohn, *Reforestation Incentives in the UK and Australia: A Comparative Evaluation*, First World Congress of Environmental and Resource Economists, Venice, 1998, p. 4. http://siti.feem.it/gnee/pap-abs/harrison.pdf accessed: 14 June 2011.

35 J.R. Crabtree and D.C. Macmillan, 'UK Fiscal Changes and Forestry Planting', *Journal of Agriculture*, 40 (1989) 3, 314-322, p. 321.

36 Sally Jeanrenaud and Jean-Paul Jeanrenaud, *Thinking Politically about Community Forestry and Biodiversity: Insider-driven initiatives in Scotland* (London: Rural Forestry Development Network, 1997), p. 8.

Policy shifts of the 1990s

In 1987 the first Scottish Community forest was established with the acquisition of Wooplaw forest in the Scottish Borders. The project originated in 1985 with Tim Stead, a wood sculptor, who worked and lived in the Scottish Borders. For aesthetic reasons he had decided to use only native British wood and this led to the idea of restoring this resource as well as using it. He conceived of the idea of 'axes for trees' and produced hundreds of handmade hardwood axe heads, which he sold to raise money to buy land to grow native trees.[37]

The publicity for this scheme attracted the attention of two people involved in the native woods movement in Scotland, Donald McPhillimy and Alan Drever. They met with Tim Stead in 1987 and teamed up to create a community woodland in the Scottish Borders. In 1987 this led to the formation of Borders Community Woodlands to take the project forward and a large public meeting was organised in Melrose. Around the same time Wooplaw, a small local woodland, came on the market and within three months the Borders Community Woodlands had succeeded in securing sufficient funds to purchase the first community woodland of its type in Scotland.[38]

The Forestry Commission realised that community forests provided a good opportunity to polish up its tarnished image. In 1989 it launched a community forest initiative, called the Central Scotland Forestry Initiative, that was designed to transform much of the landscape between Glasgow and Edinburgh, the so called Central Belt, into a complex of productive and amenity forests. In 1991 the Central Scotland Woodland Countryside Trust was established to lead the initiative.[39] Responsible for developing Central Scotland's Forest Strategy, its main objectives include creating new ways to finance, develop and manage new woodlands in the area of the Central Belt. The objectives of the Central Scotland Forest were wide-ranging and focused the creation of a multi-purpose woodland in which community participation, economic regeneration, countryside access, recreation, and heritage conservation played important roles. Local landowners and communities were seen as having an important stake in this forest project.[40]

Although the Central Scotland Forest was a successful showcase of a community focused forestry project, the Commission was reluctant to make this kind

---

37 'How Wooplaw Was Started', *Wooplaw Community Woodland*, http://www.wooplaw.org.uk/beginnings. htm Accessed: 14 June 2011.

38 Forestry Commission, *Wooplaw*, http://www.forestry.gov.uk/pdf/wooplaw.pdf/$FILE/wooplaw.pdf Accessed: 5 May 20011.

39 J.R. Crabtree, J. Rowan-Robinson, A. Cameron and A. Stockdale, 'Community Woodlands in Scotland', *Scottish Geographical Magazine*, 110 (1994) 2, 121-127, p. 122.

40 Forestry Commission, *Central Scotland Forest Strategy*, http://www.forestry.gov.uk/website/treetrunk. nsf/ByUnique/CentralScotlandForestStrategy Accessed: 6 May 2011.

of forestry an integral part of its policy. It was also contrary to the aims of grassroots community projects such as Wooplaw, which rejected the top down public sector led 'community woodlands'. The community forests envisaged by the Forestry Commission had a different level of community engagement than the community woodlands created in the grassroots community movement, with the emphasis in most cases being more on provision of a resource for recreation than active engagement in forest management. In addition these objectives gave precedence to urban interests over rural needs and ignored the need for community involvement in the Highlands of Scotland.[41]

However, the Laggan community challenged the Forestry Commission's interpretation of 'community forestry', and forced changes to the policy on forest disposals. The village of Laggan is situated in the Central Highlands of Scotland, surrounded by the Monadhliath and Grampian mountain ranges. The Forestry Commission owned Strathmashie Forest, a woodland plantation of 1400 hectares in the vicinity of Laggan. The Laggan community began lobbying for local control of Strathmashie Forest in 1992. They believed that community management of the forest and the creation of recreational facilities would provide local employment opportunities as a means to halt the decline in population and services and to revitalise the community. The Forestry Commission had not earmarked Strathmashie for disposal and the local initiative was thus entirely spontaneous in its attempt to secure the forest for the community. In addition the Forestry Commission did not consider a community as viable buyers of its forests since these groups were not regarded as proper commercial forestry operations. It also fell outside the public sector-led creation and management of community forests, such as the Central Scotland Forestry Initiative, in which the Forestry Commission was involved.[42]

In support of such expressions of interest by local communities to buy their local forests, three Scottish non-governmental organisations (NGOs), The Highland and Islands Forum, Reforesting Scotland and the Rural Forum Scotland initiated the Scottish Rural Development Forestry Program in 1994. The main aim of this programme was 'to enable local individuals and groups to realise the potential of Forestry as a land-use with environmental, social and economic benefits'.[43] The three NGOs provided information and, to a lesser extent, financial support for setting up community forest groups.

However, these initiatives were almost arrested in the middle of their development by a recession in the early 1990s when the Conservative Government under

---

41   Jeanrenaud and Jeanrenaud, *Thinking Politically about Community Forestry*, pp. 5-6; J. R. Crabtree at al., 'Community Woodlands in Scotland', p. 122.
42   Jeanrenaud and Jeanrenaud, *Thinking Politically about Community Forestry*, pp. 14-15.
43   Quoted in: Amanda Calvert, *Community Forestry Scotland. A Report for Forest Research*, (Alice Holt: Forest Research, 2009), p. 13.

John Major once more considered selling off large parts of the national forestry estate. For community forest initiatives this prospect was a double-edged sword because, on the one hand, it would have provided them with opportunities to buy forests. But on the other, the potential dismantling of the Forestry Commission would have meant the end of subsidies for the forestry industry and forestry initiatives not only to encourage better management of native trees but also community driven projects. In order to consider any privitisation efforts another forestry policy review was ordered in March 1993. It was less than a year after the United Nations Earth Summit in Rio de Janeiro and it was this global event that saved the Forestry Commission and the community forest initiatives in Scotland.

In July 1992 the world's leaders committed themselves to sustainable development at the United Nations Conference on Environment and Development known as the Earth Summit. The Earth Summit was very noticeably oriented towards empowerment through participation; rejecting the notion that sustainable development had to come about just through the 'greening' of government policy. Thus emphasis shifted from the traditional top-down perspective on environmental policy implementation, to one of bottom-up people-led initiatives?.[44] The Earth Summit produced the first global non-binding 'statement of principles' on how the world's forests should be managed sustainably, which aimed at integrating concerns for social, economic and biodiversity issues into forest policy. Earth Summit was followed by a conference in Helsinki in 1993 which was intended to take the Forestry Principles and 'interpret them for European conditions'.[45] The UK Government responded to these developments by publishing *Sustainable Forestry: the UK Programme* which brought together various elements from government policies and programmes and set them in the context of international principles and guidelines. It called for the sustainable management of existing forests, enhancing their economic value as well as seeking other gains in terms of biodiversity, to combat climate change, recreation and landscape, and for the expansion of the area of woodland in pursuit of these multiple objectives. In this document the UK Government committed the Forestry Commission to working towards the full range of forest benefits and to engaging with and empowering communities to enjoy them.[46]

This was confirmed in the ministerial statement on forest policy following the completion of the forestry review, which '...places emphasis not just on wood production but on encouraging the use of our forests for amenity and

---

44   Talib Jounis, 'Bottom up Interpretation after Rio: Rural Community Participation in Scottish Forestry', *Community Development Journal*, 32 (1997) 4, 299-311, p. 300.
45   *Sustainable Forestry: The UK Programme*. CM 2429 (London: HMSO, 1994), p. 6.
46   Colin T. Reid, 'The Changing Pattern of Environmental Regulation: British Forestry and the Environmental Agenda', *Journal of Environmental Law*, 9 (1997) 1, 23-42, p. 27.

environmental benefits'[47] and the development of community forests in line with the Earth Summit Principles. The influence of international conventions and agreements and the development of a grassroots community woodland movement initiated shifts in policy, delivery mechanisms and organisational culture that gathered pace throughout the 1990s.[48] The decision by the Government not to privatise forestry was a practical one because forestry and forest policy provided them with a vehicle for the implementation of the international environmental principles and agreements to which it had committed the United Kingdom.

The implementation of the international principles was in particular aided by the further development of community participation in Scotland. Although the Forestry Commission dragged their feet, the Laggan community got their community forest after an intervention of the Secretary of State, Michael Forsyth, in 1995. A year earlier in 1994, the Forestry Commission had established the Forests and People in Rural Areas initiative, an informal partnership between Rural Forum Scotland, development and countryside agencies and the World Wildlife Fund. The initiative was concerned with assessing and increasing the involvement of rural communities in local forestry and the mechanisms to enable them to do so. In January 1994, the Forests and People in Rural Areas held a meeting with representatives of government and non-government organisations and academics. A subsequent report by Robin Callander laid out a case for 'rural development forestry' in Scotland with a key argument that local communities should have access to the management of local forest resources, including rights to the benefits of management.[49]

The Forestry Commission's response to this was rapid, and in 1998 Lord John Sewell, the Scottish Office Forestry Minister, launched the first formal partnership agreement between the Forestry Commission and the local community at Laggan. The importance of giving communities the option of becoming involved in local woodlands was formally acknowledged by the Forestry Commission with the publications of 'Forests for people working with communities – our commitment' and 'Forests for people working with communities – our approach' a year later in 1999. In 2000 the Forestry for People Advisory Panel was convened by the Forestry Commission to encourage best practice in respect to community involvement in forestry. The establishment of the Forestry for People Panel further facilitated the process of increasing community involvement in forestry management.[50]

---

47   HC Debate, 19 July 1994, Vol. 247, Col. 177, *Forestry Review*.
48   S. Hodge and C. Maxwell, *Involving Communities in the Governance of Scotland's State Forests* (Edinburgh: Forestry Commission Scotland, 2004), p. 5.
49   S. Hodge, *Involving communities in the governance of Scotland's state forests*, Commonwealth Forestry Conference, 2005, p. 3. http://www.forestry.gov.uk/pdf/involvingcommunities.pdf/$FILE/ involvingcommunities.pdf Accessed: 14 June 2011.
50   Forestry Commission Scotland, *Community Partnerships on the National Forest Estate* (Edinburgh: FCS, 2005), p. 3.

Woodland restoration

An important aspect of the community woodland movement was their emphasis on native woodland, in contrast to the predominantly exotic softwood plantations of the Forestry Commission and commercial forestry sector. Most community and crofter woodland projects emphasised benefits of proper management of existing native woodland remnants, many of which are of great ecological significance, and the development of new native woodlands. Further benefits of better protected, and increased areas of native woodlands include protection of wildlife habitats, soils, water quality and other resources.[51] The interest in restoring and expanding the native woodlands of Scotland has been particularly focused on the native pinewoods of the Scottish Highlands, an interest that was greatly stimulated by the publication of Steven and Carlisle's seminal work *The Native Pinewoods of Scotland* in 1959. These authors mapped the remnants of the remaining ancient pinewoods and highlighted their ecological importance and that action was required to ensure pinewood conservation and regeneration.[52] Almost two decades later, these same concerns were expressed during a symposium on the native pinewoods of Scotland at Aviemore in 1975. The objective of this symposium was to discuss the ecology of the native pinewoods and the measures needed to promote their conservation. It was suggested that not only should the conservation status of pinewood remnants be improved, but that their area should be significantly expanded.[53] These events served to draw attention to the poor condition of the native pinewoods and helped to encourage some of the early conservation work carried out in places such as Glen Affric.

However, until the 1990s the Forestry Commission was not much interested in the protection of native woodlands but eventually it became an explicit part of forest policy through three independent developments. Firstly, the increase in the number of community forests with an emphasis on native woodland restoration and regeneration. Secondly, policy initiatives such as the UK Biodiversity Action Plan, which outlined a strategy for implementing the Convention on Biological Diversity, signed by the British Government at the Rio Earth Summit in 1992. The Biodiversity Action Plan laid out a plan to establish at least 35,000 hectares of native woodland by 2005. Thirdly, through the preparation of Forest Certification Standards system in the mid-1990s which placed an onus

---

51   Bill Ritchie and Mandy Haggith, 'The Push-Me, Pull-You of Forest Devolution in Scotland', in: Carol J. Pierce Colfer and Doris Capistrano, *The Politics of Decentralization: Forests, Power and People* (Oxford: Earthscan, 2005), 212-228, p. 218.
52   Adrian C. Newton, Muir Stirling and Michelle Crowell, 'Current Approaches to Native Woodland Restoration in Scotland', *Botanical Journal of Scotland*, 53 (2001) 2, 169-195, p. 171.
53   R.G.H. Bunce and J.N.R. Jeffers (eds.), *Native Pinewoods of Scotland. Proceedings of Aviemore symposium 1975* (Cambridge: Institute of Terrestrial Ecology, 1977), p. iii.

on managers to assess their Plantations on Ancient Woodland Sites (PAWS) and produce a strategy for restoration. This interest in restoration was also fuelled by the decline in the price of softwood timber during the 1990s.[54]

Figure 9.2: Restoration of an Atlantic oak wood in the Loch Awe area, ca. 2000.

Photo: Jan Oosthoek.

As a result, the removal of non-native conifers on ancient woodland sites became a major activity in many Scottish forests as part of the Commission's Native Pinewoods Initiative launched in 1992. The aim of this initiative was to double the area of native pinewood owned by the Commission to a total of 6,000 hectares by the end of the 1990s. An additional stimulus to woodland restoration efforts by non-governmental organisations and community groups has been provided by the creation of the Millennium Forest for Scotland, which received some 11 million pounds from the National Lottery to support woodland restoration projects throughout Scotland. By the end of the 1990s eighty projects were supported by the Millennium Forest for Scotland scheme, and together they aimed to restore approximately 12,600 hectares of native woodland.[55]

These initiatives and the work of the Forestry Commission to restore native woods resulted in a change in the composition of trees planted by the late 1990s. Whereas native species accounted for just over five per cent of trees planted in

---

54   S.N. Pryor and S. Smith, *The Area & Composition of Plantations on Ancient Woodland Sites* (The Woodland Trust, 2002), p.2. www.woodlandtrust.org.uk/SiteCollectionDocuments/pdf/Area_and_Comp_report2.pdf Accessed: 13 May 2011; Newton *et al.*, 'Current Approaches to Native Woodland Restoration', p. 171.
55   Newton *et al.*, 'Current Approaches to Native Woodland Restoration', p. 175.

Scotland in 1988, by 1998 this figure had risen to almost 50 per cent. This was a remarkable transformation of Scottish forestry from a single purpose approach, the production of timber, toward the adoption of broader, more inclusive philosophies of multi-purpose forestry, including community involvement, on the one hand and 'sustainable conservation' and restoration on the other.[56]

This change was also made possible by external economic and political developments related to the collapse of communist Eastern Europe. During the same period world timber prices collapsed and this created a financial crisis within the Forestry Commission. This collapse was brought about by increased timber supplies from the Baltic States and the Russian Federation desperate to generate revenue and a strong pound which made British forestry uncompetitive.[57] However, the government agreed to fund the shortfall in return for commitments by the Forestry Commission to deliver various social and environmental agendas.

When Labour came to power in 1997, it immediately placed a moratorium on further large-scale sales of forestry land. The New Labour government's social inclusion agenda placed a much greater emphasis on social forestry than the preceding Conservative government. Environmental issues were also placed higher on the political agenda as a result of the international agreements reached at the environmental summits in Rio and Kyoto. This meant that the expectations of wider society about the role of forestry was changing significantly, which required transformational change of environmental policy, which was aided by Labour's commitment to devolve government in Scotland and Wales.

As a result, the two smaller countries that make up the United Kingdom,[58] Scotland and Wales, voted for devolution in a referendum, and in 1999, the Scottish Parliament was re-established in Edinburgh. Forest policy and management was devolved to the new national administrations, and national forest strategies were prepared for Scotland, England and Wales. The devolved structure of Forestry Commission England, Forestry Commission Scotland and Forestry Commission Wales allows the organisation to focus more clearly on delivering the policies of the individual governments while still having the ability to take a United Kingdom-wide approach to cross-border issues. Despite devolved responsibility for forest policy, the Scottish national forest estate was still managed by the centralised Forest Enterprise on behalf of the United Kingdom-wide Forestry Commission.[59] This was unsatisfactory and in 2002 a

---

56 Forestry Commission, Woodland Statistics, *Time Series for New Planting and Restocking, 1976 – 2010*, http://www.forestry.gov.uk/pdf/planting1976-2010.xls/$FILE/planting1976-2010.xls Accessed: 13 May 2011.
57 Bob Crabtree, 'Cost and Benefit of UK Forestry Policy', in: David William Pearce (ed.), *Environmental Valuation in Developed Countries: Case Studies* (Cheltenham: Edward Elgar Publishing, 2006), 36-49, pp. 38-39.
58 The United Kingdom is made up of three countries: England, Scotland and Wales and one devolved province: Northern Ireland.
59 Ritchie and Haggith, 'The Push-Me, Pull-You of Forest Devolution', p. 213.

Forestry Devolution Review of the post-devolution experience was undertaken. The review considered the post-1999 administrative arrangements for delivering sustainable forestry policies in Scotland, England and Wales and the United Kingdom's international forestry commitments, including options for further devolution of these arrangements.[60] The review recommended that the Forestry Commission was to be split into sub-national branches to deliver the forestry strategies in England, Scotland and Wales and a central cross-border Forestry Commission providing shared services such as finance, research and grants administration. The Forestry Commission was decentralised in April 2003 with the creation of the Forestry Commission Scotland, answerable directly to Scottish ministers.[61] This started a process of divergence of Scottish forest policy from the rest of the United Kingdom and the development of a *de facto* independent Scottish Forestry Service.

60   Forestry Commission, *Scotland Annual Reports and Accounts 01.02* (Edingburgh: FC, 2002), p. 27.
61   Forestry Commission, *Great Britain and England Annual Report and Accounts 2003-2004* (Edinburgh: FC, 2004), pp. 25-27.

10. The past and the future

At the start of the 21st century, control of the publicly-owned forests of Scotland had been transferred to the Scottish Executive.[1] This was the beginning of a divergence in Scottish forestry policy from the rest of the United Kingdom, which was reflected in the first Scottish Forestry Strategy published in 2000. It highlighted the differences in emphasis between Scottish objectives and those of the English forestry strategy. While the English forestry strategy had a strong focus on public use of the forests, there was stronger support for commercial forestry in Scotland, reflecting both the larger forest estate in this country and its much stronger commercial forestry sector.[2]

The aim of the Scottish Forestry Strategy was to further develop multi-purpose forestry in Scotland and to increase the forest resource to cover about a quarter of Scotland's land surface. The strategy recognised five strategic policy directions for Scotland's forests including:

- the maximisation of the value of the wood that will be available during the next 20 years;
- the creation of a diverse, high quality forest resource that will contribute to the economic needs of Scotland during the 21st century;
- ensuring that forestry in Scotland makes a positive contribution to the environment;
- the creation of opportunities for more people to enjoy trees, woods and forests;
- helping communities benefit from woods and forests.[3]

Following a wide consultation process, Scottish Forestry Minister Rhona Brankin launched a revised forestry strategy in October 2006. The need for revision was in recognition of the very wide policy context in which forestry now operated and it integrated the wider land use policies and broader social and economic aims of the Scottish Executive. The Strategy's overarching principle is sustainability, through sustainable development underpinned by sustainable forest management and social inclusion. These key principles will be achieved through a culture of 'forestry for and with people' that embraces the social, economic and environmental functions of forestry. The revised strategy

---

1 The Scottish executive is the defacto regional government.
2 Crabtree, 'Cost and Benefit of UK Forestry Policy', pp. 36-37.
3 *Scotland's Trees, Woods and Forests* (Edinburgh: Forestry Commission, 2002), p. 12.

also envisages the increase in Scotland's woodland cover to around 25 per cent in the second half of the century, which involves the creation of some 650,000 hectares of new woodland.[4]

Climate change has become more important, as reflected in the extent to which the revised strategy emphasises the contributions forestry can make to climate change targets. The value of forests to local people, both rural and urban is given more emphasis, as is their potential to contribute to health and education. Forestry is no longer seen as a solitary activity but one which is fully integrated with other land uses and contributes to other policy areas such as energy, housing and health. It also envisages a broader range of forest-related businesses capturing more economic benefits of forestry.[5]

Land reform

Focus on the political hot potato of land reform sheds light on how forestry has become integrated within the wider policies of the devolved Scottish Government. At the beginning of the 21st century a relatively small number of individuals continued to own most of the land in Scotland. Historically this has led to tensions with local communities, in particular the crofters in the north and west of Scotland, who have felt that they have no control over the land and do not share the economic and social benefits of the natural resources of the land. The Land Reform (Scotland) Act 2003 attempts to address the issue of control over rural land by conferring a 'community right to buy' when land comes on the market. The aim is to create social and economic opportunities to enable rural communities to overcome high property prices, create more affordable housing, and promote the redistribution of natural resources, including forestry.[6]

The Scottish Executive has seen forestry policy as both a tool for implementing land reform and an effective way of promoting community control over rural areas. Policy is delivered through management of the public forestry estate and a variety of regulations, controls and incentive schemes, primarily the standard grant schemes. The Scottish Forestry Grants Scheme replaced the Woodland Grant Scheme in the early 2000s as the main mechanism for supporting non-state forestry activities in Scotland and helped to deliver the priorities set out in the first Scottish Forestry Strategy. The Scottish Forestry Grant Scheme

---

4   Scottish Executive, *The Scottish Forestry Strategy (Edinburgh: Forestry Commission Scotland*, 2006), pp. 9-10.

5   Ibid., pp. 9, 15, 17, 21, 31-33.

6   A. Lawrence, B. Anglezarke, B. Frost, p. Nolan and R. Owen, 'What Does Community Forestry Mean in a Devolved Great Britain?', *International Forestry Review*, 11 (2009) 2, 281-97, p. 287; Rick Rohde, 'Ideology, Bureaucracy and Aesthetics: Landscape Change and Land Reform in Northwest Scotland', *Environmental Values*, 13 (2004), 199-221, p. 200.

was closed in 2006 due to oversubscription and replaced in 2008 by the Land Management Contracts Scheme, an integrated funding mechanism that aims to deliver targeted environmental, social and economic benefits. Grant support for forests and woodlands is delivered through a number of forestry-specific options. The Scottish Government Rural Payments and Inspections Directorate, Scottish Natural Heritage (SNH) and Forestry Commission Scotland jointly administer this scheme.[7]

Native woodlands and bioenergy

Many of the schemes funded by the Scottish Forestry Grants Scheme and the Land Management Contracts Scheme are used to plant and restore native woodlands. As outlined in the previous chapter, the shift away from monoculture conifer plantations towards native species started in the 1980s and accelerated during the 1990s. In the first decade of the 21st century, the native and ancient woodlands of Scotland became a core issue in the developing national consciousness and politics that coincided with the creation of the Scottish Parliament. From its inception in the early 1990s, Scottish National Heritage (SNH) has made successful efforts to restore a Scottish collective ecology to the Highlands. The idea of a collective ecology developed from Frank Fraser Darling's argument regarding Scotland's degraded landscape that was the result of past landscape transformations that were hoisted upon Scotland by outsiders. Cast in a nationalist rhetoric, the idea saw Scottish National Heritage and other conservation organisations, such as Reforesting Scotland, call for the restoration of the Caledonian forests, to be made up of native species in general, and Scots pine and oak in particular. This rhetoric was not only used to protect funding for nature conservation but also to neutralise opposition from Highland communities who believed that the protection and restoration of native woods would not benefit them. In particular, the crofters believed that Scottish National Heritage favoured birds, mammals and native trees over the traditional farming communities. This local vision of the Highland landscape is not one of wild wood but that of a productive agricultural landscape, including the conifer plantations of production forestry.[8]

The new narrative of the 'native' forests is important but has not completely replaced the former forest plantation economy. For example, in the manifesto of

---

7 Phoebe Cochrane, *Community Involvement in Woodlands: Governance and Social Benefits*, Unpubl. PhD Thesis. Edinburgh University, 2008, p. 34; Forestry Commission Scotland, *SFGS Closure & Revisions. Q&A Document*, 13 July 2006. http://www.forestry.gov.uk/pdf/SFGSClosureRevisionsQAJul06amended.pdf/$FILE/SFGSClosureRevisionsQAJul06amended.pdf Accessed: 15 June 2011.

8 Paul Robbins and Alistair Fraser, 'A Forest of Contradictions: Producing the Landscapes of the Scottish Highlands', *Antipode*, 35, (2003) 1, 95-118, pp. 110-112.

the Scottish National Party (hereafter SNP) for the first Scottish parliamentary election in 1999 we can read that '[The SNP] will ensure a major expansion of diverse forestry stock of environmental and commercial benefit to many'.[9] This statement puts emphasis on the economic benefits of forestry, which is obvious for commercial forestry plantations, but not for the conservation and regeneration of native woodlands. Within a wider economic context, putting emphasis on the economic benefits of native woodlands makes sense. Scotland attracts over 12 million domestic and 2.5 million foreign visitors annually, contributing over 4 billion pounds to the Scottish economy. In addition, tourism is Scotland's largest private sector employer.[10] Visitors are attracted by what they perceive to be Scotland's unspoiled landscape, and not by the non-native monoculture conifer plantations that are the result of a century of single-minded forestry policy. The promotion, regeneration and restoration of native woodlands are economic necessities if the landscape that many visitors to Scotland expect to see is to continue to be provided. It is therefore not surprising that in its 2011 manifesto the SNP is not playing the nationalist card when it comes to Scotland's native forests. Rather, it is placing emphasis on economic benefits. The creation of native woodlands can be seen as an instrument with which to tap into the rich vein of green tourist capital, partly replacing timber-producing forests with Scots pine and oak woodlands as the ideal alternative forests.[11]

The emphasis on native woods should not disguise the fact that the 'old' forestry plantations cannot be part of a new green narrative. This green narrative was provided by the UK's commitment to tackle climate change and subsequent programme aimed at reducing carbon emissions. Although climate-change policy and related issues of energy were not originally part of the devolved government's portfolio,[12] the Scottish Executive has, over time developed its own climate policy. In 2006, the Executive produced a climate change programme, *Changing Our Ways*, which set out a more ambitious Scottish target for reducing carbon emissions than the UK-wide programme. The ambition to exceed UK targets was even more evident following the election of the SNP in 2007. Two years later, in 2009, an Act was passed that introduced an interim target of reducing greenhouse gas emissions by 42 per cent by 2020, and an 80 per cent by 2050 against the baseline emission year of 1990.[13]

9   *Scotland's Party. Manifesto for the Scotland's Parliament Elections 1999* (Edinburgh: SNP, 1999), p. 16.
10   Data from: Scottish Executive, http://www.scotland.gov.uk/Topics/Statistics/Browse/Tourism-Culture-Sports Based on 2009 figures.
11   Robbins and Alistair Fraser, 'A Forest of Contradictions', p. 109; *Re-elect: A Scottish Government Working for Scotland. Scottish National Party manifesto 2011* (Edinburgh: SNP, 2011), p. 39.
12   Climate change and energy policy are the responsibility of the UK Government's Department of Energy and Climate Change.
13   The baseline for CO2 and other greenhouse gas emissions is 1990; Climate Change (Scotland) Act 2009,   http://www.scotland.gov.uk/Topics/Environment/climatechange/scotlands-action/climatechangeact Accessed: 15 June 2011.

The ambitious greenhouse gas emission targets had a direct bearing on Scotland's energy policy, which is also a UK-wide policy matter and is not devolved. Nevertheless, a commitment to increase Scotland's capacity to generate electricity from renewable sources has been a key feature of Scottish climate change policy since devolution. The Scottish Government[14] has made the use of biomass from forestry one of the key elements of its forestry strategy as part of the wider policy to reduce overall greenhouse gas emissions in Scotland dramatically. Forest policy has increasingly been viewed as a conduit through which deliver wide-ranging government objectives for the Scottish Government, in particular carbon sequestration and wood fuel policies. Thus, climate change has added another layer to forest policy and 'poses significant challenges to achieving an appropriate balance of the demands placed on Scotland's forests and woodlands'.[15]

By 2006, the Scottish Forestry Strategy had outlined Scotland'scommitment to the development of a bioenergy industry based on wood resources through the continued development of commercial forestry. A Wood Fuel Task Force, that was set up to investigate how wood production for biofuels could be increased, concluded that expansion of the forest area was necessary. It also saw a new role for coppice woodlands, a traditional woodland management method that can be used effectively in native broadleaf woods. In January 2009, the Scottish Forestry Commission launched its Climate Change Action Plan, which ties together the Scottish Forestry Strategy and the Climate Change Act, Scotland. The Action Plan outlined how Forestry Commission Scotland will contribute and respond to the challenges of climate change. The most important ingredients of the plan relate to the sustainable management of existing woodland, the adaptation of forest ecosystems to climate change through the creation of forest habitat networks and the creation of new woodland to capture carbon, produce wood and aid adaptation. In line with the Forestry Strategy, the Plan envisages that

> ...woodland creation can contribute towards net emissions reduction in addition to their other well documented multi-purpose benefits. Scotland's Climate Change Programme recognises this contribution and the Scottish Forestry Strategy includes an aspiration to achieve 25% woodland cover in Scotland by the second half of this century. This will require the creation of about 10,000 ha of new woodlands each year.[16]

---

14   Prior to 2007, the formal and common name for the devolved administration was 'the Scottish Executive'. The term 'Scottish Government', was only formally (but not legally) utilised following the formation of the SNP-led government in 2007.

15   D.J. Read, P.H. Freer-Smith, J.I.L. Morison, N. Hanley, C.C. West, and P. Snowdon (eds), *Combating Climate Change – a Role for UK Forests. An Assessment of the Potential of the UK's Trees and Woodlands to Mitigate and Adapt to Climate Change* (Edinburgh: The Stationery Office, 2009), p. 9.

16   *Climate Change Action Plan 2009-2011* (Edinburgh: Forestry Commission Scotland, 2009), p. 15.

The ambitious targets for greenhouse emissions, renewable energy and forest expansion set by the Scottish Government are one indication of the divergence of Scottish, English, Welsh and UK-wide policies. In October 2010, this notion of divergence was reinforced by the proposal of the Conservative-led UK Government to sell off 15 per cent of the public forest estate in England by 2015. This would have amounted to the largest sell-off the Government could authorise without the need for an act of parliament. For this reason the Department for Environment, Food and Rural Affairs launched a consultation paper in early 2011, detailing options for the disposal of the rest of the public forest estate. On 17 February 2011, following widespread criticism of the proposals, and a petition signed by more than half a million people, the Government halted the public consultation. However, a separate sale of 40,000 hectares of Forestry Commission land in England announced by the Government as part of its Spending Review is still planned once additional 'protections on access and biodiversity' are put into place.[17]

Due to the devolved nature of forestry, Westminster's proposals for England did not apply to Scotland and Wales. Speaking at the annual Scottish Forestry Forum in Battleby near Perth in October 2010, the Scottish Environment and Climate Change Minister, Roseanna Cunningham said that 'we have no plans to dispose of the national forest estate in Scotland and there is no review of Forestry Commission Scotland being undertaken'. She added that '[t]he Scottish Government views Scotland's forests as a source of national pride and an important public asset which can help deliver many benefits in economic, environmental and social terms.'[18] These comments reinforced the notion of an increasingly Scottish identity for public forestry in Scotland operating independently from forestry in England and Wales. As it stands, the Forestry Commission for Wales will cease to exist in April 2013, when it is set to merge with other Welsh environmental bodies to form a new agency for the management of natural resources in Wales.[19] Where Scotland is concerned, the process of divergence, fuelled by a combination of nationalism, economic and social pressures, and environmental concerns is likely to increase further in the foreseeable future

---

17   Oliver Bennett, *The Forestry Commission and the Sale of Public Forests in England*. House of Commons Library, Common Note SN/SC/5734. www.parliament.uk/briefingpapers/commons/lib/research/briefings/SNSC-05734.pdf accessed: 20 May 2011; *Forest Sale Axed: Caroline Spelman Says 'I'm sorry'*, BBC News, 17 February 2011. www.bbc.co.uk/news/uk-politics-12488847 accessed: 20 May 2011.
18   Forestry Commission, 'No Forest Sale Says Scottish Government'. News Release 14143, 27 October 2010. www.forestry.gov.uk/newsrele.nsf/WebNewsReleases/8F5F9B8158F91FA5802577C90025DD88 accessed: 20 May 2011.
19   BBC News, Chief Executive Named for Merger Environmental Body, 6 October 2012. www.bbc.co.uk/news/uk-wales-politics-19844497 Accessed: 21 October 2012.

under the SNP-led government. Expansion of the national forests has become a cornerstone of Scotland's rural and resource policies, and the aim is for a further dramatic increase in forest area in decades to come.[20]

The legacy and the future

At the start of the second decade of the 21st century, the situation for Scottish forestry is in many respects very different from that of the late 1980's. Prior to 1988, new plantations consisted almost entirely of commercial coniferous species, with broadleaved species and Scots pine never exceeding five per cent of the total newly planted area. Deep ploughing has also gone out of fashion, with most planting now being carried out on clear-felled sites or the creation of new woodlands with natural regeneration.[21] The prolonged period of historically low timber prices that started in the 1990s combined with the public backlash against the silvicultural approach based upon the use of monoculture conifer plantations, clear felling and replanting has resulted in a change in woodland structure and planting practice in Scotland.

As a result of the combined activities of the Forestry Commission and private forestry, more than 900,000 hectares of new forest plantations were created or restocked in the period 1970 to 2010. A number of discernible trends were evident during this period. Firstly, the annual rate of planting and restocking declined from more than 35,000 hectares per year in the early 1970s to just over 12,000 hectares by 2010. This can largely be accounted for by the fact that new planting and restocking by the Forestry Commission which had been close to 20,000 ha per year in the early 1970s fell steadily to less than 6000 hectares per year from the mid-1990s onwards. The rate of new private planting and restocking was 15,000 ha per year in the early 1970s and more than halved by the late 1970s only to gradually increase again to over 24,000 ha in 1989 before falling below 15,000 hectares per year in the late 1990s, following withdrawal of the special tax status which forestry enjoyed during this period.[22]

---

20   In June 2012, the *Report of the Woodland Expansion Advisory Group* advised the expansion of the Scottish forest area with 100,000 hectares in the period 2014-2024. It also recommended integrating forestry with other land-use, which is a consistent with forest policy since the 1980s. See: *Report of the Woodland Expansion Advisory Group*, http://www.usewoodfuel.co.uk/news,-events-woodfuel-forums/news/report-of-the-woodland-expansion-advisory-group.aspx Accessed: 12 October 2012.
21   Jim Christie, 'Ploughing', *Forestry Journal*, 1 (2008) 3, 30-31, p. 31.
22   *Forestry Commission Annual Reports and Accounts*, 1970-1975; Forestry Commission Woodland Statistics, *Time Series New Planting and Restocking, 1976 – 2010.* www.forestry.gov.uk/forestry/infd-7aqknx accessed: 23 May 2011.

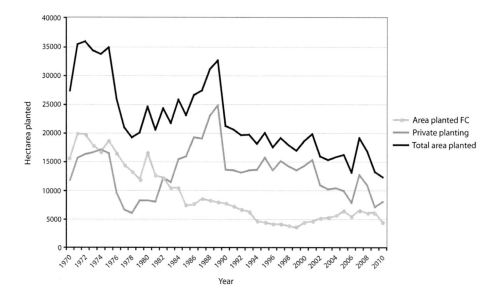

Figure 10.1: Area planted by the Forestry Commission and private sector in Scotland, 1970–2010.

Source: Forestry Commission, Time series for new planting and restocking, 1976–2010; Annual Reports 1970–75.

The second major change over the period has been in the balance of tree species planted. Up until the mid-1980s, broadleaves accounted for only a small fraction (less than two per cent of total planting) of new woodland. It was not until 1985 that the area of broadleaf planting started to increase due to the introduction of the broadleaf policy which encouraged the planting of such trees. It then steadily increased until, by the beginning of the new millennium, broadleaves accounted for more than half of all new woods being established in Scotland. A decade later, broadleaves account for 80 per cent of new woodland planted.[23]

With hindsight, the plantation forestry practised in Scotland during the 1970s and 1980s can be recognised as the end point of almost a century of forestry policy that was driven by the desire to expand the forest estate as rapidly as possible and is a prime example of the environmentally-destructive potential of single-purpose forestry. This policy was the result of the experience of two world wars and the view that the uplands represented a wasted resource, a desert in need of reclamation and cultivation, a view dominant since the time of the Enlightenment in the 18th century. The afforestation of the Flow Country can be regarded as the last expression of that perspective in Scotland.[24]

---

23   Forestry Commission Woodland Statistics, *Time Series New Planting and Restocking, 1976 – 2010*.
24   Warren, 'Significance of the Flow Country Debate', p. 331.

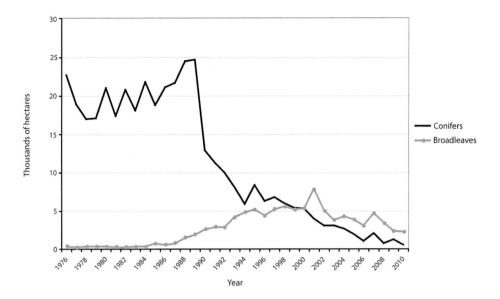

Figure 10.2: Area planted with conifers and broadleaf trees in Scotland, 1976–2010.

Source: Forestry Commission, Time series for new planting and restocking, 1976–2010.

The harsh criticism of the commercial afforestation programme led Scottish forestry to refocus and rebrand itself as a provider of public goods. Since the late 1980s, the shift towards a broader, more inclusive multi-purpose focus for forestry on the one hand and sustainable conservation on the other has dramatically reshaped Scottish forestry. Improved practices are rectifying the environmental mistakes of the past; the poor species choice, poor plantation design and excessive ground preparation that has had detrimental effects on landscape, water quality and biodiversity. This was aided considerably by the pre-existing attitudes of foresters who believed in holistic forestry balancing production with amenity, conservation, and the social function of forestry. The shift was made possible by a younger generation of more conservation-minded foresters who had wanted to create more diverse and productive forest ecosystems but had been prevented from doing so by government policy and economic imperatives. After all, a concern for landscape and ecology is hardly new in forestry circles and goes all the way back to the interwar period and the work of pioneers such as Anderson, Steven, Carlisle and many others.

Nevertheless, the dense post-war conifer plantations established in many parts of Scotland have left a negative perception of commercial forestry and as a result the Forestry Commission still struggles to get its case across to the public. However, critics often overlook the fact that the Scottish forest plantations were created in upland areas that had not seen any woodland cover for hundreds if not thousands of years. The nature of the plantation forests was partly a response to the absence of forest conditions, but the creation of these conifer plantations has changed this and provides the basis for developing a more diverse forest estate in the Scottish uplands. In many areas, the conifer plantations have been ecologically destructive but this also provides new opportunities for creating more robust, diverse and dynamic ecosystems that will be able to cope with a changing climate and can help to mitigate its impact. It is therefore not surprising that the recent justification in the Scottish Forestry Strategy for increasing the area under woodland is partly driven by climate change considerations.

Thus, Scottish forest policy has seen a shift over the last thirty years from the creation of commercial forestry plantations through environmental and amenity goals to one of combating climate change. It is a measure of the multi-functionality of forestry that the sector has been able to successfully accommodate these changes in forest policy. However, a range of issues face forestry in Scotland, many of them global, some more local. Balancing the demands for local access, nature conservation and land reform as well as the impact of climate change, increasing global demand for timber products and the resultant changing policies on forest utilisation and function, and the requirement to develop robust adaptation policies, will provide a major challenge.

List of people interviewed

The following were interviewed or provided written and/or oral comments:

- Mr R.A. Allison, 21 July 1999, at his home in Fochabers.
- Jim Atterson, 13 August 1999, at the University of Stirling.
- Mr John Berry, Correspondence, 28 April and 29 may, 1999.
- Mr Roger Bradley, 27 August 1998, at the University of Stirling and written comments.
- Mr John Davies, 22 September 1999, at his home in Dumfries.
- Mr F.J. Donald, 13 July 1999, at his home in Edinburgh.
- Dr. William E.S. Mutch, 12 August 1998, at his home in Edinburgh.

Mr Allison was Chief Instructor for the Women's Timber Corps for Scotland during the Second World War. From 1946-1950 he was Foreman in charge at Auchtermuchty. From 1950 until his retirement in 1970 worked in the Speymouth forests and was appointed Head forester in 1953.

Mr Atterson read forestry at Edinburgh University. After graduation he joined the Forestry Commission and posted to the Research Branch in Edinburgh he was then transferred to the Dornoch District in the North of Scotland Covering Sutherland Catithness and the Northern Isles. Atterson was there seven years as a District Officer before he was appointed and as principal silviculturist North at the start of the 1970s. At the beginning of the 1980s he became Assistant Conservator harvesting and marketing for West Scotland Conservancy before becoming the Conservator for Scotland.

Mr Berry was chairman of the Scottish Committee of the Nature Conservancy from 1949 until his retirement in 1967.

Mr Bradley graduated from Oxford in 1960. Then the Forestry Commission employed him as a Research Officer at Alice Holt Research station, Surrey. There he was responsible for research in planning and economics. From 1970 to 1983 he occupied the posts of District Officer in Argyll, Scotland, Assistant Conservator in South Wales, Conservator N. Wales and Director Wales. From 1983 to 1985 he was director of Harvesting and Marketing of the Forestry Commission before becoming Forestry Commissioner. After the reorganisation of the Forestry Commission in 1992 he was made Head of the Forestry Authority for Great Britain. In 1996 he left the Forestry Commission to become President of the Institute of Chartered Foresters. Mr Bradley has also been Chairman of the UK Forestry Accord.

Mr Davies graduated in 1949 from the University of Edinburgh and joined the Forestry Commission in 1950 as an acquisition officer. He was then promoted to assistant conservator Conservancy West, Scotland and then he became conservator. In 1971 he became the senior forestry officer for Galloway and stayed there until his retirement in the 1980s.

Mr Donald graduated in forestry from Aberdeen in 1950 and was then employed on survey work. Worked from 1951 until 1957 as private woodlands officer in Banff before he was appointed as a district officer, a position he held in several places before he retired in 1980.

Dr Mutch graduated from Edinburgh in 1946 and then went to Nigeria in the Colonial Forest Service. After his return in the UK he became a research assistant in Oxford. In 1953 he was appointed as a lecturer in forestry at the University in Edinburgh. From 1981 until 1987 he was head of the Department of Forestry and Natural Resources. Dr. Mutch is now retired.

Glossary of terms

Afforestation – The creation of a new forest by seeding or planting on previously unforested land.

Aspect – orientation of a slope to the sun.

Blanket peat – Blanket peat is found in areas with cool, wet, typically oceanic climates. Under these conditions peat mosses and other plants break down very slowly and gradually form a layer of peat that expands over large areas of undulating ground.

Bronze Age – A cultural period that is characterised by the use of weapons and implements made of bronze, approximately 2,500–700 BC.

Brown earth – Brown earth, called brown forest soil in Scotland, is a rich forest soil associated with areas where the natural vegetation is, or was, deciduous woodland. This kind of soil is very suitable for agriculture.

Catchment area – The area drained by a river or body of water, for example the River Spey and its tributaries.

Clear felling – A logging practice in which all trees in an area are uniformly cut down. Sometimes an entire forest is harvested in this way altering the landscape in a dramatic way.

Collective ecosystem – An ecosystem that is regarded typical for a certain region or country and is often closely lined with a national or regional identity. For example the Alpen meadows in Switerland or the Claledonian pine forests in Soctland. These ecosystems are often the result of sustained human interference over long periods of time.

Coppicing – Coppicing is a traditional method of woodland management technique in which young tree stems are cut down to near ground level. Subsequently, new shoots will emerge, and after a number of years, the newly grown branches are harvested again. The cycle is repeated periodically when the coppiced tree, or stool, is ready to be harvested again. The wood is used as building material, firewood and for many household purposes such as weaving baskets.

Dauerwald – A German term that translates as 'continuous forest cover' or 'permanent forest'. *Dauerwald* is a set of forestry principles that aims to abolish clear-fells, encourage mixed species and ages within stands and ensure harvestable timber occurred over the entire stand.

Forest – There is no precise definition of 'forest' in Britain. During the 20th century it tends to be associated with forest plantations. In the context of this book forest is only used to refer to plantations.

Glaciation – The process of the growth of glaciers and ice sheets but it also refers to a period when large areas of land are covered in ice, often described as an ice age.

Gley – Gley soils form in waterlogged conditions, reducing the oxygen supply, and anaerobic micro-organisms flourish by extracting oxygen from ferric. This process gives a greenish-blue-grey colour to the soil. Gley soils are sticky and hard to work.

High forest – A forest consisting of tall trees that are planted or raised from seed. These forests are often even aged in structure.

Holocene – The present geological period that started at the end of the last ice age 10,000 years ago and still continues to the present and which is characterised by a warm climate and the development of modern human culture.

Hygrophilous plant species – A plant species growing in or preferring moist habitats.

Iron Age – A cultural period that is characterised by the introduction of iron metallurgy, approximately 700 BC–400 AD.

Loch Lomond stadial (10,900–9,400 BC) – Cold period that occurred towards the end of the last ice age in Scotland characterised by the development of small ice-caps and glaciers in the Scottish Highlands.

Mesolithic – The Middle Stone Age. A cultural period that is associated with hunter-gatherers, approximately 10,000–4,000 BC.

Mid-Holocene Climate Optimum – A term referring to a sub-interval of the Holocene period from 5000–7000 years ago when summer conditions were probably warmer than today in the North Atlantic.

National Nature Reserve (NNR) – National Nature Reserves are areas of land set aside for nature, where the main purpose of management is the conservation of habitats and species of national and international significance. NNRs are designated under the National Parks and Access to the Countryside Act 1949 and the Wildlife and Countryside Act 1981. All NNRs are also SSSIs but often much larger and other activities are often excluded and public access restricted.

Nachhaltigkeit – A system to secure forest resources for the future. More generally it can be translated as 'sustainability'.

Neolithic – The New Stone Age. A cultural period that is associated with the arrival of agriculture, approximately 4,000–2,500 BC.

Podzols – Podzols are leached soils that form in cool and moist climates and are generally associated with acid parent material and semi-natural heath or coarse grassland vegetation and coniferous woodland. Podzols are generally not very fertile.

Pollarding – Pollarding is a traditional woodland management method of encouraging lateral branches by cutting off a tree stem or minor branches two or three metres above ground level. Subsequently, new branches will appear and these are periodically cut and used for firewood or building material. This management technique is used in areas where cattle grazing will prevent the regrowth of shoots from coppice stools.

Ring-barking – Ring-barking is the practice of remove a ring of bark from a tree trunk in order to kill the tree.

Silviculture – The art and science of the cultivation of forest trees.

Site of Special Scientific Interest (SSI) – Sites of Special Scientific Interest (SSSI) are areas of land considered to be of special interest with regard to features such as flora and fauna, geology or shape and form of the landscape. SSSIs were enshrined in the 1949 National Parks and Access tot he Countryside Act and is based on the idea of habitat conservation through site designation. Unlike nature reserves where conservation is generally the primary objective, the conservation interest defined by the SSSIs has to co-exist with other land uses. Under the 1947 Act it was assumed that agriculture and forestry were compatible with nature conservation objectives.

Under planting – The practice to plant young trees, under an existing stand of trees. In Scotland the practice was used to underplant native trees with fast growing conifers with the aim to outgrow the original trees to deprive them of light and kill them. This was cheaper than removing the original trees. Many of these underplanted native woodlands survive in conifer plantations and are now 'restored' by removing the conifers.

Woodland – The term 'woodland' refers to land under stands of trees, both semi-natural and planted, with a canopy cover of 20% or the potential to reach this, but with no minimum height. The term 'woodland' includes shrub as well as production forests and is much more inclusive than the term 'forest'. In the context of this book woodland refers to all types of forest cover in Scotland, including forest plantations when not mentioned specifically.

Glossary of common and scientific names of tree species

ash (Fraxinus)

birch: two species are native to Scotland, silver birch (Betula pendula) and downy birch (Betula pubescens)

Corsican pine (Pinus nigra)

Douglas fir (Pseudotsuga menziesii)

European larch (Larix decidua)

European silver fir (Abies alba)

Japanese larch (Larix kaempferi)

lodgepole pine (Pinus contorta)

Norway spruce (Picea abies)

oak (Quercus)

Scots pine (Pinus sylvestris)

Sitka spruce (Picea sitchensis)

sycamore maple (Acer pseudoplatanus)

western hemlock (Pinaceae tsuga)

western red cedar (Thuja plicata)

Archival collections consulted

The National Archives, London (TNA)

F1	Forestry Commission: Minutes of Meetings
F18	Forestry Commission: Headquarters Divisions
F19	Assistant Commissioner for England and Wales, and English Directorate: Correspondence and Papers
FT3	Nature Conservancy: General Matters
T224	Treasury: Agriculture, Transport and Trade Division

The National Archives of Scotland (NAS)

AF79	Afforestation files, 1909-1995
FC11	South (Scotland) Conservancy: General Files, 1930-1979
FC7	Forest histories and working plans, 1841-1974
SNH1/1	The Nature Conservancy Scottish Committee: Minutes, 1949-1973

Glasgow City Archives (GCA)

GB243/T-PM	Records of the Maxwells of Pollok
TD 454	Records of the Glasgow Tree Lovers Society

Highland Council Archives (HCA)

HCA 538	Munro of Novar Papers

Stirling Council Archives (SCA)

PD60   MacGregor Papers

Cumbria Record Office (CRO)

WDSO 117   Friends of the Lake District

University of Edinburgh Special Collections

GEN 1971; GEN 2158

Papers of Professor Mark Louden Anderson. Miscellaneous papers Department of Forestry, not catalogued.

Other archives

Archive of the Association for the Preservation of rural Scotland

Archive of the National Trust for Scotland

Select bibliography

Anderson, Mark Louden, *A History of Scottish Forestry* (2 vols, London & Edinburgh: Thomas Nelson and Sons, 1967)

Avery, Mark and Roderick Leslie, *Birds and Forestry* (London: Poyser, 1990)

Crone, Anne and Coralie M. Mills, 'Seeing the Wood and the Trees: Dendrochronological Studies in Scotland', *Antiquity*, 76 (2002) 293, 788-794

Crowe, Sylvia, 'The Multi-purpose Forest', *Scottish Forestry*, 26 (1972) 3, 213-216

Davies, John, *The Scottish Forester* (Edinburgh: Blackwood, 1979)

Dickson, J.H., 'Scottish woodlands: Their Ancient Past and Precarious Future', *Scottish Forestry*, 47 (1993) 3, 73-78

Dunn, Malcolm, 'Forestry in Scotland in the Reign of Her Most Gracious Majesty Queen Victoria', *Transactions of the Royal Scottish Aboricultural Society*, 15 (1898) 2, 109-132

Foot, David, *Woods and People: Putting Forests on the Map* (Stroud: History Press, 2010)

Forbes, A.C., *The Development of British Forestry* (London: E. Arnold, 1910)

Fraser Darling, Frank, and Morton Boyd, *The Highlands and Islands* (Revised edition; London: Oliver and Boyd, 1969)

Fraser Darling, Frank, *West Highland Survey: An Essay in Human Ecology* (Oxford: Oxford University Press, 1955)

Jeanrenaud, Sally and Jean-Paul Jeanrenaud, *Thinking Politically about Community Forestry and Biodiversity: Insider-driven initiatives in Scotland* (London: Rural Forestry Development Network, 1997)

Lambert, Robert, 'Therapy of the Green Leaf': Public Responses to the Provision of Forest and Woodland Recreation in Twentieth Century Britain', *Journal of Sustainable Tourism*, Vol.16 (2008) 4, 408-427

Lindsay, J.M., 'The Iron Industry in the Highlands', *The Scottish Historical Review*, 56 (1977) 161, part 1, 49-63

Macdonald, James, 'Forestry Research and Experiment in Scotland 1845-1953', *Scottish Forestry*, 8 (1954) 3, 127-141

Mackay, Donald, *Scotland's Rural Land use Agencies. The History and Effectiveness in Scotland of the Forestry Commission, Nature Conservancy Council and Countryside Commission* (Aberdeen: Scottish Cultural Press, 1995)

Mather, Alexander S. (ed.), 'Afforestation in Britain', In: Alexander Mather (ed,), *Afforestation: Policy Planning and Progress* (London: Belhaven Press, 1993), pp. 13-33.

Maxwell, John Stirling, 'A Decade of State Forestry and its Lessons', *The Scottish Forestry Journal*, 44 (1930) 1, 1-6.

Miller, Robert, *State forestry for the axe a study of the Forestry Commission and de-nationalisation by the market* (London: Institute of Economic Affairs, 1981)

Nairn, David, 'Notes on Highland Woods, Ancient and Modern', *Transactions of the Gaelic Society of Inverness*, 17 (1891), 170-221

Oliver, Susan, 'Planting the Nation's "Waste Lands": Walter Scott, Forestry and the Cultivation of Scotland's Wilderness', *Literature Compass*, 6 (2009) 3, 585–598

Rackham, Oliver, *Trees and woodland in the British landscape: the Complete History of Britain's Trees, Woods and Hedgerows* (London: Phoenix Press, 2001)

Robbins, Paul and Alistair Fraser, 'A Forest of Contradictions: Producing the Landscapes of the Scottish Highlands', *Antipode*, 35, (2003) 1, 95-118

Rowe, W.H., *Our Forests* (London: Faber & Faber, 1947)

Ryle, George B., *Forest Service. The First Forty-five Years of the Forestry Commission of Great Britain* (New Abbot: David and Charles, 1969)

Sansum, Philip, 'Argyll Oakwoods: Use and Ecological Change, 1000 to 2000 AD - a Palynological-Historical Investigation', *Botanical Journal of Scotland*, 57 (2005) 1, 83-97

Smout, T.C., *The Highlands and the Roots of Green Consciousness, 1750-1990* (Edinburgh: Scottish National Heritage, 1993)

Smout, T.C., *Scotland Since Prehistory. Natural Change & Human Impact* (Aberdeen: Scottish Cultural Press, 1993)

Smout, T.C., *Nature Contested. Environmental History in Scotland and Northern England since 1600* (Edinburgh: Edinburgh University Press, 2000)

Smout, T.C. (ed.), *People and Woods in Scotland: A History* (Edinburgh: Edinburgh University Press, 2003)

Smout, T.C., Alan R. MacDonald and Fiona Watson, *A History of the Native Woodlands of Scotland, 1500-1920* (Edinburgh: University Press, 2005)

Smout, T.C., 'Oak as a Commercial Crop in the Eighteenth and Nineteenth Centuries', *Botanical Journal of Scotland*, 57 (2005) 1, 107-114

Smout, T.C., 'The Pinewoods and Human Use, 1600-1900', *Forestry*, 79 (2006) 3, 341-349

Steven, H. M., 'The Forests and Forestry of Scotland', *Scottish Geographical Journal*, 67 (1951) 2, 110 -123

Stirling Maxwell, John, *Loch Ossian Plantations* (Glasgow, 1913)

Tipping, Richard, 'Blanket peat in the Scottish Highlands: Timing, Cause, Spread and the Myth of Evironmental Determinism', *Biodiversity and Conservation*, 17 (2008) 9, 2097-2113.

Tipping, Richard, 'The Form and Fate of Scotland's Woodlands', *Proceedings of the Society of Antiquaries of Scotland*, 124 (1994), 1-54

Tittensor, Ruth, *From Peat Bog to Conifer Forest: An Oral History of Whitelee, its Community and Landscape* (Chichester: Packard Publishing, 2009)

Tompkins, Steve, *Forestry in Crisis: The Battle for the Hills* (London: Christopher Helm, 1989)

Tsouvalis, Judith and Charles Watkins, 'Imagining and Creating Forests in Britain, 1890-1939', in: Mauro Agnoletti and Steven Anderson (eds), *Forest History: International Studies on Socioeconomic and Forest Ecosystem Change* (Wallingford, 2000)

Tsouvalis, Judith, *A Critical Geography of Britain's State Forests* (Oxford: Oxford University Press, 2000)

Warren, Charles, '"Birds, Bogs and Forestry" Revisited: The Significance of the Flow Country Controversy', *Scottish Geographical Journal*, 116 (2000) 4, 315-337

Zehetmayr, J. W. L., 'Afforestation of Upland Heaths', *Forestry Commission Bulletin* 32 (London: HMSO, 1960)